Modeling Religion

Scientific Studies of Religion: Inquiry and Explanation

Series editors: Luther H. Martin, Donald Wiebe, Radek Kundt
and Dimitris Xygalatas

Scientific Studies of Religion: Inquiry and Explanation publishes cutting-edge research in the new and growing field of scientific studies in religion. Its aim is to publish empirical, experimental, historical, and ethnographic research on religious thought, behaviour, and institutional structures. The series works with a broad notion of scientific that includes innovative work on understanding religion(s), both past and present. With an emphasis on the cognitive science of religion, the series includes complementary approaches to the study of religion, such as psychology and computer modelling of religious data. Titles seek to provide explanatory accounts for the religious behaviors under review, both past and present.

The Attraction of Religion, Edited by D. Jason Slone and James A. Van Slyke
The Cognitive Science of Religion, Edited by D. Jason Slone and William W. McCorkle Jr.
Connecting the Isiac Cults, Tomáš Glomb
The Construction of the Supernatural in Euro-American Cultures, Benson Saler
Contemporary Evolutionary Theories of Culture and the Study of Religion, Radek Kundt
Death Anxiety and Religious Belief, Jonathan Jong and Jamin Halberstadt
Gnosticism and the History of Religions, David G. Robertson
The Impact of Ritual on Child Cognition, Veronika Rybanska
Language, Cognition, and Biblical Exegesis, Edited by Ronit Nikolsky, Istvan Czachesz, Frederick S. Tappenden and Tamas Biro
The Learned Practice of Religion in the Modern University, Donald Wiebe
The Mind of Mithraists, Luther H. Martin
The Minds of Gods, Edited by Benjamin Grant Purzycki and Theiss Bendixen
Naturalism and Protectionism in the Study of Religion, Juraj Franek
New Patterns for Comparative Religion, William E. Paden
Philosophical Foundations of the Cognitive Science of Religion, Robert N. McCauley with E. Thomas Lawson

Religion, Disease, and Immunology, Thomas B. Ellis
Religion Explained?, edited by Luther H. Martin and Donald Wiebe
Religion in Science Fiction, Steven Hrotic
Religious Evolution and the Axial Age, Stephen K. Sanderson
The Roman Mithras Cult, Olympia Panagiotidou with Roger Beck
Solving the Evolutionary Puzzle of Human Cooperation, Glenn Barenthin
The Study of Greek and Roman Religions, Nickolas P. Roubekas
Understanding Religion Through Artificial Intelligence, Justin E. Lane
*A Social Cognition Perspective of the Psychology of Religio*n, Luke Galen
Imagining the Cognitive Science of Religion, E. Thomas Lawson

Modeling Religion

Simulating the Transformation of Worldviews, Lifeways, and Civilizations

Wesley J. Wildman and F. LeRon Shults

BLOOMSBURY ACADEMIC
LONDON • NEW YORK • OXFORD • NEW DELHI • SYDNEY

BLOOMSBURY ACADEMIC
Bloomsbury Publishing Plc, 50 Bedford Square, London, WC1B 3DP, UK
Bloomsbury Publishing Inc, 1359 Broadway, New York, NY 10018, USA
Bloomsbury Publishing Ireland, 29 Earlsfort Terrace, Dublin 2, D02 AY28, Ireland

BLOOMSBURY, BLOOMSBURY ACADEMIC and the Diana logo are trademarks of
Bloomsbury Publishing Plc

First published in Great Britain 2024
Paperback edition published 2026

Copyright © Wesley J. Wildman and F. LeRon Shults, 2024

Wesley J. Wildman and F. LeRon Shults have asserted their right under the Copyright,
Designs and Patents Act, 1988, to be identified as Authors of this work.

For legal purposes the Acknowledgments on p. xxi constitute an extension of this
copyright page.

Cover image © Shutterstock

All rights reserved. No part of this publication may be: i) reproduced or transmitted in
any form, electronic or mechanical, including photocopying, recording or by means of
any information storage or retrieval system without prior permission in writing from the
publishers; or ii) used or reproduced in any way for the training, development or operation
of artificial intelligence (AI) technologies, including generative AI technologies. The rights
holders expressly reserve this publication from the text and data mining exception as per
Article 4(3) of the Digital Single Market Directive (EU) 2019/790.

Bloomsbury Publishing Plc does not have any control over, or responsibility for, any
third-party websites referred to or in this book. All internet addresses given in this
book were correct at the time of going to press. The author and publisher regret any
inconvenience caused if addresses have changed or sites have ceased to exist,
but can accept no responsibility for any such changes.

A catalogue record for this book is available from the British Library.

Names: Wildman, Wesley J., 1961– author. | Shults, F. LeRon, author.
Title: Modeling religion : simulating the transformation of worldviews,
lifeways, and civilizations / Wesley J. Wildman and F. LeRon Shults.
Description: London ; New York : Bloomsbury Academic, 2024. |
Series: Scientific studies of religion: inquiry and explanation ; vol. 27 |
Includes bibliographical references and index.
Identifiers: LCCN 2023051594 (print) | LCCN 2023051595 (ebook) |
ISBN 9781350367302 (hb) | ISBN 9781350367340 (paperback) |
ISBN 9781350367319 (epdf) | ISBN 9781350367326 (ebook)
Subjects: LCSH: Religion and civilization–History.
Classification: LCC BL55 .W56 2024 (print) | LCC BL55 (ebook)
LC record available at https://lccn.loc.gov/2023051594
LC ebook record available at https://lccn.loc.gov/2023051595

ISBN: HB: 978-1-3503-6730-2
PB: 978-1-3503-6734-0
ePDF: 978-1-3503-6731-9
eBook: 978-1-3503-6732-6

Series: Scientific Studies of Religion: Inquiry and Explanation

Typeset by Newgen KnowledgeWorks Pvt. Ltd., Chennai, India

For product safety related questions contact productsafety@bloomsbury.com.

To find out more about our authors and books visit www.bloomsbury.com
and sign up for our newsletters.

For Nicholas Gibson, tireless champion of the scientific study of religion.

Contents

List of Illustrations		xi
Foreword *David Voas*		xvi
Preface		xviii
Acknowledgments		xxi
1	Why Model Religion?	1
	Religion Matters	1
	Studying "Religion" Through Transdisciplinary Human Simulation	4
	The Modeling Religion Projects	6
	Worldviews and Lifeways	10
	Preview	13
2	Civilizational Transformation	17
	What Drives Civilizational Transformation?	19
	Ideological-Political Theories	22
	Material-Social Theories	27
	Cognitive-Coalitional Theories	32
	Can Theories of Civilizational Transformation Be Synthesized?	38
	A Heuristic Matrix for Theoretical Integration	41
3	Computational Simulation	43
	From Narratives to Formal Models to Computational Simulations	43
	The Conversion Paradigm	46
	The Promise and Peril of Computational Humanities and Social Sciences	52
	Artificial Ethics	56
	Artificial Ontology and Epistemology	62
	Next Steps	64
4	Modeling the Neolithic Transition	67
	Why Model the Neolithic Transition?	67
	Synthesizing Theories	71
	NSIM: The Neolithic Social Investment Model	75

	Simulation Experiments	89
	How Religion Mattered in the Neolithic	95
5	Modeling the Axial Age Transition	101
	Why Model the Axial Age Transition?	102
	Synthesizing Theories	104
	MAxiM: A Computational Simulation of the "Axial Age"	113
	Simulation Experiments	116
	How Religion Mattered in the Axial Age	138
6	Modeling the Modernity Transition	143
	Why Model the Modernity Transition?	144
	Synthesizing Theories	146
	The FOReST Model	152
	Simulation Experiments	164
	How (Non)Religion Matters in Modernity	181
7	Insights and Prospects	189
	Transition Dynamics	193
	Likely Futures for Religion and Spirituality	205
	Likely Futures for the Human Project	209

Repositories Containing Model Details	215
References	217
Index	232

Illustrations

Figures

3.1	Six pathways through the conversion model	47
3.2	Flow rates within the conversion model	47
3.3	The conversion model with origins and destiny of the two subpopulations as cloud icons	48
3.4	The conversion model taking account of resource scarcity	48
3.5	The conversion model with the main output variable, the ratio of the new subpopulation to the old subpopulation (B:A Ratio)	49
3.6	The conversion model showing the critical role of the six flow-rate variables (top)	50
3.7	The conversion model showing the role of tuning parameters (top left)	50
3.8	The conversion model showing the "Causal Nexus" (top) that is required to specify the "Flowrate Variables" (center), which then drive the conversion model (bottom), as tuned by the parameters (left)	51
4.1	Stock-and-flow diagram for conversion model between low-investment (LI) and high-investment (HI) lifestyles	76
4.2	The core of the Causal Nexus for the Neolithic transition	78
4.3	Six outputs from the Causal Nexus	87
4.4	Closest solution to the Target transition pathway for the growing population of Çatalhöyük	91
4.5	The behavior of Social Intensity (socialInt) as the simulation runs through the best approximation to the Target transition pathway	92
4.6	The impact on HI_prop of varying the Stress parameter while holding other parameters at the values they have in the best approximation to the Target transition pathway	93
4.7	The impact on HI_prop of varying the Technology parameter while holding other parameters at the values they have in the best approximation to the Target transition pathway	93
4.8	Probability distribution function (PDF) and cumulative distribution function (CDF) for the proportion of people adopting high-intensity lifestyles (HI_prop variable)	94

5.1	The ideological-political pathway	106
5.2	The material-social pathway	109
5.3	The cognitive-coalitional pathway	110
5.4	Integrating the ideological-political and the cognitive-coalitional paths	112
5.5	Conceptual integration of three theories about the emergence of Axial Age civilizations	113
5.6	The conversion component of the model, showing the role of six key variables related to birth rates of people	114
5.7	The Causal Nexus of MAxiM, which expresses the theoretical synthesis	114
5.8	The Causal Nexus of MAxiM, illustrating the way it produces the six flow rates that feed into the conversion component of the model	127
5.9	The number of people with traditional and Axial worldview-lifeways over time	128
5.10	Key transition period during the Axial transition	129
5.11	Many virtual societies (represented by a dot) pictured in terms of their equilibrium state with energy capture (shading) as the input variable and both proportion of Axial people (vertical axis) and degree of axiality in institutional form (horizontal axis) as the two output variables	132
5.12	Many virtual societies (represented by dots) pictured in terms of their equilibrium state with energy capture (shading) as the input variable and both proportion of Axial people (vertical axis) and degree of axiality in institutional form (horizontal axis) as the two output variables	134
5.13	Many virtual societies (represented by dots) pictured in terms of their equilibrium state with cultural differentiation (shading) as the input variable and both proportion of Axial people (vertical axis) and degree of axiality in institutional form (horizontal axis) as the two output variables	135
5.14	Many virtual societies (represented by dots) pictured in terms of their equilibrium state with supernatural punishment (shading) as the input variable and both proportion of Axial people (vertical axis) and degree of axiality in institutional form (horizontal axis) as the two output variables	136
5.15	Many virtual societies (represented by dots) pictured in terms of their equilibrium state with the importance of priestly elites (shading) as the input variable and both proportion of Axial	

	people (vertical axis) and degree of axiality in institutional form (horizontal axis) as the two output variables	137
6.1	Conceptual model of the Meaning Maintenance Path	147
6.2	Conceptual model of the Subjectivization Path	147
6.3	Conceptual model of the Existential Security Path	148
6.4	Conceptual model of the Human Development Path	149
6.5	Conceptual model of the Cultural Particularity Path	150
6.6	Conceptual model of the Supply-Side Path	150
6.7	Conceptual model of synthesis of six theories of religious and secular change	151
6.8	Conversion model for FOReST	154
6.9a	The conversion process shows an emerging equilibrium between traditional supernaturalist religious (black) and post-supernaturalist secular (gray) people	155
6.9b	The conversion model's emerging equilibrium with parameters set to yield more post-supernaturalist secular people than supernaturalist religious ("traditional") people	155
6.10	The main looping structure within the Causal Nexus of FOReST	158
6.11	The Causal Nexus of FOReST	159
6.12	The derivation of six flow rates from FOReST's Causal Nexus	162
6.13a	FOReST response surface for the proportion of the post-supernaturalist secular population (postProp) as a function of the level of technology (Technology) and the pro-Modernity influence of supernaturalist religious worldviews-lifeways (PM)	165
6.13b	FOREST response surface for the difference between the post-supernaturalist secular population and the traditional supernaturalist religious population as a function of the level of technology (Technology) and the pro-Modernity influence of supernaturalist religious worldviews-lifeways (PM)	166
6.14a	Equilibrium state for the post-supernaturalist secular (postProp, in black) and supernaturalist religious (1−postProp, in gray) population percentages plotted against the Technology parameter, showing sensitive dependence on technology at the boundary between the two equilibrium regimes	168
6.14b	The same as Figure 6.14a with population numbers instead of percentages, which shows that a dominantly post-supernaturalist secular population is significantly smaller overall, with important sustainability and ecological implications	169

6.15	FOReST scatter plots illustrating the impact of the destabilization parameter (horizontal axis) on the proportion of post-supernaturalist secular people (vertical axis) for different levels of technology (shade intensity) and the pro-Modernity influence of supernaturalist religion (PM in the panels)	170
6.16	FOReST's artificial societies, with the degree of modern institutional form (Modernity) on the horizontal axis, the proportion of post-supernaturalist secular people on the vertical axis, and 3 percent random jitter added to improve readability	173
6.17	FOReST's artificial societies, with the degree of modern institutional form (Modernity) on the horizontal axis, the proportion of post-supernaturalist secular people on the vertical axis, the freedom variable determining shading, and 3 percent random jitter added to improve readability	174
6.18	FOReST's artificial societies, with the degree of modern institutional form (Modernity) on the horizontal axis, the proportion of post-supernaturalist secular people on the vertical axis, the pluralism variable determining shading, and 3 percent random jitter added to improve readability	175
6.19	FOReST's artificial societies, with the degree of modern institutional form (Modernity) on the horizontal axis, the proportion of post-supernaturalist secular people on the vertical axis, the existential security variable (security) determining shading, and 3 percent random jitter added to improve readability	176
6.20	FOReST's artificial societies, with the degree of modern institutional form (Modernity) on the horizontal axis, the proportion of post-supernaturalist secular people on the vertical axis, the existential security variable (security) determining shading and faceting, and 3 percent random jitter added to improve readability	177
6.21	FOReST simulation results showing the effect of (1) strengthening key conditions (years 0–400) and (2) a destabilizing event that weakens key conditions (after year 400)	177
6.22	A summary of the consensus of four experts in modern religious history of Norway, estimating the change in six dimensions of religiosity over the past 120 years	180
7.1	Word clouds for the four latent factors	200

7.2	Sankey diagram showing our projection of estimated flows among four cultural packages of spirituality at 2000 (left), 2050 (center), and 2100 (right)	204
7.3	The effects of Modernity on spirituality and on religions that seek to adapt to secular, post-supernaturalistic worldviews-lifeways	208

Tables

2.1	Schema for interpreting the role of religion in major episodes of civilizational change	41
4.1	Causal Nexus parameters and variables constituting the causal architecture of the model	81
4.2	Additional parameters impacting output variables but not Causal Nexus variables	88
4.3	Parameter settings yielding the closest approximation to the target transition pathway through the model's parameter space from a low to a high proportion of HI people	91
4.4	Matrix for neolithic transition	97
5.1	Parameters for MAxiM	116
5.2	Variables in MAxiM, together with attached links from other variables, parameters, and output variables	117
5.3	Flowrate definitions in MAxiM	127
5.4	Multiple regressions examining the association between three key variables—energy capture, cultural differentiation, and supernatural punishment	131
5.5	Axial Age matrix	140
6.1	Definition of FOReST's parameters	157
6.2	Definition of the variables involved in the main looping structure within FOReST's Causal Nexus	158
6.3	Definition of the variables within FOReST's Causal Nexus	160
6.4	Definition of six flow rates driving FOReST's conversion model	163
6.5	ANOVA comparing the four key variables across two groups	172
6.6	Modernity matrix	186
7.1	Rotated component matrix, disclosing four latent factors	199

Foreword

It is said that Erasmus was the last man who knew everything, though the label has been applied to a number of others. Sadly, our brains would explode if we tried to absorb even a small fraction of the current stock of knowledge, but a few polymaths still walk among us. Wesley J. Wildman and F. LeRon Shults are two of them.

It is rare to find scholars who know so much about so much: simultaneously foxes who know many things and hedgehogs who know one big thing, as Isaiah Berlin might have put it. And how that breadth and depth is needed here! How else could we comprehend, in a single work, the Neolithic transition to agriculture, the Axial Age, and the onset of secularization in Modernity? It is an immense achievement.

Wildman and Shults do not claim to be experts on all of the topics they cover, though I know from experience that they are too modest. Their contribution comes from theoretical synthesis allied with skills in model building and the power of contemporary computing. I am reminded of how Richard Feynman explained his ability to solve problems that had resisted the best efforts of colleagues at MIT and Princeton: "I got a great reputation for doing integrals, only because my box of tools was different from everybody else's, and they had tried all their tools on it before giving the problem to me." Feynman was also too modest, of course, but the point is that creative application of new or unusual tools can produce remarkable results.

Computational social simulation is both well established and still fairly novel. The progress that has been made over the past few decades is astonishing. For my PhD research at Cambridge in 1978–81, I used simulation in conjunction with historical research to try to explain the persistence of low fertility in equatorial Africa. At that time it was possible for even an ungifted novice to know most of what had been done previously. I wrote code in FORTRAN and put stacks of punch cards into the jaws of a machine that would read them into the mainframe. I'd then wait nervously for hours, if not overnight, to see whether a misplaced comma had brought the job to a halt. In the end I did obtain some answers, and they shed light on a phenomenon that had puzzled demographers for decades. I was sold on simulation.

I promptly defected from the academy, however, and only returned in middle age after making some money, pondering the meaning of life, and wandering from the City of London to Bulgaria via many points in between. Since my return to the world of academic research, I have received numerous grants, large and small, but the very first funded a project entitled "Computer Simulation and the Study of Religious Change." My experience a couple of decades earlier had convinced me that the approach was fruitful. The field had become enormously more sophisticated, though, and I emerged from the experience with little more than an appreciation for how much remedial education I would need in order to contribute anything useful. I veered off the road less traveled and back onto the highway of conventional social science.

Another two decades on, the literature on computational models has developed beyond all recognition, along with the hardware and software available for this work. In Boston, Wesley J. Wildman founded the Center for Mind and Culture, which has played a leading role in the use of modeling and simulation to explore the interaction of psychological, cultural, and sociological factors that lead to social goods, ills, and change. In Kristiansand, Norway, F. LeRon Shults established the Center for Modeling Social Systems to develop conceptual and computational models for analyzing and predicting psychological and societal change. I have had the good fortune of serving as a subject matter expert on a couple of their projects, and it has been fascinating to observe this research at first hand.

Faced with the tension between lumpers and splitters, between scholars in search of generalizations and those who focus on particularity, Wildman and Shults have achieved a synthesis: there is a forest (see Chapter 6!), but they observe the trees as well. Actual history is singular and gives us scant leverage when trying to understand complexity. Computational social simulation enables us to rewind the past again and again, under varying conditions, to see what matters.

We are lucky to have such good guides to our past, present, and future. I continue to learn from them, and I am delighted that this book will enable others to share that good fortune.

David Voas
University College London

Preface

What kind of book is this? At one level, this is a book about human worldviews and lifeways and how they change. That means it is also a book about religion, its varied roles in human life, and the shape of secular worldviews and lifeways after the decline of religion in certain cultural settings. At another level, this book tells a story about human civilizations, charting how they transition by destabilizing one equilibrium arrangement and eventually regathering around a new stable equilibrium. At yet another level, this book is about how computers can help us understand human life through a powerful methodology called computational social simulation (CSS). We believe CSS can generate novel insights into both human history and the challenges facing human societies today.

We're not alone in working at any of these levels. Many scholars have sought to understand religious and nonreligious views of reality and ways of life. A fascinating group of intellectuals have attempted to chart the development of human civilizations. And, in the past several decades, as the power and flexibility of computing machines has increased, many researchers have turned to CSS to capture the complexity of human social life, to explore policy options, and to extend cognitive control over social systems that can be difficult to comprehend in their intricate complexity.

Combining these three levels of research is where this book makes a distinctive contribution. Our overarching goal is to ask and answer a deceptively simple question. What role does religion play in the seismic transformations of civilizational form? This book offers an interpretation of the long history of human beings, as a suite of other books have done. But it makes a case for how to move beyond speculation in talking about the deep past, as well as more recent periods of human history, and even the not-so-distant future.

The book also tackles the urgent question of what sort of civilizational transformations might be possible in a world where the influence and significance of religion continues to decline wherever technology, education, freedom, and cultural pluralism are most advanced. Will this trend spread globally? Will it reverse course? How do moral frameworks and social stability arise in post-religious cultures? What does the past teach us about our likely futures?

Theories represented in the scholarly literature as competing explanations are not always mutually exclusive. The consistency demands of computational models are helpful for evaluating the degree to which putatively competing models can be rendered as complementary perspectives on a more complex process. When integrated in a theoretical architecture it may turn out that key elements of competing theories are in fact consistent. Each of the models considered in this book takes advantage of deep complementarity between explanations, thereby benefiting from numerous theoretical perspectives, including newer empirical findings from the scientific study of religion.

The three main models we discuss in Chapters 4 to 6 have already been presented and discussed in other contexts. We are grateful to the publishers for permission to reuse ideas from these papers, though little remains of the originals.

- Shults, F. L., & Wildman, W. J. (2018). Simulating religious entanglement and social investment in the Neolithic. In I. Hodder (Ed.), *Religion, history and place in the origin of settled life* (pp. 33–63). University of Colorado Press.
- Shults, F. L., Wildman, W. J., Lane, J. E., Lynch, C., & Diallo, S. (2018). Multiple axialities: A computational model of the Axial Age. *Journal of Cognition and Culture*, 18(4), 537–64.
- Wildman, W. J., Shults, F. L., Diallo, S. Y., Gore, R., & Lane, J. E. (2020). Post-supernaturalist cultures: There and back again. *Secularism & Nonreligion*, 9.

Our presentation of these computational simulations clusters technical and mathematical material into a single section of each chapter, so bored or desperate readers can easily bracket those details and still follow the flow of the book's argument.

At several points throughout the book we also weave in ideas that we have articulated in other ways in other contexts. We discuss ideas related to the importance of ethical considerations and stakeholder engagement when attempting to utilize CSS to address societal challenges (e.g., Wildman & Shults, 2018; Shults & Wildman, 2019, 2020a, 2020b; Shults, 2020). We also discuss the meaning of spirituality in secularizing settings (Wildman et al., 2023).

The book as a whole illustrates the explanatory power of CSS methods applied to the complex case of the role of religion in the transformation of human worldviews, lifeways, and civilizations. However, we are interested in more than an explanation of the past. We also tentatively move into territory that more angelic scholars have feared to tread, and thus have tended to avoid: speculation on the future role of religion in civilizations transformed by secularization.

We want to be up front that our approach is guided by methodological naturalism and methodological secularism. That is, we prefer academic arguments that optimize the use of theories, hypotheses, methods, evidence, and interpretations that do not appeal to supernatural agents, and we prefer academic practices that optimize the use of scholarly strategies that are not tied to the idiosyncratic interests of supernatural coalitions (Shults, Wildman, Taves, et al., 2020; Taves et al., 2022; Shults & Wildman, 2023). Moreover, for reasons we explain throughout the book, we ourselves in fact embrace *metaphysical* naturalism and secularism. In other words, we argue that supernatural entities independent of human minds do not exist, and we argue that we cannot rely on purported supernatural authorities as resources for organizing the social field in pluralistic contexts. These may appear to be overly bold claims, but we think there are good reasons for making them and good reasons for being explicit about their importance as we pursue questions about the transformation of human worldviews, lifeways, and civilizations.

Acknowledgments

We are grateful to the magnificent members of many research teams with whom we have had the privilege of working. For their roles in NSIM (Chapter 4), MAxiM (Chapter 5), FOReST (Chapter 6), and the Dimensions of Spirituality project (Chapter 7), we express our warm appreciation to Saikou Y. Diallo, Nicholas DiDonato, Ross Gore, Justin E. Lane, Christopher J. Lynch, Aimee Radom, David Rohr, and Steven Sandage. We also acknowledge funding from the John Templeton Foundation for the Modeling Religion Project, and funding from the Research Council of Norway for the Modeling Religion in Norway project. We are grateful for the excellent production support we received from Bloomsbury, and to David Rohr for creation of the index. Finally, we note the use of AnyLogic's multimodal simulation platform as the main simulation software and SPSS and R as the main statistical analysis and visualization packages.

1

Why Model Religion?

This chapter outlines some of the key concepts that will guide our modeling of religion in this book, including contentious terms such as religion and secularity. These issues are conceptually vital for the argument and require a transdisciplinary approach that integrates the sciences of cognition and culture with an understanding of the evolutionary development of the human species. It prepares the ground for explaining how we will be able to move beyond mere speculation by relying on a technique within computational humanities and computational social science known as computational modeling and simulation. These tools can help explicate the vital roles that religions have played in civilizational transformation and even help us peer a little way into the future.

The final section of this chapter offers a preview of the remainder of the book. First, however, let's provide an initial rationale for including religion in our interpretation of civilizational transformation in the first place. Why model religion?

Religion Matters

For our purposes, there are at least two senses in which religion matters. First, because religion has played such a significant role in past transformations of human civilization (a claim for which we will need to argue in some detail), it matters that it is appropriately included in any more or less comprehensive *explanation* of such transformations. Our interest is in the role that religion has played in the major civilizational transformations associated with the Neolithic Revolution, the Axial Age, and Modernity. Each of these transitions was marked by a series of nonlinear changes in human relationships with nature and one another, changes that resulted in radically new social structures and behavioral norms. Within and across the various fields that study these transformations, including archaeology, evolutionary biology, cultural anthropology, sociology, and economics, scholars disagree over the extent to which religiosity—as opposed to other factors such as energy capture, social structure, or political ideology—had a causal function in these processes.

What role does religion play in the seismic transformations of civilizational form? Given what is discussed in the literature, some scholars are supremely confident they know the answer: religion is a mere detail, riding on the coattails of larger forces that do the real work of change. It is energy and organization, technology and security that drew us out of roving extended family groups of hunters and gatherers and into towns of farmers who domesticated animals and crops and figured out how to cooperate with nonkin. The same factors created mega civilizations with the emergence of priestly and educated classes to contest the centralized god-like power of monarchs. And those factors also gave birth to the upheaval we know as Modernity. Religion had nothing to do with it. At most, it was decoration on the cake, comforting rationalizations for transformations of civilizational form that were changing everything, whether religious people were ready or not.

As scholars of religion, we have a different perspective. We're in no doubt about the critical role that guns, germs, and steel—as well as calories, politics, and economics—play in the way human beings order their civilizations. But we suspect that religion has been more than a decorative frill. We think that supernaturalist religious worldviews have been crucial to catalyzing civilizational change and stabilizing newly emergent civilizational equilibria. We have concluded that religious worldviews and lifeways interact in intricately complex ways with extraction of energy from the environment, political organization, cultural creativity, and technologies of war. So we will argue that religion did matter and try to show how and why it mattered in the three major shifts in worldviews, lifeways, and civilizational form identified above.

How, you might well ask, could an argument of this kind be anything more than one more speculative reconstruction of the complex history of our species during the past several thousand years? Will we rely on the findings of archaeologists? Will we engage the work of paleo-anthropologists? Will evolutionary theory make an appearance? What about sociology and psychology? History and political economy? What's our angle? We'll be drawing on all that has been mentioned to make our case—as many disciplinary perspectives as might be relevant. And we'll be deploying computational social simulation (CSS) as well. Specifically, we'll present computational simulations to explicate the vital roles that religions play in civilizational transformation. These computer models will explain precisely what we mean about the interactions between religious worldviews and the many other forces that impact civilizational change—far more precisely than is possible in theories stated merely verbally or narratively. There is so much interpretative slippage in critical terms of theory. Methods from computational humanities and computational social science, including simulation, used wisely, can enhance precision and clarity, and thereby encourage focused debate using terms that really connect instead of talking past one another.

But there is a second sense in which religion matters for our argument. We also believe that a lot is at stake in the religious impulse within human beings, both for understanding the past and for coming to grips with what's coming next. In other words, religion (or the lack thereof) will matter in future transformations of human civilization and is therefore an important element of any speculation about the conditions under which—and the mechanisms by which—such transformations will occur in secularizing societies. If we're right about the past role of supernaturalist religious worldviews in catalyzing cooperation, destabilizing and restabilizing civilizational forms, and helping people navigate sometimes distressing transitions, then we're also flagging an unprecedented challenge for our species. The civilizational changes afoot in our own time hint at an era in which supernaturalist worldviews are no longer experienced as convincing by increasingly large numbers of people. Whatever the ultimate outcome of the civilizational transition we are currently navigating, it will need to be handled differently than in the past. Supernatural resources, real or imagined, will not be universally effective for guiding or even easing the journey.

It is worthwhile explicitly naming two radically opposed perspectives in this debate: religious supernaturalists versus secular naturalists. The former are worried that humanity can't make it without beliefs in invisible spirits that provide social glue, while the latter are worried that we won't make it if we cling to supernaturalist beliefs. The former are large but shrinking in developed nations; the latter are no longer small and still growing fast. The former charge the latter with having no record of accomplishment at running civilizations; the latter charge the former with having an abysmal record at running civilizations.

Our species has never before needed to navigate a civilizational transition when polarized between religious supernaturalists and secular naturalists. It is far from obvious how it is going to turn out. For example, we know with complete confidence that there are supernaturalist religious extremists who would happily deploy weapons of mass destruction to wipe the abomination of Modernity from the face of the earth, if they could get their hands on such weapons—and they'd do it with a breathtaking degree of zealous confidence in the rightness of their actions, buttressed by belief in a life hereafter that is more real than anything in this world. Fortunately, most religious supernaturalists are peace-loving citizens who aim to make the world more beautiful rather than turn it into a smoldering ruin. To date, however, neither the peaceful religious folk nor the secular naturalists have been able to regulate violent supernaturalist religious extremists without resorting to military force. The journey ahead, we surmise, is guaranteed to be complicated and conflicted.

Although we (the authors) often disagree about the value and even the meaning of "religion," as well as the sense in which religions can become naturalized and demythologized, we agree that human beings have to take responsibility for regulating their own behavior. We (all humans) have to learn to do this, with or without religion, because supernaturalist views are drying up and dying out. Data supporting the latter are outlined in the chapter on the Modernity model, which (spoiler alert) suggests that supernaturalist beliefs will continue to decline so long as existential security, education, pluralism, and freedom of expression increase. Because most people rather like cultures blessed with existential security, education, pluralism, and freedom, as a species we are unlikely to choose a future without such features, unless it is forced upon us by violent ideologues determined to trigger a reversion to a world in which supernaturalism will once again seem credible.

Studying "Religion" Through Transdisciplinary Human Simulation

We have been using the term "religion" relatively vaguely. Authors discussed in the following chapters do not agree on how to define religion, and do not always operationalize the term in the same way, or at all, in their conceptual models. Phenomena commonly referred to as "religious" are enormously complex, and understanding them calls for a transdisciplinary method that integrates approaches from the natural sciences, social sciences, and humanities. We have found the shared territory between the sciences of cognition and the sciences of culture particularly valuable for making sense of religion. This leads directly to the "bio-cultural" study of religion, in which the interpretation of minds and cultures are both taken seriously, neither reduced to the other.

Why is this important? As will become clear in the explication of the computer models mentioned further on, we want to account for both cognitive and cultural dynamics in these transformations. The bio-cultural study of religion can help us do this, and also incorporate other factors from fields such as history, peace studies, sociology, political science, and many others.

In humanities disciplines that include research on religion, including religious studies, some scholars emphasize the importance of avoiding essentialist and colonialist definitions of religion. We agree. However, for the sake of clarity in formalizing theories, computational models require careful operationalizations of all key terms involved. We see this as an opportunity. Without claiming that any particular usage of the term is best, we do our best to surface our assumptions and provide a rationale for whatever operationalization we utilize in a particular model. In the context of the models themselves, we will lean toward definitions that emphasize the role of supernaturalist beliefs and behaviors in religion. This makes sense, on the one hand, because that is the way most scholars in the scientific study of religion, and especially the bio-cultural study of religion, utilize the term. It also makes sense for our distinctive purpose of exploring what sort of civilizational transformations lie ahead of us as such supernaturalist beliefs and behaviors wane in secularizing societies.

What do we mean exactly by transdisciplinary, and why do we think social simulation can help? We were among the coeditors of a book titled *Human Simulation*, which set out the rationale for such an approach and the general methodology that has guided our computational modeling efforts here and elsewhere (Diallo et al., 2019). This approach is committed to involving scholars from the humanities and the social sciences, along with subject-matter experts, policy professionals, and other stakeholder change agents in the process of constructing computational simulations that address pressing societal challenges (Shults, 2023). Of course, the method can also be used (and indeed we use it here) for exploring complex scientific hypotheses about the past, or understanding human behavior for its own sake (basic science). However, we strive to incorporate vital human factors into computer architectures and artificial societies in order to account more adequately for the cognitive and cultural complexity of our species. In the next chapter, we will explain in more detail why computer modeling is a uniquely useful methodology for this sort of transdisciplinary work.

It is important to acknowledge that not everyone who researches religion will be equally enthusiastic about admitting computer modeling to the methodological club. One of the many distinctions within the academic fields that study religion, especially from a bio-cultural perspective, is between those who prefer the methodological tendencies of scholars such as Talal Asad over scholars such as Scott Atran—or vice versa. Their approaches are well illustrated in works such as *Genealogies of Religion* (Asad, 1993) and *In Gods We Trust* (Atran, 2002). We can use these author's names metonymically to indicate two distinctive approaches to the study of religious and nonreligious worldviews and lifeways: one (Asad) that is primarily grounded within qualitative, social, anthropological, and historical research, and another (Atran) that is primarily grounded within quantitative, psychological, cognitive, and evolutionary research.

Of course, the Asad and Atran camps in the scientific study of religion overlap and interact, but there is a core methodological (and often a political and even psychological) tension between them. Those who prefer Atran-like approaches have been far more likely to embrace CSS methodologies. In fact, the *Journal of Cognition and Culture* hosted a special issue on computer models of religion (Lane & Shults, 2018), and social simulation was included in a special issue on methodology in the *Journal for the Cognitive Science of Religion* (Lane & Shults, 2020), as well as in a target article with commentaries in *Religion, Brain & Behavior* (Whitehouse et al., 2012).

CSS has been embraced far more vigorously within the Atran camp than it has within the Asad camp in the academic study of religion. However, it is important to emphasize that qualitative and hermeneutical research on religion is not at all excluded (much less replaced) by the use of CSS methods. On the contrary, insights that can only be generated by Asad-like approaches and theories (and the humanities in general) are increasingly incorporated within the construction of computer simulations of complex and changing social systems. This is the case in the three system-dynamics models described in Chapters 4 to 6, each of which was designed to simulate the transformation of civilizational forms at key turning points in human history. CSS methods employ both qualitative and quantitative data and are both interpretative and analytical in character. Asad-style religion scholars may not like CSS methods, but their objections should not be because CSS sells out to quantitative approaches in the scientific study of religion because that would be a misunderstanding of the method itself.

The Modeling Religion Projects

The general approach to human simulation and the specific system-dynamics models outlined in Chapters 4 to 6 are part of a wider series of modeling religion projects in which the authors have played key roles. Understanding this context will be valuable both for grasping the value of modeling religion in general and for making sense of our rationale for applying such methods to the shifts in civilizational form during the Neolithic, Axial, and Modernity transitions. What follows in this subsection is a summary of the wider context provided in (Shults, 2021).

This work occurs within the context of the joint efforts of several transdisciplinary teams within a growing international collaborative network of scholars of religion. It all began with the Modeling Religion Project (MRP), led by Wesley at the Center for Mind and Culture (CMAC) in Boston. The MRP project was funded by the John Templeton Foundation (JTF), and CMAC's main partners for this grant were the Virginia Modeling, Analysis and Simulation Center (VMASC) and the Social Simulation Research Group at the University of Agder (UiA), which later became linked to the NORCE Center for Modeling Social Systems (CMSS). It was during MRP that we began developing the radically transdisciplinary and policy-oriented participatory modeling approach mentioned earlier (Diallo et al., 2019).

MRP ran from 2015 to 2018 and provided the context for the development of several computational models of religion. These included a model of the role of religiosity in terror management, which was able to simulate the emergence of increased population-level anxiolytic ritual behaviors in the wake of threats related to contagion, natural hazards, predation, and cultural others (Shults, Lane, et al., 2018). The architecture of that model was also expanded to include behaviors and interactions informed by social identity theory and identity fusion theory, enabling the simulation of the mutual escalation of xenophobic anxiety between religious groups that is observed in the real world (Shults, Gore, et al., 2018).

One of the MRP models that was most directly related to the subject of the current book, especially the last two chapters, we refer to as the "Non-Religiosity Model" or NoRM (Gore et al., 2018). The computational architecture of NoRM was based on an integration of several empirically grounded theories that show how nonreligious worldviews emerge and expand in a population as critically thinking individuals learn about natural causes and human capacities within a wider social field in which they feel safe and secure. In other words, religiosity is "prevented" (or lowered) in a population as education and existential security are increased. These are not the only relevant mechanisms in the secularization process, but their effects in lowering religiosity are among the most well documented (Ellis et al., 2017; Hungerman, 2014; Inglehart & Welzel, 2005; McLaughlin & McGill, 2017; Norris & Inglehart, 2011; Shults, 2018; Strulik, 2016; Zuckerman et al., 2013).

The goal of NoRM was to understand and explain factors that influence changes in average religiosity and existential security in a population. The artificial society was populated with networked heterogeneous agents having cognitive architectures and distributed levels of the relevant variables such as supernaturalist beliefs, religious formation, and religious practices (dependent variables); and education and existential security (independent variables). Data for initializing the model were derived from factor analysis and structural equation models of the International Social Survey Programme, and from the Human Development Index for multiple countries. The simulation experiments explored the conditions under which—and the mechanisms by which—the dependent variables were affected.

Validating NoRM required us to determine whether the model could simulate the emergence of macro-level shifts in religious practices and existential security within its artificial populations (in a way that matched their change over time in real-world datasets) from micro-level agent behaviors and interactions. We calibrated the model to predict the (real-world) shifts in the relevant variables over a ten-year period (1990–2000) within eleven countries. Using that calibrated model, we then predicted shifts in the relevant variables for twenty-two countries (including eleven for which the model was not initially calibrated) during a subsequent ten-year period (2000–10). NoRM's predictions were significantly more accurate than its closest competitor, which used linear regression, lending plausibility to its theoretical synthesis and causal architecture.

After the successful launch of MRP, the team applied for another grant from the Research Council of Norway, which led to the Modeling Religion in Norway (MODRN) project. Based at UiA, this project was led by LeRon and ran from 2016 to 2019. MRP and MODRN overlapped both conceptually and temporally and included many of the same team members who collaborated in the development of a variety of computational models for studying (non) religion. One of the most interesting and complex was a model of minority integration in a Western city (Puga-Gonzalez et al., 2019), which was based on a more generic platform for simulating societal changes such as secularization (Shults, Wildman, Diallo, et al., 2020).

In the context of the current book, however, perhaps the most relevant MODRN computer models were those that emerged out of a 2018 seminar at UiA's Metochi Centre in Lesbos, Greece. This seminar brought together three teams of computer scientists and subject matter experts for a week to work on three different models designed to explore cognitive variables and mechanisms involved in the increase of religious disbelief (analytic atheism), the growth of pro-social attitudes and behaviors among the nonreligious (altruistic atheism), and the role of social networks in exiting religion (affiliated atheism). Two of these models have now been published (Galen et al., 2021; Cragun et al., 2021).

The third major funded project in this series of collaborations was the Modeling Religious Change (MRC) project, which began in early 2020 and ended in 2023. MRC was made possible by a grant from JTF and was also led by Wesley, with several collaborating institutions including VMASC and CMSS. One of the main goals of the MRC project was to develop and execute a new approach to the demography of religion and non-religion that builds on and expands agent-based modeling and social simulation techniques developed in the team's prior work. Traditional approaches in the demography of religion tend to focus on self-reports of religious identity or affiliation, in part because these are variables on which longitudinal data are most readily available. Such approaches often employ cohort-component methodologies to make population projections. MRC aims to enhance demographic projections of religion (and secularization) by using computational methods that will allow us to take account of other dimensions of religiosity such as supernaturalist belief, private religious practice, religious service attendance, and personal importance of religion (see https://mindandculture.org/projects/modeling-social-systems/modeling-religious-change/ardemis/). Moreover, linking cohort-component methods to simulations within artificial societies could also help demographers take account of nonlinear feedback loops and interaction among variables, produce narrower error estimates, and integrate a rich array of disciplinary insights relevant to religious and nonreligious change.

The "Religion, Ideology, and Prosociality" (RIP) project was also launched in 2020 and ran through 2023. This project was funded by EEA-Norway (a European Economic Area grant) and is a collaboration between CMSS and the University of Bialystok in Poland. RIP is led by Konrad Talmont-Kaminski whose work on religion and secularization incorporates theories and data from a wide variety of disciplines (Talmont-Kaminski, 2014). Four main models are currently being developed, each of which will contribute to the task of simulating secularities. The first model aims to simulate the role of the growth and decline of "fuzzy fidelity" within a secularizing population, a process hypothesized and first demonstrated by David Voas (Voas, 2009), one of the main subject matter experts on the team. The second is a model of the relationships among anxiety, religiosity, and secularization as these engender (or enervate) pro-social behaviors within and across groups. The third will attempt to implement error (note: not "terror") management theory within a computational model in order to simulate the function of some evolved cognitive biases in religiosity. The architecture of the fourth model will include the mechanisms articulated in epistemic vigilance theory, which hypothesizes that source vigilance and content vigilance play a dominant role in religious and scientific thinking respectively.

The unique capacities of computer modeling tools, outlined and illustrated further on, provide exciting new opportunities for the study of religion and non-religion. As programming and participatory techniques—perfect for incorporating Asad-like insights derived from qualitative research and hermeneutical analysis, and Atran-like insights derived from quantitative research and evolutionary anthropological analysis, into computer modeling and simulation—continue to improve, it will become increasingly easy for scholars of secularism in the social sciences and humanities to take advantage of these methodologies (Diallo et al., 2019).

Worldviews and Lifeways

One way to tackle the controversies billowing around the use of the term "religion" is to switch to "worldviews," which may or may not be religious. This is the approach championed by Ann Taves and Egil Asprem, an approach we will follow, adapt, and expand in what follows. One of our main adaptations is to explicitly include "lifeways," a point to which we will come momentarily. The proposed shift toward "worldviews" as a replacement for "religion" flowed out of Taves and Asprem's earlier work on what they call the "Building Block Approach" (BBA) which, as we will see further on, fits naturally with the processes of CSS, especially agent-based modeling methodologies.

Taves and Asprem see BBA as providing a method for analyzing and explaining "complex cultural phenomena in terms of the constituent parts that interact to produce them" (Taves & Asprem, 2020, p. 1). The first step in this approach is "reverse engineering," a process they unpack with the help of the "new mechanism" framework developed by William Bechtel and others within the philosophy of science. Given the historical divide between the natural (explanatory) sciences and the human (interpretive) sciences, many scholars operating in the latter will likely be suspicious of suggestions that they should incorporate "mechanistic" kinds of "explanation" into their work. However, Taves and Asprem argue that this approach can contribute to healing the unfortunate divide between those who study religion (and other complex cultural concepts) within fields such as cognitive science and evolutionary psychology (Atran-types), on the one hand,

and those who approach such phenomena from humanities perspectives as historians or religious studies scholars, on the other (Asad-types).

Why are they optimistic? Unlike early modern mechanistic philosophy, which searched for universal and fundamental physical causes, the new mechanism approach that inspired Taves and Asprem explores local interactions among entities (or forces) and, because it is grounded in evolutionary biology, its explanations are also meant to apply to goal-oriented or intentional behaviors. This makes it far more tenable to humanists than early modern notions of mechanism. This approach is also far more holistic and dynamic. As Bechtel puts it, the focus on goal-oriented or intentional behaviors in the new mechanism approach can foster robust explanations of a complex phenomenon by combining a reductive "looking down" to identify the component parts with a wider "looking around" at the way they are organized and a "looking up" at the situation in which they are embedded (Bechtel, 2009).

For Asprem and Taves, this kind of explanation can play an important role in the study of religion because mechanisms "can be conceived vertically as nested levels of mechanisms and horizontally in terms of causal chains distributed along spatiotemporal lines" (2018, p. 12). Each of these authors has stressed in their own work that reverse engineering must include synthetic reconstruction as well as reduction. In the context of reverse engineering the concept of esotericism, for example, Asprem argues that BBA, far from being a form of essentialism or reductionism, explicitly aims "to reconstitute the objects of study through vertical and horizontal integration" (Asprem, 2016, p. 183). As Taves puts it elsewhere, "To build effective bridges between the historical and the scientific study of religion we need not only to break religion down into its parts but also to test to see if the parts can be reassembled into wholes" (Taves, 2015, p. 192).

This first step in the BBA comes naturally for scholars working with CSS methodologies because reverse engineering is central to many of its most popular techniques. The construction of multi-agent artificial intelligence models, for example (Lane, 2013, 2021), typically begins by "looking down" in order to identify some of the key mechanisms at work in the production of the emergent dynamics of the target phenomenon. But making sense of these dynamics also requires "looking around" at the way in which the component parts are organized and interact. Because varying conditions may alter the way in which the parts interact, computer modelers must also learn to "look up" in order to determine which parameters or social network effects to include in the artificial societies they construct.

How might this work in the study of religion? Computer modeling of phenomena deemed religious can begin by "looking down" at some of the key mechanisms—for example, naturally evolved cognitive and coalitional biases—that empirical research suggests play a role in shared imaginative engagement with supernatural agents. However, we should also "look around" at the way these biases are evoked differently in relation to other relevant factors such as mortality salience, social identity, and the fusion of individual and group identities. Such factors can impact the way the constituent parts of religion are expressed as minds organize themselves in groups. Moreover, cultural and physical variations in environments also impact the way religious tendencies are manifested in human populations, so we also need to "look up" at the environmental parameters that shape the situations within which these biases are expressed (or contested). Simulation experiments on such models can identify some of the conditions under which—and the mechanisms by which—religious variables emerge and increase or decrease. In this way, computer modeling enables scholars to reverse engineer and then synthetically reconstruct the religious phenomenon in question and simulate it within an artificial society. For a fuller discussion of the connection between the BBA and CSS, see Shults, 2020.

So what exactly do Taves and Asprem mean by *worldviews*? They mean ways of answering, implicitly or explicitly, the "big questions" facing all human individuals and groups (Taves & Asprem, 2020, p. 19):

1. What exists, what is real? (Ontology)
2. Who are we, where do we come from, and where are we going? (Cosmology)
3. How do we know what is true? (Epistemology)
4. What is the situation in which we find ourselves? What is our nature? (Situation)
5. What is the good (or goal) that we should strive for? (Axiology)
6. What actions should we take? What path should we follow? (Praxeology)

Taves has outlined and defended her proposal for replacing "religious studies" with "worldview studies" in several places (Taves, 2015, 2020; Taves et al., 2018). The advantages of this approach include overcoming theoretical problems in the study of religion by highlighting fundamental big questions and providing a pan-human basis for designing comparative studies. It also might help to overcome the academic polarization between the humanities and natural sciences, including what we have referred to as the tension between Asad-style and Atran-style scholars in the academic study of religion. It even provides an opportunity for developing a new approach for studying scientific worldviews (Taves & Asprem, 2018), which will be particularly important for our proposals in the final chapter of this book.

We adapt and expand their approach in three ways. First, for our purposes, we can simplify their six categories into three. We collapse ontology, cosmology, and situation into "ontology," and axiology and praxeology into "ethics." The reason for this simplification is not that there are no important differences here, but only that, given our limited purposes, these three suffice: ontology, epistemology, and ethics. We will spell out how and why we use these three categories in Chapter 2 and then operationalize them as a heuristic device in the chapters that remain.

Our second adaptation is to expand beyond worldviews and explicitly link to "lifeways." Asad-style scholars of religion are quick to point out that the way we live together in civilizations is not just about how we *view* the world but also about how we make our *way* in life. Religion, in particular, is not merely a matter of ideas and beliefs but also of ritual practices and behavioral choices integrated with the rhythms of life. Religion is not merely believed; it is also lived. Indeed, as the "lived religion" movement has rightly argued, in some settings, for understanding the practical meaning of religion, living out religion is a lot more important than what people may (or may not) believe (Ammerman, 2007; Hall, 2020; Orsi, 2002). Individual differences of temperament also matter here. For some people, beliefs are vital in defining their relationship to religion, while beliefs are almost irrelevant for others. Most people live somewhere between these two extremes. Surely, we don't need to choose between believing and living; both are important. This is why we speak of worldviews *and* lifeways.

Finally, as explained in more detail in the following chapter, we believe that understanding worldviews and lifeways cannot be separated from understanding shifts in *civilizational forms*, which supply critical contexts for making sense of big questions in life. Most answers to the latter have traditionally involved "religion," but increasingly this is no longer the case in some secularizing contexts. Simulation can help us get a conceptual grip on what has happened in the past, what is happening now, and what is likely to happen in the future under varying civilizational conditions.

Preview

While we may appear to be articulating an impossibly broad agenda for a single book, in fact our approach to this swirling vortex of issues is focused, deliberate, and tractable.

In Chapter 2 on civilizational transformation, we address the main object of our study, namely, the large-scale shifts in the organization of human life. These have long fascinated interpreters of the human condition—anthropologists, sociologists, historians, political scientists, economists, among them—in part because they are stunning transformations seemingly without a sufficient explanation. Why, in a world of so many stable continuities, should there be radical discontinuities in the transformation of civilizational form? How did we end up with grocery stores instead of hunting parties? With democracies instead of centralized absolute political power? With world wars instead of regional skirmishes? With cyber currency instead of bartering? With global video communication instead of smoke signals? With dangerous overpopulation instead of struggling for enough calories to make reproduction possible? What can we say about the species that generated these changes, for better and worse? And what would it take to control the direction of future transformations of civilizational form rather than leave everything to chance—which is to say, leave the future to the mysterious outworking of complex causal systems that have consistently defeated our most gifted interpreters?

Our approach to episodes of civilizational transformation benefits from countless scholarly exertions aiming to address such questions but operates with a clear focus and important limitations. The focus is on the role of what many people are willing to call religion within such episodes. The limitation is the consideration of only three key instances of civilizational transformation, albeit important phase changes: the Neolithic agricultural transformation (Chapter 4), the Axial Age (Chapter 5), and Modernity (Chapter 6). These limitations in focus and scope will keep the study tractable while supplying enough theoretical framing to enable us to draw some general conclusions and to peer into the future at least a short way (Chapter 7).

In Chapter 3 on computational simulation, we present the main tool utilized in our work throughout the book. In the most general terms, computational simulations are techniques for extending and stabilizing cognitive grasp over vast amounts of information and otherwise unfathomably complex causal systems to enhance understanding and to render interpretations concretely answerable to demanding constraints from theory and data. We're accustomed to fortifying our knowledge base using encyclopedias and databases and to enhancing our conceptual modeling capabilities using diagrams and mathematics. Computational simulations allow us to do both, thereby extending our cognitive reach all the way into the heart of complex causal systems that routinely defeat our best prognosticators and interpreters.

There are many types of computational simulation. We and others have used agent-based models to create artificial societies that are useful for understanding the functions of religion in human worldviews and lifeways. This book focuses on computational modeling of the dynamics of systems interpreted as complex wholes, abstracting away from the human agents whose interactions underlie those dynamics. In fact, each of the models presented in Chapters 4 to 6 tries to capture a shift in civilizational form as the destabilization of one equilibrium state and the subsequent coalescing around a new equilibrium state. Of course, the context for these transformations is critically important, and the causal architectures of the three computational simulations are very different as a result. But the fundamental contribution of complexity theory is evident in all three cases.

The payoff of using computational simulations to extend our cognitive reach is already evident in the insights reaped in relation to each of the three episodes of civilizational transformation treated in Chapters 4 to 6. But the cumulative benefit of those simulation-afforded insights also permits us to peek a little way into the future, which we attempt to do in Chapter 7.

2

Civilizational Transformation

One of the main goals of this book is to contribute to the scholarly discussion around the ways in which, and the extent to which, religion matters in the emergence, stabilization, maintenance, disruption, transformation, and restructuring of civilizational forms. In Chapter 1 we suggested that the use of computer modeling in general, and the transdisciplinary *human simulation* approach in particular, has a special role to play in this conversation. In Chapter 3 we will spell out our computational approach, setting the stage for simulating the major civilizational shifts that will occupy our attention in Chapters 4 to 6.

The current chapter explains in more detail exactly what we plan to model. As noted earlier, religion is a complicated subject, and there is always the danger of losing our way in endless definitional debates. Computational modeling encourages and enables scholars to be precise about how they use key terms and then to move on to the formalization of theories about the phenomena in which they are interested. For reasons that we tried to make clear in the previous chapter, we think that discussing worldviews and lifeways is a fruitful approach to what has traditionally been studied under the rubric of religion. Here we link that discussion about worldviews and lifeways to debates over the causes and dynamics of civilizational transformation. The bulk of this chapter presents a typology of theories that attempt to explain what drives these processes of transformation. As we will see, these theories often overlap, and we suggest that they are not as incompatible as many of their proponents seem to believe. We also indicate how considerations related to worldviews and lifeways fit within each type of theory. We conclude the chapter by outlining a heuristic to guide our efforts both in theoretical integration and in implementation of integrated theories in computer simulations.

In the context of this book, the phrase "civilizational transformation" refers specifically to a change within its inhabitants, exchanging one kind of civilizational form (with associated worldviews and lifeways) for another. As the next chapter explains, all three of our models use a "conversion" conceptuality to express this change, though there is nothing particularly religious about it. By "civilizational form," we refer to the socioeconomic and axiological structures and dynamics by which human groups cohere and persist over time.

There is no normative content in these concepts. We are certainly not arguing for a simplistic linear evolution of civilizational forms, or that one form is better than another, or that forced transformation under colonial pretensions to cultural supremacy is the way civilizational change should occur. Rather, we are interested in how civilizational forms can and do shift—in various directions—and what role worldviews and lifeways (some of which some people are willing to call religious) play in those shifts.

We are modeling three transformations of civilizational form: the Neolithic, Axial, and Modern transitions. To be more precise, we will be considering three pairs of high-level forms of civilization and the transition pathways between them: hunter-gatherer and sedentary-agricultural; pre-Axial and Axial; premodern and modern. We are not claiming these are the only high-level civilizational forms or that these shifts occurred at concrete times that are easily determined. We'll dive into these possible objections and concerns as we go along. The main point at this stage can be expressed using the sciences of complex dynamical systems: each civilizational transformation involves a movement from one equilibrium regime, through a process of destabilization, to another equilibrium regime, along determinate pathways within a vast space of possibilities for civilizational form. The human experience of this type of transformation might take several generations to unfold but it always involves the emergence and maintenance within a human population of one relatively stable view of the world (and associated ways of life) from the destabilized ruins of an older equilibrium arrangement.

What is actually changing (in reality and in the models) is the *large-scale organization of the mind-culture nexus*. By "large-scale organization," we mean not families or communities (micro) or even social and institutional networks (meso), though relevant dynamics from these levels will be included in the simulation architectures. Rather, we mean the economic, legal, political, military, ecological, energy-capture, and other dynamics operative at the macro-level, holding together the group as a whole. By "mind-culture nexus," we refer to human reality in a very particular way, stressing both that minds are interacting in networks and enmeshed in practices that give rise to cultures and social norms and that cultures condition minds in a process of social construction (Wildman, 2009). We interpret interaction between the levels of minds and cultures as bidirectionally irreducible: minds and their interactions can't be reduced to cultural influences, and cultures can't be reduced to the minds that help give rise to them. The mind-culture nexus is the playground of human evolution, the possibility space through which human individuals and groups move, cooperating and competing as they go. It is a landscape of transitory niches within which distinctive selection pressures act both on organisms—in this case human bodies and minds—and on cultures, thought of nonreductively as the accumulation of individual organisms' influence and the reciprocal influence of emergent norms on individuals.

To understand principles underlying the transformation of civilizational form, we will attend to some of the major equilibrium regimes in human history, as well as the transition pathways between them. In particular, we are studying the functions of religion, including especially supernaturalist worldviews and lifeways, in facilitating those transitions between equilibrium regimes. We are claiming that religion plays a nontrivial role in facilitating those inter-regime transitions, alongside many other factors. Each type of transition involves instability in worldviews, lifeways, and social forms, so a transitional period can feel profoundly unsettling to individuals and may be highly disruptive for groups of individuals—particularly those with something large at stake in preserving the status quo. In other words, we intend to model the dynamics within a population that alter the conditions under which people within populations transition from one set of civilization-forming worldviews and lifeways to another.

We approach this as scholars of religion who know something about the way social realities are constituted by networked minds operating within material contexts, including the complex interactions across levels of emergent complexity. Thus, we cannot overemphasize that this involves multidirectional causation and nonreductive system elements: each fundamental component of the complex system—minds, networks, cultures, material conditions—is irreducibly critical for understanding the dynamics of civilizational change.

We turn now to an overview of some of the main classes of theories that bear on the mechanisms and conditions for these transitions.

What Drives Civilizational Transformation?

Laborers in the vineyards of cognitive science, moral psychology, evolutionary anthropology, and historical sociology have plucked wondrous clusters of insights into the emergence and transformation of human civilizations. In the process, they have taught us a great deal about the nature and functions of religion at the individual (cognitive, emotional) and social (cultural, economic) levels. Nevertheless, our method of blending varieties of fruit differs slightly from most traditional vintages. In the following chapters we argue and provide computational demonstrations for the claim that *shifts in religious worldviews and lifeways are one of several necessary-but-not-sufficient conditions for the transformation of civilizational form*, along with energy capture, technologies of war, cultural-political imaginaries, and other factors.

This proposition implies two corrections to the current main lines of scholarly argument about transformations of civilizational form.

First, religion does not merely ride on the coattails of calories, weapons, and political power, as many experts assume; religious change itself has been a critical causal condition for changes in civilizational form. For students of religious worldviews and lifeways, this is a vitally important and unsurprising addition. For much of the literature in other fields on civilizational change, however, religion is not necessary and certainly not sufficient for civilizational change. So, there is quite some work to be done to make the case that religious worldviews and lifeways really are the potent necessary conditions we claim, making possible transformations in civilizational form that guns, germs, and steel could not have achieved by themselves.

The key insight here is that religion is peculiarly capable of generating both social glue and disruptive energy. The bio-cultural study of religion, by uniting the sciences of cognition and the sciences of culture, has demonstrated that religion links individual motivation with large-scale social effects in an extremely efficient way. For example, believing that an invisible moral judge with unlimited power to reward or punish is watching your every move is powerful motivation to behave in prescribed ways and effectively solidifies trust with strangers who appear to believe and behave similarly. This establishes a direct connection from personal structures of motivation to emergent socioeconomic effects, all facilitated by religious worldviews and lifeways. Moreover, such motivational structures are robust, powered by a degree of personal commitment that is difficult to generate in other domains of life.

The religion-afforded linkages between personal motivation and emergent socioeconomic behavior need to be incorporated into scholarly analyses of the dynamics of civilizational change. We believe the importance of these linkages has been generally underestimated in much of the extant literature. We aim to make the needed correction.

A second correction to the main lines of debate in the field that is implied in the central hypothesis of this book emerges out of our observation that many theories of civilizational change champion one or another necessary condition, treating that condition also as sufficient, thereby provoking needless conflict over what drives such processes of transformation. It is not surprising that claims about the drivers of civilizational transformation are diverse and shaped by disciplinary context. But we find it more credible that the various identified drivers of civilizational change are all individually necessary conditions and that no one condition is sufficient by itself to trigger a transformation in civilizational form. In effect, by including religious worldviews and lifeways in the story, we are expanding a list of necessary-but-not-sufficient conditions by one.

Demonstrating the complementarity of competing theories of civilizational transformation is a nontrivial undertaking. Our approach has two aspects. On the one hand, computer modeling invites us to make explicit relevant interconnections among competing theories about drivers of civilizational change. Even before we write any code, therefore, we endeavor to harmonize multiple competing theories about drivers of change. But merely narrating a possible interdisciplinary synthesis is not enough; computational models also require clear algorithms that determine every postulated theoretical integration, enabling concrete arguments about the hypothesized causal interactions. Thus, on the other hand, we integrate existing classes of theories into causal architectures that simulate these transitions in artificial societies. If we can reconstruct *in silico* the central dynamics of the revolutionary transitions in the Neolithic, the Axial Age, and Modernity, then we will have supplied one important kind of support for the causal architecture of those models, which expresses the integration of multiple drivers of change.

The payoff of this approach goes well beyond demonstrating the possibility of a theoretical synthesis of large tracts of competing classes of theories; we also generate new insights into the episodes of civilizational transformation that we examine. And we provide a new way of thinking about the revolution in human history that is already underway: the shift toward a post-supernaturalist world—provided our species survives the transitional upheavals.

For analytic and heuristic purposes, we identify three broad (and partially overlapping) classes of theories of civilizational change:

- ideological-political theories
- material-social theories
- cognitive-coalitional theories

Unfortunately, most theorizing involves a primary focus on one of these and all too often a partial (or total) dismissal of insights from the other two. This is how what we see as needless and actually misleading conflict arises. The computational simulation methodology invites and enables us to integrate the most reasonable and compelling parts of these classes of theories into a single causal architecture, facilitating testing to see whether the hypothesized theoretical integrations can actually simulate the transformation of civilizational forms.

The next three sections introduce and illustrate these three classes of theory. Each attempts to trace the causal factors at work in the transformation of civilizational forms. We believe we need not, and ought not, choose between them, but instead should forge a synthesis of the best insights of each.

Ideological-Political Theories

We call the first sort of theory in our typology "ideological-political" because it emphasizes the role of reflective thought in orienting new political visions of the organization of civilization. This type of theory is most often championed by scholars from disciplines such as sociology, history, and political science. Ideological-political theories contend that ideas are a primary driver of the transformation of civilization, ideas held initially by leaders or political elites before catching on more broadly and spreading throughout a population.

One of the strengths of this type of theory is that it captures the role of ideas, political and personal, in the transformation of civilizations. Given our interest in world *views*, we definitely want to include insights from this type of theory in our analysis. One of the weaknesses of this approach is its neglect of the biological and cultural evolution of humanity prior to the Bronze Age, which is when most of its theorists begin their narratives in earnest, typically with only vague references to what preceded it.

If we were to look for a philosophical inspiration or forebear for such theories, Georg Wilhelm Friedrich Hegel would be an obvious choice. Of course, debates about civilizational forms and the role of ideas and politics go back (in the West) at least to the ancient Greeks (e.g., Plato's *Republic*) and Romans (e.g., Cicero's *De Republica*). But Hegel provides a good launching point because he is well-known for claiming that the transformation of civilizations or cultures follows a dialectical path expressing the logical meaning of key ideas. This link between concrete historical events and the logical structure of ideas is striking, and for Hegel the entire historical process is the self-actualization of Spirit (or

"Geist," sometimes translated as Mind). The following excerpt allows us to see Hegel's reasoning about this. No contemporary reader will fail to see the deeply problematic aspects of this way of reasoning, but this passage still affords a glimpse into Hegel's hypothesis about the dialectical linkages between the conceptual structure of ideas and historical events.

> [Universal History] is the exhibition of Spirit in the process of working out the knowledge of that which it is potentially... The Orientals have not attained the knowledge of that Spirit—Man *as such* is free; and because they do not know this, they are not free. They only know that *one is free* ... The consciousness of Freedom first arose among the Greeks, and therefore they were free; but they, and the Romans likewise know only that *some* are free—not man as such ... The German nations, under the influence of Christianity, were the first to attain the consciousness, that man, as man, is free: that is the *freedom* of Spirit which constitutes its essence. (Hegel, 1894, pp. 18–19; emphases in the original)

For Hegel, then, the transformation of civilizational forms is driven by (and toward) the self-realization of "Spirit." For our purposes, the main point is not what he meant by "Spirit" or the obvious ethnocentric and masculinist bias, but that Hegel represents a philosophy of history that downplays the material and ignores the role of human evolution (Hegel had the excuse of living before Darwin; many of his followers do not).

As we will see in more detail in our chapter on the Axial Age, the twentieth-century scholar Karl Jaspers was certainly close to Hegel in this sense. He argued that the origin and goal of history is "the One of transcendence ... thus this deepest unity is elevated to an invisible religion, to the realm of spirits, the secret realm of the manifestation of Being in the concord of souls" (1953, p. 265). This approach is ruthlessly resisted and even mocked by proponents of the other two types, especially those who prefer material-social theories, but despite its idealism it still has much to offer. And, indeed, most of those who followed in the wake of Jaspers were far more circumspect and less theological in their analyses. A good example is S. N. Eisenstadt, who explores not only the Axial Age but also Modernity in his "multiple modernities." He does emphasize the role of ideological premises, broadly speaking, but avoids linear development or Western-centric problems (Eisenstadt, 2002).

The examples further on are certainly not Hegelian in a technical sense, but they do emphasize the role of ideas in altering political fields and human social life. In each case, they are aware of and sometimes even emphasize Darwin, and equally importantly, they attempt not to fall into the culturally self-aggrandizing triumphalism of the Germanic present found in Hegel.

One example of a theorist who fits primarily into this category is sociologist Charles Taylor. Although he has developed his view in earlier works, also focusing on sense of self in the modern world (Taylor, 1992), for our purposes it is best to focus on his magnum opus *A Secular Age* (Taylor, 2007), which has been more influential on the topics we are discussing. The main question he sets out to answer in that book is "Why was it virtually impossible not to believe in God in, say, 1500 in our Western society, while in 2000 many of us find this not only easy, but even inescapable" (p. 25). His answer has to do with "an acceptable form of exclusive humanism" that "had to be imagined" in order to replace the enchanted view of the universe in which the cosmos testified to divine purpose and God was implicated in the fabric of society. Ancient and medieval social imaginaries filled with supernatural agents were slowly, through phases, replaced by a modern social imaginary in which the "buffered self" can thrive in a "secular age."

Taylor is clearly aware that some critics (from what we call here the material-social types of theories) will accuse him of idealism, so he devotes an entire chapter to ward off the objection. He acknowledges that major changes of this sort will always involve "materialist" explanations but challenges the idea that this excludes the role of ideas. He also makes clear that he will argue for a causal claim that makes sense of the way in which "the new idea of moral order [in modernity] came to acquire the strength which eventually allows it to shape the social imaginaries of modernity" (p. 214). The bulk of the book tells this story. What happened between 1500 and 2000?

> The intervening centuries have seen the dissipation of the enchanted cosmos (some elements of belief in enchantment remain, but they don't form a system, and are held by individuals here and there, rather than being socially shared). Then there came the introduction, within the context of the modern moral order, of a viable alternative to belief, of forms of exclusive humanism, in turn followed by a multiplication of both believing and unbelieving positions ... This all generated the challenge, undermining, and dissolution of the early social forms which embedded God's presence in social space. (p. 531)

The details of Taylor's story are not important for our purposes, but it is important to note that his focus is on the effect of ideas (especially about transcendence and immanence) on political engagement through the social imaginary.

We noted earlier the danger, following Hegel, of being too idealistic and Western focused. Some appreciative critics of Taylor worry that he is guilty of this (Calhoun et al., 2011; Warner et al., 2013). At any rate, Taylor himself seems to betray a certain "idealism" when he argues at the end of his magnum opus that "the Radical Orthodox are right that we need some Plato-type understanding of what we are made for," and finally makes explicit his own (very Hegel-like) assumption that "all people have a sense of fullness" and that "our sense of fullness is a reflection of transcendent reality (which for me is the God of Abraham)" (Taylor 2007, pp. 769, 775).

Another more recent example of what we are calling an "ideological-political" theorist is Yuval Noah Harari, who has published several best sellers dealing with broad developments in human evolution and culture (Harari, 2016, 2018). For our purposes, the most relevant is his first and most influential book, *Sapiens: A Brief History of Humankind* (Harari, 2015). While Taylor was primarily interested in the shift of civilizational form during Modernity, Harari is interested in the long evolutionary history of humanity and engages far more disciplines. So he has chapters dealing with what he calls the Cognitive Revolution and Agricultural Revolution, which fit into the time period we simulate in our computational model of the Neolithic shift in civilizational form in Chapter 4. Harari's key question is what was the Sapiens' secret of success? He argues that the most likely answer "is the very thing that makes the debate possible: *Homo sapiens* conquered the world thanks above all to its unique language" (p. 21).

Like Taylor, Harari's methodological-theoretical nemeses are in the "material-social" camp. Scientists, he notes, "usually seek to attribute historical developments to cold economic and demographic factors. It sits better with their rational and mathematical models." However, Hariri insists that, at least in the case of modern history, "scholars cannot avoid taking into account non-material factors such as ideology and culture" (p. 100). Even in ancient history it is sometimes possible to find clues to the role of such factors. He points to the complex monumental structures of Gobekli Tepe (around 9500 BCE) and argues that "only a sophisticated religious or ideological system could sustain such efforts" (p. 101). Hariri emphasizes the way in which humans created "imagined orders" that made cooperation possible beyond what would be expected by what we are calling "cognitive-coalitional" theories alone. Myths, he insists, are stronger than most traditional historians and sociologists have imagined.

Harari spends a significant amount of space in the book dealing with the period often called the "Axial Age," which is connected to the emergence of large-scale religions, and the slow rise of science during Modernity, both of which are understood in large part as ideas that drive political behaviors. He defines religion as "a system of human norms and values that is founded on a belief in a superhuman order" (p. 234) and traces how Axial Age religions impacted the various regions in which they emerged and thrived. This applies to science as well. "One of the things that has made it possible for modern social orders to hold together is the spread of an almost religious belief in technology and in the methods of scientific research, which have replaced to some extent the belief in absolute truths" (p. 283). Why has the West thrived more than other cultures? It is not because those other cultures did not have inventions such as steam engines, which (as he points out) they could have copied or bought. Rather what they lacked was "the values, myths, judicial apparatus and sociopolitical structures that took centuries to form and mature in the West and which could not be copied and internalized rapidly" (p. 314). Hariri clearly has proponents of material-social theories in mind when he insists that "we have to take into account the ideological, political and economic forces that shaped physics, biology and sociology, pushing them in certain directions while neglecting others. Two forces in particular deserve our attention: imperialism and capitalism. The *feedback loop* between science, empire and capital has arguably been history's chief engine for the past 500 years" (p. 306, emphasis added).

Our final example here is an even more recent volume by Graeber and Wengrow titled *The Dawn of Everything: A New History of Humanity* (Graeber & Wengrow, 2021). Their provocative, and somewhat overstated, overall claim is that the traditional view of civilizational development as following relatively discrete stages (e.g., from tribes to clans to states) is incorrect and that from the dawn of humanity members of our species have been imaginative, intelligent creatures playing with new concepts and ways of organizing social life. "Living in unbounded, eternal, largely imaginary groups is effectively what humans had been doing all along" (p. 282). "As we've been showing throughout this book, in all parts of the world small communities formed civilizations in that true sense of extended moral communities" (p. 433). Cities and all social forms are "in our heads," and this capacity for political imagination is the main driver of social and cultural transformation.

These authors illustrate the emphasis of what we are calling the ideological-political type of theorist when dealing with fundamental questions about the nature and evolution of human civilizational forms. For them, the "ultimate question of human history is not our equal access to *material* resources (land, calories, means of production), though these things are obviously important, but our equal capacity to contribute to *decisions* about how to live together" (p. 8, emphasis added). Graeber and Wengrow argue that we humans are projects of collective self-creation. Scholars often ask "what ultimately determines the shape a society takes: *economic* factors, *organizational* imperatives or cultural meanings and *ideas*?" They follow the lead of the anthropologist Mauss in suggesting a fourth option, asking rhetorically: "Are societies in effect *self-determining*, building and reproducing themselves primarily with reference to each other?" (pp. 183–4, emphasis added).

The key point for Graeber and Wengrow is that human groups emphasize cultural meanings and ideas with the aim of protecting and enhancing the self-determining or self-creative role of self-conscious political ideological debates. "The process by which cultures define themselves against one another is always, at root, political, since it involves *self-conscious arguments* about the proper way to live" (p. 203, emphasis added). They also offer another somewhat novel and controversial claim: that the shift we call the Enlightenment, Modernity, and so on, was shaped in large part by the ideological critique of European culture by indigenous North American philosophical thinkers. In particular, they credit Kandiaronk, through debate with Westerners, with critiquing the unequal and unfree social structures of Europe, challenging them with the superiority of his own culture's self-conscious ideals of equality and freedom. They even argue that Rousseau's key work on the idea of a "social contract" was a response to this indigenous critique. "Indigenous North American ideas—from the advocacy of individual liberties to skepticism of revealed religion—certainly had an impact on the European Enlightenment" (p. 473).

In the view of Graeber and Wengrow, therefore, it was *political self-consciousness* that has led humans to play with various forms of civilization since the dawn of humanity. Our models allow for and incorporate this nuance. Findings from the models also suggest that today we have lost this playfulness and political self-consciousness, so that many believe we are stuck in one mode of civilizational form and don't have the capacity to invent new ones. This is relevant for our final chapter. At this stage of the journey, however, the next step is to outline the other two classes of theories that aim to identify the main drivers of the transformation of civilizational form.

Material-Social Theories

Proponents of what we are calling material-social theories insist that thinkers of the type briefly reviewed in the last subsection put the ideological cart before the materialist horse. They will have none of this idealism. They prefer *materialist* explanations of the development of more complex *social* forms, emphasizing factors such as energy capture, war-making capacity, information technology, and city size. The most basic driver of cultural change, they claim, was energy capture, which led to new forms of social organization, which fueled more energy capture, and so on. This type of theory has been more than popular; it has been dominant for at least the past half century. Although many theorists in this camp note the roles of the natural environment, geography, earthquakes, climate change, water flow, warfare technologies, and subsistence technologies, and so on, they tend to stress the role of economics and modes of organizing material resources.

Earlier we suggested that Hegel can be seen as an important philosophical precursor for ideological-political theorists. Here we can suggest a similar role for Karl Marx, who famously claimed to "turn Hegel on his head," and has been inspirational for many material-social theorists. Marx maintained the notion of an overarching world-history dialectic, but it was dialectical *materialism* (not *idealism*). In other words, material and socioeconomic factors are the dominant drivers of the transformation of civilizational form in world history. The point here is not the failure of Marx's predictions about the political revolution of the proletariat, but rather the way he theorized that material-social forces are the drivers of social change. Marx's perspective continues to shape many noted theorists today. These theorists are not necessarily Marx-ist in the technical sense, but they share his philosophical emphasis on the importance of the material over the ideational.

Advocates of "world-systems" theory illustrate this type. Chase-Dunn and Lerro, the authors of *Social Change: Globalization from the Stone Age to the Present*, for example, refer to their preferred approach as "institutional materialism," which they explicitly argue involves a synthetic combination of what they call "culturalist" and "materialist" theories of social change. These are the only options they consider, not engaging the cognitive-coalitional theories we discuss later. For them, "the master variables" driving social change "can be broadly categorized as either cultural or material" (Chase-Dunn & Lerro, 2014, p. 12). Like proponents of the first type of theory we mentioned earlier, they are quite aware of the opposing theoretical approach and do not deny it has some validity. They acknowledge and even attempt to include in their approach "culturalist" intuitions about the role of values, ideas, and beliefs, but it is clear that their view is predominantly "materialist." Human sociocultural evolution is "an adaptive response to demographic, ecological, and economic forces in which people devise institutional inventions to solve emergent problems and to overcome constraints" (p. 13).

Elsewhere, in *From Earth Spirits to Sky Gods*, Lerro makes it far more explicit that "material conditions" enable the rise of (ideological) cultural and religious traditions. Embracing a materialist perspective, he sees his task as showing "how a change in thinking processes in history is dependent on *material social factors*" (Lerro, 2000, p. 145, emphasis added). In fact, in a chapter titled "Matter over Mind," he explains that his approach to understanding the shift builds on Vygotsky's "dialectical materialist" theory of the human mind, which "finds its origin, function, and future destiny in the social and historical relations of labor" (p. 181). Here we can see the influence, at least indirectly, of Marx. For our purposes here, however, the key point is that, for Lerro, the question of whether ideological (religious) change is a cause or consequence of material-social evolution is to be answered clearly on the side of consequence. All forms of sacred cultural systems "rather than leading or causing social evolution, are instead improvised adaptation strategies which legitimize *already existing* changes in material culture" (p. 57, emphasis added).

Many scholars of this type emphasize the role of demographics, subsistence, and warfare technologies in driving civilizational transformation (Johnson & Earle, 2000; Scheidel, 2017). This can be illustrated clearly in the work of historian Peter Turchin. Like most theorists of this type, Turchin emphasizes quantitative methods. He argues that historical sociology must develop such approaches because "the history of science is emphatic: a discipline usually matures only after it has developed mathematical theory" (Turchin, 2018, p. 1). He calls his own approach a "demographic-structural" theory, whose hypotheses he has tested on empirical data from various time periods (Turchin & Nefedov, 2009; Turchin, 2016). Social change can mainly be explained by the historical dynamics in feedback loops between demographic shifts (especially rising populations) and structural shifts in factors related to, for example, elite dynamics, economics, and instability. Warfare plays a key, and admittedly surprising, role.

As we will see in more detail in Chapter 5 on the Axial Age, Turchin proposes that war-making technology and capacity is the main driver of the changes in the social environment during that period (Turchin, 2015, p. 193). "Warfare is the chief selective force for increased society size" (2010, p. 13). Larger societies have a better chance of successful defense (or predation) because they can mobilize greater resources to support bigger armies. Forces as diverse as commerce, feminization, cosmopolitanism, and the escalation of reason "*do indeed* share a single cause. The key process in the decline of violence has been the increase in the scale of human cooperation." And what drives that increase? Paradoxically, "It was violence—societies making war on each other—that drove the evolution of ultrasociality, and it was ultrasociality that ultimately made violence decline" (2015, p. 219, emphasis in the original; see also Turchin, 2007).

The influential work of Jared Diamond also fits well into what we are calling the material-social type of theory. As he puts it in the 2003 afterword to his bestselling *Guns, Germs, and Steel*:

> My main conclusion was that societies developed differently on different continents because of differences in continental environments, not in human biology. Advanced technology, centralized political organization, and other features of complex societies could emerge only in dense sedentary populations capable of accumulating food surpluses ... The most valuable domesticable wild species were concentrated in only nine small areas of the globe, which thus became the earliest homelands of agriculture. The original inhabitants of those homelands thereby gained a head start toward developing guns, germs, and steel. The languages and genes of those homeland inhabitants, as well as their livestock, crops, technologies, and writing systems, became dominant in the ancient and modern world. (Diamond, 2003, p. 426)

Like Lerro and Turchin, Diamond sees material conditions as the most important, though certainly not the only, factors shaping the emergence of more complex societies. Like them, he recognizes factors such as warfare and subsistence technology, along with centralized organization, as drivers in this process. It is not that smaller groups decide to cooperate through a contract. Rather, amalgamation into larger groups occurs in one of two ways: "by merger under threat of external force, or by actual conquest" (p. 289).

Diamond formulates the main question we are exploring in this chapter as follows: "How did small, noncentralized, kin-based societies evolve into large, centralized societies in which most members are not closely related to each other? Having reviewed the stages in this transformation from bands to states, we now ask *what impelled societies thus to transform themselves?*" (p. 282, emphasis added). For him, the answer lies in the capture and manipulation of energy. Food production and growing human populations mutually reinforce one another, sparking societal competition that yields more complex organizational forms. "Thus, food production, and competition and diffusion between societies, led as ultimate causes, via chains of causation that differed in detail but that all involved large dense populations and sedentary living, to the proximate agents of conquest: germs, writing, technology, and centralized political organization" (p. 292).

As he puts it in his more recent *The World Until Yesterday: What Can We Learn from Traditional Societies?*, the explanation for differences in types of societies "depends on environmental differences. Increases in political centralization and social stratification were driven by increases in human population densities, driven in turn by the rise and intensification of food production (agriculture and herding)" (Diamond, 2013, p. 19). He explicitly rejects Rousseau's social contract theory and the hydraulic theory of states, in part because these do not explain what drove the progression from bands to tribes to chiefdoms prior to large-scale irrigation and states. His own answer starts with the fact that

> the size of the regional population is the strongest single predictor of social complexity ... there is a finer trend, within each of those categories [bands, tribes, chiefdoms, states] between populations and societal complexity ... These correlations suggest strongly that regional population size or population density or population pressure has *something* to do with the formation of complex societies. But the correlations do not tell us precisely how population variables function in a chain of cause and effect whose outcome is a complex society. (p. 284)

The key causal factor, for Diamond, is the diverse ways in which populations, in various geographic reasons, grow in density and manage food production.

Our final example of a theorist in the material-social category is Ian Morris, who also emphasizes the role of energy capture in the shift toward more complex civilizational forms. In *The Measure of Civilization: How Social Development Decides the Fate of Nations*, Morris explicitly comes down "strongly on the materialist side" in the debate over the relative importance of material and cultural forces in shaping history. Morris proposes that shifts toward "high end states" were made possible by increases in energy capture, mediated through increases in war-making capacity, information technology, and complexity of social organization. Ideological developments, such as those we will explore in more detail related to the Axial Age, are not the secret ingredient driving social change. Its influence only came later, when the great states learned to "tame it, making it work for them" (2011, p. 262).

For Morris, the ideological peculiarities that emerged in the middle of the first millennium BCE were consequences, not causes: "Axial thought was just one of the things that happened when people created high-end states, and disenchanted the world" (Morris, 2011, p. 263). Morris suggests that the same argument applies to Modernity: while there may be significant cultural or geographical differences among contemporary nation-states, "there is just one path to modernity" and that involves "an explosion in energy capture, provided by an industrial revolution tapping into the power of fossil fuels, followed by the application of energy to new walks of life" (258).

This suggests that the real motor behind the changes we see in civilizational forms such as the Axial Age "was the same as it had been since the end of the last Ice Age. Lazy, greedy, and frightened people found easier, more profitable, and safer ways to do things, in the process building stronger states, trading farther afield, and settling in greater cities" (263). Morris makes even stronger claims in *Foragers, Farmers and Fossil Fuels*, where he argues that "energy capture *determines* values" and that "culture, religion, and moral philosophy play only rather *small causal roles* in the story of human values" (Morris et al. 2015, pp. 5, 10, emphases added). He posits that the relation between energy capture and human ideas about values "is in fact causal" and that causality is in fact directional: "Changes in energy capture drive changes in human values" (2015, p. 223).

In our review of these first two classes of theory, we have seen that there are many differences between scholars within each type and that, in general, they are at least open to the other type of theory having something to contribute, although they clearly see the superior explanatory power lying in their own approach. In later sections and chapters, we will note examples of additional crossover and critique between and among ideological-political and material-social theorists. Our next step, however, is to outline a third class of theories, which can also be brought into dialogue with the others and, in fact, integrated into computational causal architectures for experimenting with their varying claims.

Cognitive-Coalitional Theories

This final type of theory that addresses transformations of civilizational form we refer to as "cognitive-coalitional." Proponents of the third type of theory often operate within academic disciplines such as cognitive science, psychology, and anthropology. Cognitive-coalitional theories interpret arrangements of human groups, large or small, as local equilibria inside a multidimensional fitness landscape, within which stability is achieved through a strong fit between cognitive capacities and coalitional requirements. Destabilization of an equilibrium zone for any reason—new forms of energy capture, an aspirational vision of a revolutionary kind of politics, a climate catastrophe, or the drift into new regimes of the fitness landscape through exploring new potentialities for human minds and groups—leads to migration through the landscape and restabilization around a new energy-efficient equilibrium better suited to the new contextual constraints. The restabilization process typically involves activating novel aspects of our cognitive abilities while deemphasizing others and discovering new ways of gluing societies together.

The all-important concept here is the fitness landscape, which contains the secrets of both the human past and the human future. It encompasses all possible matches between minds and cultures, including forms of fit that heavily rely on architectures of learning that make possible forms of sociality that are unstable without intensive brain training. For example, some civilizational forms critically depend on literacy for exchanging information, so human minds need to be bent toward learning to read and write, and cultures to the associated forms of brain training. Human brains have that potential, but it has not always been activated in our species. When it is activated, new possibilities for civilizational form are realized. All of this is comprehended in the fitness landscape, which is only ever partially understood because of the monumental complexity of evolutionarily stabilized human minds, the vastness of the space of possible cultural forms, and the manifold ways in which fit between the two can be achieved. In the case of the cognitive-coalitional family of theories, therefore, the focus is less on the ideological or material conditions and more on the emergence of new modes of cultural cohesion made possible by more or less close fits with human cognitive capacities, which can be selectively enhanced or suppressed.

If Hegel and Marx are touch points for the first two types of theory, we can single out Charles Darwin as a key figure in the emergence and spread of the third type of theory. Darwin does not deal in any detail with what has come to be called cultural evolution, though some of his followers famously did so (e.g., social Darwinism); he focused instead on biological evolution. Nevertheless, he offers a touchstone for "bio-cultural" approaches to studying changes in societies in general, including understanding tensions reflective of mind-culture misfits, which tend toward destabilizing social equilibria and provoke migration in the direction of newly adequate forms of social stability.

In a way that the other two families of theories do not, the cognitive-coalitional family of theories is particularly useful for making sense of the role of religion in social bonding. This is because religion is a classic example of both a close fit between the reflective operations of evolutionarily stabilized human minds (e.g., the ease with which we embrace the belief that we are watched by morally concerned invisible beings with power over us) and the production of social glue sufficient to support some forms of social organization (e.g., the ease with which we embrace the identification of "safe" in-group members and "unsafe" out-group members based on whether they believe as we do about invisible moral watchers, and thus earn low-energy default judgments of trust). Religion can also be a major factor in the destabilizing of civilizational forms by giving cosmic significance to the moral critique of an existing sociopolitical order while inspiring highly motivated people in large numbers to strain for a better form of social organization.

One ongoing debate within this camp is between those who emphasize the role of cognition (e.g., biologically based biases or tendencies in cognition) and those who emphasize the role of culture or coalition (e.g., naturally arising problems and solutions within human groups). Of course, all theorists in this family agree that both matter—hence "bio-cultural"—but emphases can still persist. For example, there has been a vibrant debate about the role of belief in "big gods" or "morally interested" supernatural agents in driving civilizational transformation and complexity. One line of debate holds that human minds are biased in the direction of believing in morally interested invisible beings, which generates ever-stronger social glue through widening circles of trust, thereby sparking larger and larger civilizations (e.g., Norenzayan, 2013). An opposed line of debate is that the formation of larger and larger agglomerations of human beings in connected socioeconomic systems drove people to tell stories about big gods in an attempt to stabilize their civilizational orders (e.g., Turchin et al., 2023). As an intra-family debate, the question is one of emphasis rather than decisive causal priority, and the adjudication of this intriguing bio-cultural tussle depends on careful parsing of historical data. A third view (ours) is that both dynamics are causally relevant and it is impossible to trigger one without triggering the other in a reinforcing cycle that ratchets up both big-god beliefs and large-scale civilizations.

Another significant debate relates to the way features of human life evolve and is triggered by significant uncertainty about the far past of our species. On the one hand, aspects of cultural complexity may be evolutionary byproducts of more basic adaptations, byproducts that may or may not become secondarily adaptive in novel cultural contexts. For example, Terrence Deacon sees language as a byproduct of changes in vocal-tract physiology and in the capacity for symbolic thinking, with stunning secondarily adaptive force (Deacon, 1997). On the other hand, aspects of cultural complexity may be interpreted as direct adaptations selected for their fitness in the era of evolutionary adaptation. For example, Michael Tomasello sees the capacity to cooperate as directly selected (Tomasello, 2009, 2010). These are relatively noncontroversial examples but not everything is so straightforward. There are strong advocates on both sides, with some seeing religion as an evolutionary byproduct that can be both adaptive and maladaptive depending on social context (Atran, 2002; Boyer, 2002) and others seeing it as directly selected for its function in promoting cooperation (Bulbulia, 2004; Sosis & Alcorta, 2004). It is difficult to resolve such debates, given the murkiness of the deep evolutionary past of our species, but there is a rough consensus: most researchers regard most central elements of religious worldviews and lifeways as evolutionary byproducts and only a few elements as directly adapted. For example, our interest in invisible beings and minimally counterintuitive stories about them are widely regarded as side effects of more basic cognitive capacities and biases, whereas the ability of religious practices to promote altered states with healing potential is often interpreted as directly adapted.

One of the important early proponents of the cognitive-coalitional approach was Merlin Donald, whose *Origins of the Modern Mind* (1993) is important for thinking about the transformation of civilizational forms. Donald takes us much farther back in history than is common in either the ideological-political or the material-social families of theories—all the way back to early hominid evolution. He recognizes that developments in cognition and culture go together. Cognitive capacities influence the kinds of "culture" produced by all animals, and at least for humans it goes the other way, too: different forms of human culture have effects on individual cognition through activating potentialities that may otherwise have remained latent. Against that background, Donald identifies three major evolutionary shifts by which the structure of the primate mind "was gradually surrounded by new representational systems and absorbed into a larger cognitive apparatus" (p. 4).

The first major shift was the movement from the kind of culture produced by apes and australopithecines to that of *Homo erectus*. The former produced what he calls "episodic" culture, shaped by a representational strategy involving social behaviors that are immediate and short-term responses to changes in the environment. In *Homo erectus*, however, there emerged the ability to mime (or reenact) events, which Donald takes to be the most basic level of human representation. Here representational acts are intentional but nonlinguistic. This supported what he calls "mimetic" culture, which allowed for new forms of social control, and practical effects such as tool making, coordinated seasonal hunting, and group mimetic acts (primitive ritual).

The second major transition was from *erectus* to *Homo sapiens*, whereby the latter developed the cognitive capacity to construct and decode narrative and symbols, which enabled the emergence of what Donald calls "mythic" culture. He links language to mythic invention and to the construction of conceptual models of the universe and the place of humans within it. "Mythic culture tended rapidly toward the integration of knowledge. The scattered, concrete repertoire of mimetic culture came under the governance of integrative myth" (p. 267).

The third and more recent transition involved the emergence of new modes of visual symbolism, external memory, and theoretic thought, which had a major effect on cognitive architecture and the structure of the human mind. Given the main cognitive innovations at work, Donald calls this new form of culture "theoretic." Theoretic cultures organize themselves through the management of symbols, from mathematics to a host of specialized technical languages, extending our cognitive reach with technology wherever we can. If Donald were to revisit his thinking on this question, he might regard the era of generative AI as so revolutionary as to demand its own designation, with newly distinctive socioeconomic forms of organization. However that goes, on his view, we are not standing still.

Neither have we left behind earlier representational strategies, according to Donald. Modern human minds are hybridizations, highly plastic combinations of episodic, mimetic, mythic, and theoretic elements that are the traces of increasing complexity within hominid evolution, carried in the minds of every human being. For our purposes, the key point here is that Donald's understanding of the role of the reciprocal reinforcement of cognitive changes and cultural coalitional strategies illustrates the driving intuition of scholars who fit into this category of theorizing about civilizational transformation.

Another topic that commonly functions as an integrative concept within the cognitive-coalitional class of theories is "ritual." In his "ritual modes" theory, Harvey Whitehouse sets out two modes of ritual, each of which has a distinctive relation to cognitive memory functions, though they cannot be cleanly separated from one another (Whitehouse, 2004). "Imagistic" rituals are high arousal and low frequency and facilitate the initiation of individuals into relatively egalitarian small-scale societies. These rituals primarily utilize episodic or flashbulb memory, and the ritual meaning is internally generated through the intense experiences that they provoke. Moreover, imagistic rituals lead to relatively potent forms of social cohesion, tend to be exclusive, and cooccur with noncentralized sociopolitical structures.

"Doctrinal" rituals, by contrast, are low arousal and high frequency. They are characteristic of larger-scale societies and require more complex hierarchies to maintain orthodoxy of belief and practice. These types of ritual primarily utilize semantic schemas and implicit scripts in memory, and ritual meaning must be taught and acquired. They also tend to produce more diffuse forms of social cohesion, be more inclusive, and have centralized structures. Where imagistic rituals create intense bonds in local communities, doctrinal rituals foster identification with larger and more extended social groups. Whitehouse illustrates a common approach within the bio-cultural study of religion that focuses on the dynamic interrelation between cognitive capacities and coalitional structures as a way of understanding the driving forces of transformations of civilizational form. As we will see further on, this theory has been applied to the Neolithic transition and Çatalhöyük in particular, which provides a point of contact with our model of that transition in Chapter 4.

The central point here is that those who primarily defend what we are calling cognitive-coalitional theories of civilizational transformation, contrary to the first two types of theorist, centralize the concept of a fitness landscape in the interpretation of crucial periods of transition in the organizational form of human cultures. The mind-culture fit is all-important in determining what counts as a stabile equilibrium and what functions as sufficiently potent disruption to drive the mind-culture system out of one equilibrium state in search of another. Cognitive-coalitional theories tend to be wide open to proposals from the ideological-political and material-social families of theories for what might be sufficiently disruptive to provoke destabilization of an equilibrium state but they also add distinctive drivers of their own. These are the cultural-evolutionary equivalent of genetic drift in biological evolution, in which exploration of the fitness landscape opens up new possibilities for human minds and human societies. These migrations through the fitness landscape may create deeper fits, strengthening existing social forms. But they can also create misfits that provoke the need for disruption, transformation, and reconsolidation around newly evident stable equilibria.

An example of drivers of transformation distinctive to the cognitive-coalitional family of theories—one that is vital for understanding the near future of our civilizations—is the way we human beings discovered and explored our ability to train ourselves out of reliance on cognitive defaults related to belief in supernatural agents and forces. We always had this capability to resist the associated cognitive biases, but very few human beings activated it for want of supportive social conditions and for fear of dissolving the social glue that seemed necessary for socioeconomic stability. But Modernity created supportive social conditions, and now this variety of cultural-evolutionary drift is taking off wherever those conditions exist, driving us toward forms of sociopolitical organization that are compatible with people who desire to contest their built-in cognitive tendencies to embrace supernatural beings, forces, explanations, and authorities. This type of driver is adequately comprehended in neither the ideological-political nor the material-social families of theories because it critically depends on concepts such as the bio-cultural fitness landscape furnished by the cognitive-coalitional family of theories.

Can Theories of Civilizational Transformation Be Synthesized?

Most of the authors we have considered in the foregoing have crossed the boundaries between the three families of theories about drivers of transformations in civilizational form. This is due partly to the complex phenomena in question, which seem to demand grasping insights wherever they arise, and it is also partly due to the creative interdisciplinary instincts of the theorizers themselves. We appreciate those integrative instincts and want to take them further. *Not only is there no reason to choose between these classes of theories; any such choice damages the explanatory power of any theory that results.* Aspirational ideas matter. Material conditions matter. Fitness landscapes matter. Theoretical synthesis, therefore, is essential.

We are not the first to argue that these families of theories overlap, mutually implicate one another, and cry out for integration. Each of these theories has robust empirical support, so it is no surprise that advocates of one would be tempted by features of another. But some readers might object that theoretical synthesis is not possible even if it is desirable.

Let's address the issue of desirability first. While there are proponents of each approach who see their views as excluding others, there is a general temperament in the debates that is at least open to the possibility of synthesis to some extent. We'll see more examples in later chapters, but here we provide just a couple of examples of scholars in each camp to further illustrate this desirability of this kind of openness to theoretical integration. For the sake of brevity and simplicity, we'll use examples of authors who engage with the question of the drivers of civilizational transformation during the Axial Age.

Most scholars who favor *ideological-political* theories are not ignorant of the material and social conditions at work in the Axial Age (e.g., Eisenstadt, 1986).

Robert Bellah, who generally fits in this category, was clearly aware of some of the cognitive and coalitional factors that contribute to axiality; he borrowed heavily from Donald's conception of "theoretic culture" in his magnum opus on the evolution of religion through the Axial Age (Bellah, 2011). Another example of such openness is Seth Abrutyn who, though he emphasizes the role of priestly elites or "religious entrepreneurs" and strongly resists "materialist" interpretations of axiality, still ends up acknowledging that a "confluence" of various technological and economic forces, population growth, and social inequality contributed to the "theorized disjunction between the mundane and the transmundane, the 'age of criticism,' the strain towards historicity and agentiality, and all of the other ways Axial Age scholars characterize symbolic change during that time period" (Abrutyn, 2014, p. 124).

Advocates of *material-social* theories also typically recognize the relevance of other factors that played a role in the emergence of Axial civilizations. Ian Morris, for example, observes that there is something like a feedback loop in the dynamics of the Axial Age, acknowledging that rising energy capture is "itself an almost-inevitable *cultural adaptation* to changing environments and the growing stock of knowledge" (Morris et al. 2015, p. 170, emphasis added). A similar attitude is displayed by Stephen Sanderson, who clearly identifies the main causal mechanisms in the evolution of human civilizations as population demographics (especially larger groups), advances in subsistence and warfare technology, and new modes of economic exchange such as writing and record keeping. Although he insists that the "principal causal factors" driving the Axial Age transition were "material forces," Sanderson acknowledges that there is a sense in which Axial religions can be viewed as "bio-cultural" adaptations (2019, pp. 219–20). He emphasizes the primary role of demographic, technological, and economic factors in a "socioecological context" for determining which ideas catch on among large numbers of people; still, new religious ideas did have to emerge before they could spread in the Axial Age (2019, p. 201).

Most proponents of the *cognitive-coalitional* type of theory are also aware that the causal relations between key variables contributing to axiality sometimes appear to be reciprocal. For example, Norenzayan and colleagues stress the "causal processes that link the adoption of certain religious beliefs to group success," but also allow for the possibility of bidirectional influence in some historical cases (Norenzayan et al., 2016, pp. 14, 18). Many other theorists whose work relates to the cognitive-coalitional pathway are also quite comfortable with aspects of the material-social hypothesis. Based on an analysis of environmental bioclimatic data and global distribution of belief in moralizing high gods, some researchers suggest that "the emerging picture is neither one of pure cultural transmission nor of simple ecological determinism, but rather a *complex mixture of social, cultural, and environmental influences*" (Botero et al., 2014, pp. 16784–9, emphasis added). Does "materialist" intensification drive "sociopolitical" hierarchy, or vice versa? A phylogenetic study of 155 Austronesian-speaking societies provided "support for a reciprocal coevolutionary relationship between the two variables … highlighting the importance of social as well as material factors as drivers of cultural evolution" (Sheehan et al., 2018, p. 3628).

This cursory survey already indicates why researchers have found integration of the three families of theories *desirable*. But mere openness to theoretical synthesis, insofar as it exists in these transdisciplinary debates, does not establish that it is *possible*. Our argument for its possibility, and the explicit formalizations that enable testing of such theoretical integrations, will be presented in detail in the following chapters. Arguably much of our published work could most easily be slotted into the third type, cognitive-coalitional theories. Here, however, we want to emphasize our long-term commitment, more or less successful, to transdisciplinary theoretical synthesis. We have attempted for a long time to cross the boundaries and link to other types of theory, long before we developed the typology discussed here and long before we extensively utilized computational methodologies to address such issues. Our own approaches (together and individually) in other authored works have tried to incorporate multiple theories arcing across the three families we have discussed here (e.g., Wildman, 2009, 2011; Shults, 2010a, 2012).

Two of our goals in this book are to press for deeper integration of relevant theories about the transformation of civilizational form and to set the bar higher for what counts as adequate theoretical synthesis and integration. The computational methods outlined in the next chapter are critical for achieving both goals. On the one hand, computational simulation promotes deeper theoretical integration by explicitly modeling bidirectional causation and looping feedback and dampening mechanisms, which are precisely what is needed to express what theorists notice about the different kinds and levels of causal forces at play in episodes of civilizational transformation. On the other hand, computational modeling demands detailed expression of theory, including integration of multiple elements of theory, in a way that far exceeds in precision what can be accomplished in narrative integration alone. The models we present in Chapters 4 to 6 use computational methods to express a more radical, more formal, and more useful approach to theoretical integration.

A Heuristic Matrix for Theoretical Integration

Throughout our discussion in the following chapters of three major transitions of civilizational form, we will incorporate discussions of all three families of theories. At the same time, we will weave in a discussion of some of the philosophical assumptions and practices (worldviews and lifeways) that are involved in the transition under review. As explained in more detail in the next chapter, we operationalize transformations of civilizational form as inherently connected to and emerging out of shifts in worldviews and lifeways. Here we outline the heuristic matrix that will guide those discussions (see Table 2.1).

Table 2.1 Schema for interpreting the role of religion in major episodes of civilizational change

	Ontology	Epistemology	Ethics
Ideological-political			
Material-social			
Cognitive-coalitional			

The matrix facilitates an exploration of the ways in which each of the sorts of theory in our typology play a role in the ontological, epistemological, and ethical shifts in worldviews and lifeways in each of the major transformations of civilizational form that we model in Chapters 4 to 6. We will use a chart like this in each case, filling it out in relation to the civilizational shift under review.

We have already outlined the typology of theories, which correspond to matrix rows, but we need to say a bit more about the columns in this matrix. As noted in Chapter 1, we have collapsed the six big questions treated by Taves and Asprem into these three.

In this context, the concept of "ontology" is meant to capture all the concerns expressed in what Taves and Asprem call cosmology and situation as well as ontology. The latter has to do with what exists, what is real. Cosmology, which deals with the big questions of where we came from and where we are going, can be seen as a subcategory of ontology because the origin and future of humanity and the universe as a whole are intimately connected with what exists (space, time, being, becoming, values, histories, etc.). Similarly, "situation" or the "nature" of humanity is also a question of what is real. "Epistemology" remains the same as it is in Taves and Asprem: how do we know what is true? Finally, "ethics" for us captures the issues in what they call axiology and praxeology: what is the good (or goal) we should strive for and what actions should we take to realize desired goods and to achieve desired goals?

Each of the major shifts in civilizational form—the Neolithic, Axial, and Modern transitions—involves fundamental changes in how the majority of individuals in the population answer questions (explicitly or implicitly) related to the ontological, epistemological, and ethical dimensions of their worldviews and lifeways. In many cases, shifts in attitudes and behaviors toward supernatural agents (animal spirits, ancestor ghosts, gods, etc.) and associated changes in the social glue generated by imaginaries related to morally interested invisible watchers play key roles. This is the basis for the long-range hypothesis we seek to support in this book: that religious worldviews and lifeways matter in processes of civilizational transformation. Important questions here include What kinds of supernatural agents (if any) are included in one's ontological inventory? What role (if any) does revelation or intervention by supernatural agents play in constituting or regulating human knowledge or claims about what is true? Are supernatural agents the source of ethical norms or does their potential punishment or reward shape human moral behavior?

A potential objection here is that by deciding to model conversions of worldviews and lifeways, we are inherently favoring "ideological-political" theories, because the latter are somewhat more apt to explain or connect to such conversions. As will become clear later, however, our causal architectures also involve measuring changes in variables related to cognition-coalition and material-social factors. What exactly is being transformed? As explained earlier, we are interested in the conversion of worldviews and lifeways that support (and are buttressed by) distinctive modes of civilizational form, or modes of social cohesion. Worldviews and lifeways are taken as a kind of proxy for, or as indicative of, a civilizational form (structure or mode-of-cohesion) that characterizes the population.

As part of our analysis of each episode of civilizational change in Chapters 4 to 6, we will explore the extent to which religion mattered, and this 3×3 matrix will help us be more consistent and complete in our evaluation. First, however, we need to spell out our general approach to computational social simulation. This will provide a scaffold both for our theoretical syntheses and for testing of hypotheses about the causes and consequences of civilizational transformation.

3

Computational Simulation

This chapter introduces the main tool deployed in this book to articulate the meaning of civilizational change: computational simulation. While this tool is routinely used in many hard sciences and has been employed for several decades in some corners of the empirical social sciences, it is less familiar in the interpretative social sciences and humanities, which is home to much of the intensive reflection on civilizational origins and structural social transformation. We therefore set out to explain computational simulation for the audience of teachers, students, and researchers in the interpretative social sciences and humanities, being careful to acknowledge the disadvantages as well as the advantages of this method.

We use the "conversion model" as a case study to explain fundamental concepts in computational simulation. Each of the models discussed in Chapters 4 to 6 are elaborations of this conversion model, rendered specific to a particular group of cultural and historical contexts. Thus, the presentation of simulations presupposes a grasp of the conversion model presented in this chapter.

From Narratives to Formal Models to Computational Simulations

Most books about civilizational origins and change are narrative accounts. Some weave in hard data and illustrative graphs, but the narrative still carries the burden of making the case about what causes societies to change, to emerge, to stabilize and destabilize. The informal models implicit within these narrative accounts are hermeneutically fluid, with plenty of room for interpretative flexibility. For example, it is difficult to determine whether, to what degree, or in what respects two narrative accounts disagree with one another, which obscures assessment of the possibility of a theoretical synthesis. And it is rarely straightforward to decide whether a theory expressed in narrative terms is conceptually coherent and internally consistent. Greater precision about causal claims would be useful—and, we dare say, necessary—for a full and fair evaluation of any causal account of civilizational origins and change.

Formal models, by contrast, are very useful for evaluating internal consistency of a theory as well as the logical fit between competing theories. By formal models, we mean mathematical or logical models that eliminate semantic ambiguity and have the potential to be implemented in a computational environment. Formal models call for explicit definitions of operational concepts, which can lead to less messiness in the model than is present in the phenomenon under study. But the gain in clarity is certainly an improvement for interpreting, evaluating, and comparing conceptual models, so the associated tradeoff might be regarded positively, as least for some applications.

What kind of formal model would be required to articulate and evaluate a theory of civilizational change? To begin with, it would need to be a time-dependent model. It would also need to be a causal model in the sense that the causal dynamics within the time-dependent model directly represent the causal dynamics that are thought to obtain within the phenomenon under study. This is the territory of simulations, where a time-dependent model expresses a causal architecture or "nexus." Finally, it would be particularly convenient if this time-dependent, causal model could be realized in a computing machine and then executed, thereby explicitly representing the way a civilization changes over time and yielding outputs that can be analyzed quantitatively. This is computational simulation—and, when the subject matter is related to social life, computational social simulation.

There are several kinds of computational simulation modalities. One is event-driven, in the way a factory assembly line is event-driven: there's a starting event, then one thing happens, then another thing, then another, and finally there's a stopping event. There may be conditional branching along the way. These are called discrete-event simulations: time-dependent and causal, yes, but best for analyzing a process of change where the events are already well understood, which is not the case for civilizational change.

A second type of computational simulation is agent-driven, and thus is called agent-based modeling. In this agent-oriented domain of CSS, agents are typically individual artificial people, and through agent interactions the model produces emergent effects in much the way we see that occurring in social life. If this type of computational simulation is to be more than a game, a mere amusement, it requires the modeler to know a great deal about agent minds, agent interactions, and agent behaviors, as well as the conditions affecting the artificial societies inhabited by the agents. When thinking about civilizational change in the far past, this is a very difficult standard to meet. Moreover, agent-based models are difficult to validate against real data when we're talking about the far past. In other settings, agent-based models can be superb tools for analyzing social phenomena, including religion (see, e.g., Lane, 2021), but this kind of tool is ill suited to the application we're interested in here.

A third modality of computational simulation is the system-dynamics model (SDM). Like the other two modalities, SDMs are time-dependent, causal models but they have no artificial agents in artificial societies, and they are typically not marked by discrete events. Rather, the causal architecture of an SDM expresses the causal dynamics of the real-world system, on the scale of the entire system. For example, an SDM could represent the way a population of human beings interacts with a contagious disease. In any given period of time, a portion of the population is susceptible to the infection, and some of that portion changes state from being not exposed to exposed, from exposed to infected, and from infected to dead or recovered. Environmental conditions such as virulence of the disease and degree of interaction between people would determine the strength of flow from one state into another. Even compliance with public health advice could make a difference. In an SDM, these state changes are expressed not as decisions or events in the life of individuals but as a percentage of the population in a given state at a given time. The states are called "stocks," and the causal transitions from one state to another are called "flows"; what flows is a proportion of a population. Fittingly, the characteristic diagram describing the causal architecture of an SDM is called a "stock and flow" diagram. The thing that flows between stocks might not always be people; it might be money or power or energy or whatever is most relevant for describing the causal dynamics of the system under study.

SDMs are more promising for our purposes because they don't require us to know unknowable details about past individuals or events and they register mechanisms of change that are conceptually rather close to the way the existing literature describes causal processes of civilizational change. In our case, the thing that flows is people (thought of as a fluid quantity, rather than individuals); stocks would be the percentage of a population in a given state at a given time, and flows would be the causal pathways by which people move between states. Like all computational simulations, SDMs are formal models whose causal architecture is executable over time, so they possess the advantages of formal models described earlier.

Importantly, the validity of an SDM needs to be assessed in terms of two levels of matching: between the simulation's causal architecture and prevailing causal theories of civilizational change, and between the simulation's behavior and whatever data we possess about the process of change being studied. Think about population-health simulations: we often have population-level data and need to explain state changes, so SDMs are routinely used in public health research. When studying phenomena in the far past, by contrast, we often lack the detailed population-level data we would use to validate an SDM in the ideal way. In such cases, SDMs can still be useful by establishing internal consistency of components in the causal architecture and by creating qualitative matches between simulation behavior and our best guesses about the behavior of the real-world phenomenon of interest. That's our situation for the simulations in this book. The SDMs we will be presenting are designed not to be perfect empirical matches with real-world episodes of civilizational change but to serve as aids for reasoning about such episodes in a way that helps us to detect consistency and inconsistency, forces us to be clear, and supports arguments about the causal architecture of episodes of civilizational change.

The Conversion Paradigm

We conceive of a transformation in civilizational form as a kind of conversion, exchanging one kind of worldview (with associated lifeways) for another. For example, in the Neolithic setting, a percentage of the population might decide to surrender the worldviews and lifeways of hunting and gathering in small bands of extended family groups and take up the worldviews and lifeways of living in farming townships and working with domesticated plants and animals. Naturally, in principle, conversion can occur in both directions.

Whether such a conversion is possible depends on whether people have been exposed to the alternative worldviews and associated lifeways, and on whether people actually convert after being exposed to an alternative. Thus, we have several pathways through the causal architecture of a model that expresses conversion between two states, A and B.

- Starting in State A, people are never exposed to an alternative and remain in State A.
- Starting in State A, people are exposed to State B but do not convert and remain in State A.

- Starting in State A, people are exposed to State B and convert to State B.
- Starting in State B, people are exposed to State A and convert to State A.
- Starting in State B, people are exposed to State A but do not convert and remain in State B.
- Starting in State B, people are never exposed to an alternative and remain in State B.

We can depict these six pathways in a simple diagram (Figure 3.1).

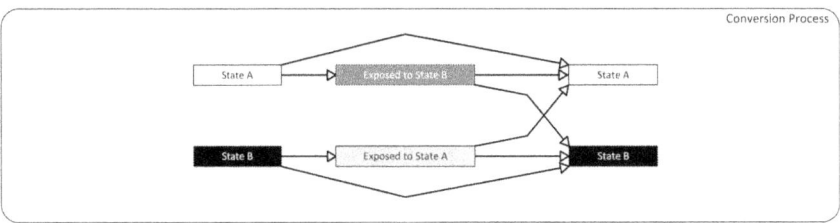

Figure 3.1 Six pathways through the conversion model.

Figure 3.1 nicely expresses logically alternative pathways through a causal architecture but does not yet express anything about how much of the population flows from one state to another along those various paths. For that we require "flow rates" on each flow, akin to faucets on a water pipe, allowing a lot of water to move through the flow, or a trickle, or nothing at all. We represent flow rates as double triangles and place them somewhere along each flow, as in the more elaborate depiction of the conversion process in Figure 3.2.

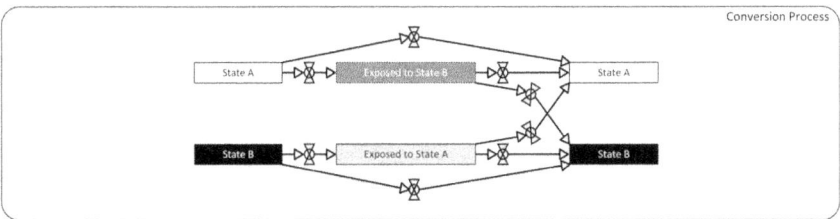

Figure 3.2 Flow rates within the conversion model.

At this point, we have the beginnings of a stock-and-flow diagram. Since a population is flowing through this diagram, it is fair to ask from where the portion of the population in the left-side "State A" stock arrive, and same for the left-side "State B" stock. The answer is that they are born at some point. We should also ask what happens to the portion of the population in the right-side State A and State B stocks. The answer is that they die. Because we are not modeling at the level of individual agents (people), all we care about is that the population flows into State A and State B on the left at a certain rate, and that the population flows out of State A and State B on the right at a certain rate. We use cloud icons on one end of flows to express this, as in Figure 3.3.

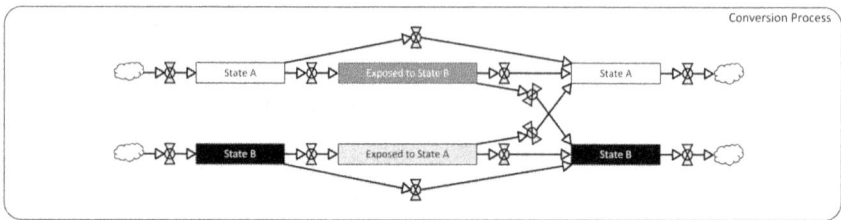

Figure 3.3 The conversion model with origins and destiny of the two subpopulations as cloud icons.

The birthrates of real-world populations are affected by resource scarcity: the more people, the more resource scarcity, and if resource scarcity is high enough, the two birthrates will plummet. Moreover, we can assume that the population in State A impacts birthrates for the incoming State A population, and the population in State B impacts birthrates for the incoming State B population. These kinds of impacts are not flows of the population between states; rather, they express mathematically formalizable influences on flow rates. They are called flow rate adjustment factors and are graphically represented with thin curving arrows, as in Figure 3.4. The way flow rate adjustment factors combine with one another is recorded in mathematical equations.

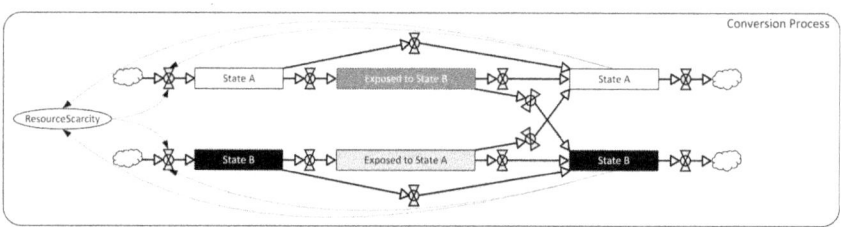

Figure 3.4 The conversion model taking account of resource scarcity.

For analytical purposes, we are deeply interested in the relative proportion of the population in State A versus State B at any given time. This single ratio summarizes the complex dynamics of civilizational change between the two states in question. Figure 3.5 adds this ratio ("B:A Ratio") into the diagram.

To go further, we need to express how the flow rates are set. One part of this is simple mathematics: we say that the flow rate is the rate of change in the difference between what is in the stock on the receiving end of the flow and what

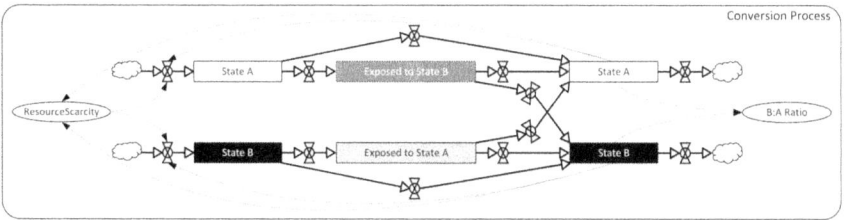

Figure 3.5 The conversion model with the main output variable, the ratio of the new subpopulation to the old subpopulation (B:A Ratio).

is in the stock on the originating end of the flow. Calculus can be used to express this rigorously:

d/dt(any given stock) = sum of inflows − sum of outflows.

So, for example, considering the "Exposed to State B," the corresponding differential equation is:

d/dt("Exposed to State B") = (inflow from the left-side "State A") − (outflow to right-side "State A" + outflow to right-side "State B").

It follows that, if we know the flow rates, we know what will be in the stocks. So the remaining puzzle on the way to an executable computational simulation is how to set the flow rates.

Figure 3.5 already illustrates the way variables and stocks can affect flow rates. For example, the ResourceScarcity variable and the right-side State A stock affect the flow rate corresponding to the birthrate for the left-side State A portion of the population. But other variables, not pictured in Figure 3.5, could play a role as well. This is true for all of the flow rates. Consider the portion of the population that is in State A on the left side of Figure 3.5: some are exposed to the alternative State B and some are not. Those two flow rates add up to 100 percent of the portion of the population that flows out of the left-hand State A stock, but the proportion of those exposed to the alternative State B could be affected by a lot of considerations, including the prevalence of the population in State B, the eagerness of the State B subpopulation to recruit, and the intrinsic attractiveness of State B to the State A subpopulation. All of these influences need to be combined in a mathematically unambiguous way to set the various flow rates. Figure 3.6 shows the result: variables with curving arrows that determine the various flow rates. The two death rates are 100 percent, since we're not entertaining immortality in these models.

The next challenge is to introduce the concept of tuning parameters. Parameters are fixed for a given run and adjusting them retunes the simulation, producing

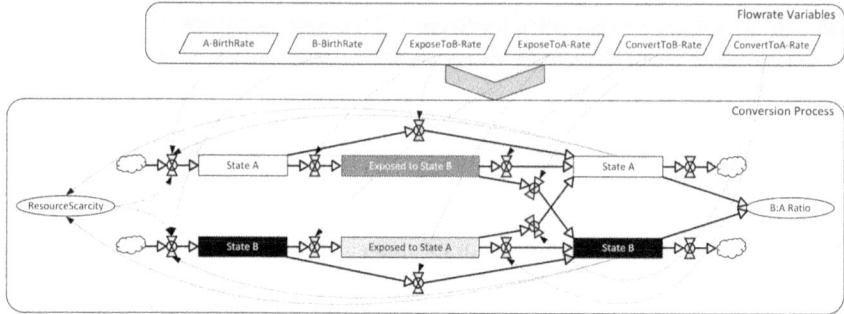

Figure 3.6 The conversion model showing the critical role of the six flow-rate variables (top).

potentially quite different behavior. Much of the analysis of any simulation consists in exploring the space of tuning parameters to identify meaningful regimes of behavior. Figure 3.7 adds four parameters to the conversion model.

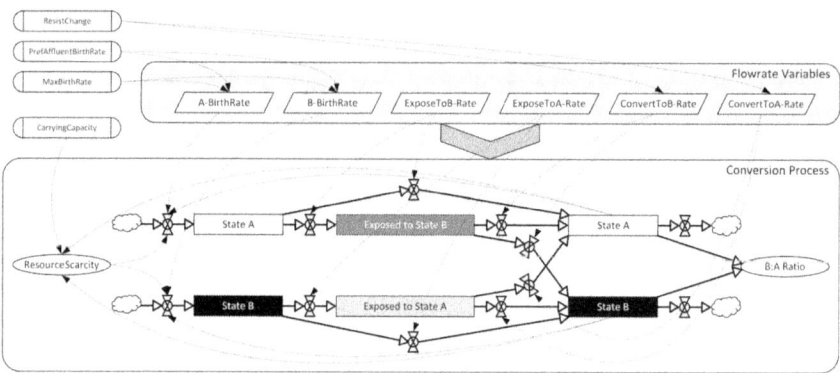

Figure 3.7 The conversion model showing the role of tuning parameters (top left).

- ResistChange is a population characteristic akin to stubbornness; it describes the extent to which any conversion will be resisted on principle.
- PrefAffluentBirthRate describes the culturally preferred birthrate for the most affluent portions of the population and affects the two birthrates.
- MaxBirthRate is a biologically based parameter setting the maximum birthrate for the population; it also affects the two birthrates.
- CarryingCapacity determines how large a population can be supported in the relevant ecological setting and affects the ResourceScarcity variable.

That is as far as we can go with the conversion model itself. The remaining question is how to set the six variables in the "Flowrate Variables" region of

Figure 3.7: the two birthrates, the two exposure rates, and the two conversion rates. These determine the flow rates, which determine the stocks, which makes the conversion model executable over time as a simulation. We cannot specify those six key variables unless we know what we are converting from and to. Figure 3.8 expresses this by adding in a "Causal Nexus" frame, which specifies the six flow rate variables and which is influenced in turn by the "B:A Ratio" variable from the "Conversion Process."

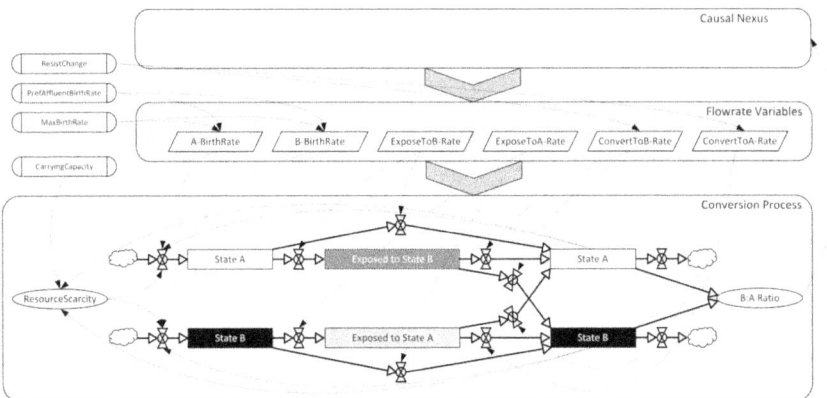

Figure 3.8 The conversion model showing the "Causal Nexus" (top) that is required to specify the "Flowrate Variables" (center), which then drive the conversion model (bottom), as tuned by the parameters (left).

Getting specific about a "Causal Nexus" or architecture requires us to confront the theoretical debates swirling around the episodes of civilizational transformation that we'll consider in this book. That is the task of the next three chapters. Chapter 4 will take up the Neolithic transformation from a millennium either side of 10,000 BP (before the present). Chapter 5 will consider the Axial Age from a few centuries either side of 2,500 BP. Chapter 6 will tackle Modernity, a monumental transformation that is still underway, beginning about 300 BP. In each case, our strategy is the same. We examine the best theoretical understandings of each transformation in civilizational form, we synthesize those understandings wherever possible (being careful to specify what we're excluding to preserve consistency), we extract from that synthesis the variables needed to determine the six flow rates in the conversion model, and we identify the parameters that tune the entire simulation and push its dynamics into a variety of behavior regimes.

The remainder of this chapter explains in more detail the rationale for applying a humanities-guided, social-science-informed, computer-engineering methodology to the questions examined in the book.

The Promise and Peril of Computational Humanities and Social Sciences

Both authors are trained primarily in the humanities, secondarily in the interpretative social sciences, and tertiarily in the empirical social sciences. One of us has specific training in mathematics, hard sciences, and computing and data sciences. The other has specific training in educational psychology. Our home professional identities are in the humanities and social sciences, and we use methods drawn from computing and data sciences when we discern a benefit in doing so. We see such benefits in several computational methods: natural-language processing for content analysis of texts, machine-learning algorithms for classifying data, computational affect analysis of video and audio, network analysis, and computational social simulation. We also use traditional humanities methods such as textual, historical, conceptual, contextual, and comparative analysis. And we use traditional social science methods such as ethnographic, qualitative, quantitative, survey, and experimental analysis. Sometimes we need to learn unfamiliar methods, for which our collaborations with (endlessly patient!) experts have been vital. In short, we make use of whatever methods seem relevant and useful for understanding a particular problem area.

We acknowledge that the problem-focused approach to determining which methods to use sometimes sits awkwardly with university academic traditions that tend to associate a specific range of methods with specific academic disciplines. We appreciate the deep methodological expertise that such structured traditions yield but we're concerned about the associated limitations, particularly when thinking about complex real-world problems that seem to defy comprehension through a single methodological lens. Indeed, most of the important problems in our time cannot be solved within a single discipline, so at least some academics need to be both expert in their home-field disciplines and agile enough to learn new methods—and learn them well enough to collaborate with experts outside their home fields, if not to deploy them independently.

In fact, universities can display a high degree of responsiveness to this challenge of problem-focused determination of research methods. In the humanities, religion scholars work with historians and political scientists. In the sciences, biomedical engineering and neuropsychology and a host of other cross-disciplinary ventures have become routine. Multidisciplinary adventures that cross the humanities-science divide are less common, however, and sometimes resisted. Since this is what we are doing in this book, we need to pause to address this problem.

Let us address an extreme version of this resistance at the outset. Some scientists don't take the humanities and interpretative social sciences seriously, treating it all as unintelligible nonsense. Some humanities scholars don't take the sciences seriously, treating it all as socially constructed invidious reductionism. We are quite sure that representatives of these views will not be reading this book, since we take both sides with great seriousness, so we'll go right ahead and dismiss such views as aggressively ignorant and not worthy of our, or anyone's, time, aside from object lessons in failure of empathic connection with the unfamiliar.

More interesting to us are legitimate concerns about the future of university disciplines. The so-called crisis of the humanities is much more than mere paranoia about moving the crown of university prestige from the humanities to the sciences. This crisis is also reflected in materially significant ways: faculty hiring, recruitment of PhD students, grant-funded research, media coverage, public impact, employment prospects, and existential survival of disciplines are all at stake. Admittedly, humanities scholars have not always responded in constructive or productive ways to this fundamental, large-scale challenge to their legitimacy and value. Resentful withdrawal is a tempting response to being left out of the party.

A more helpful response would be to engage in research across the humanities-science divide and demonstrate the value of the hermeneutical sophistication of scholars in the humanities and interpretative social sciences—value not only for home-field research problems but also for improving the quality of research in the empirical sciences. For example, religion scholars know a lot about worldviews and lifeways that many are willing to call religious, in a host of manifestations all over the world. This knowledge is badly needed by researchers studying the health effects of religious beliefs and practices, who often settle for simplistic operationalizations of key concepts related to religion. Closing this gap would demonstrate the power of the humanities and interpretative social sciences in a most welcome way.

Be that as it may, the kind of computational methods on display in this volume can feel like a hard sell to scholars in the humanities and interpretative social sciences. Isn't this just one more encroachment of the technical disciplines on the interpretative disciplines? Isn't it one more exhibition of the sacrifice of hard-won hermeneutical skills on the altar of computational oversimplification? We think these questions are worth taking seriously, not least because they point to genuine limitations of the methods of computational humanities and computational social sciences, including the kinds of computational simulation used in this book. But there are also important answers to these challenges that exhibit the possibilities implicit in these less familiar methods. So let us consider the possibilities and perils of computational social simulation.

Any method that wins the title of "the third pillar of science" alongside theory and experimentation must be doing something right (Benioff & Lazowska, 2005; Tolk, 2015). Computational simulation is so good at supporting the analysis of nonlinear complex dynamical systems that it has become a mainstay of the physical and biological sciences, and is increasingly being adopted and adapted within the social sciences (Alvarez, 2016; Barceló & Del Castillo, 2016; Squazzoni, 2012). What is it about CSS specifically, as against computational simulation more generally, that has succeeded in capturing the attention of humanities and social science researchers?

- CSS encourages "generative social science" (the phrase of Epstein, 2006). This refers to gaining new insights into complex social systems by generating emergent phenomena from the ground up, thereby causally replicating the phenomena under study. This strengthens causal inference, demonstrates the deep causal meaning of theoretical proposals, and inspires novel ideas for testing and evaluation.
- CSS forces conceptual clarity about assumptions, inferences, and consequences. Every variable must be explicitly defined and operationalized. This can yield greater clarity than we might want at times, artificially simplifying real-world vagueness, but that problem can be managed, and most of the time the demand for clarity helps us discover when and where scholars are talking past each other or utilizing concepts that are too broad (or too narrow) for the purpose at hand.
- CSS allows the integration of multiple theories at all levels of complexity. So much of the time, the humanities and social sciences treat perspectivally related theoretical edifices as a forced choice between uncompromising competitors. Scholars who see resonance between the competitors can be drowned out by the internecine battles. CSS offers a way to demonstrate the consistency of large tracts of theory that are routinely taken to be sharply contrasting alternatives.
- CSS is empirically grounded, able to make use of both quantitative and qualitative data to inspire design features, validate simulations, and calibrate

simulations to real-world experiences. In fact, CSS is remarkably supportive of, and hungry for, all kinds of data, from ethnographic to experimental, and from qualitative to survey.
- CSS can shift the burden of proof in complex debates within the social sciences, driving a richer discussion. This occurs because simulations can advance debates even when they are stalled using more traditional methods, thereby setting forth new types of support for certain lines of theory and inviting those with contrasting guesses to make their cases as well as they can using the more demanding method.
- CSS offers greater transparency about assumptions made in theoretical design. All such assumptions are present in the code of a computer model. From there, they can be discovered and challenged. Narrative theories, by contrast, often bury assumptions so deeply that even their proponents cannot identify some of them.
- CSS can change the tone and methods of debate. This can happen by democratizing theoretical discussions, empowering younger researchers who might normally be marginalized to use their simulation-based research for inserting new ideas into discussion based on demonstrable merit. It can also happen through encouraging participatory modeling processes, in which experts and non-scholarly stakeholders most directly affected by the topic of discussion can work together to determine the optimal way to design a simulation.

At the same time, CSS comes with increasingly well understood perils that need to (and can) be managed with appropriate awareness and experience (some items on this list derived from Edmonds & Aodha, 2019).

- Institutionalized and theoretically ossified assumptions can be a problem, with simulation designers thoughtlessly replicating those assumptions and thereby failing to grasp the opportunity for novel insights. The mitigating strategy here is to be explicit about assumptions through stakeholder engagement, including alternative perspectives, and documenting everything carefully so design decisions can be audited.
- CSS researchers can be confused over the precise purpose of the simulation they themselves are building, moving ahead with design and building before winning clarity about what they are trying to achieve. One mitigating strategy is a brutal demand for clarity of purpose, tested in discussions with diverse experts and on-the-ground stakeholders. Another is to assess critically extant models, even those that are taken-for-granted and used

frequently, noting what they're good for and using those insights to clarify the purpose of any new model.
- Failing to be fully aware of the conceptual and functional limitations of a simulation can lead to significant confusion. To mitigate this problem, researchers need to continually review a new model as (and after) it is built, performing extensive exploration and analysis of models and of any sub-models that it may contain.
- Excitement around new simulations can lead to a false sense of security and a minimization of uncertainty, particularly among those desperate to find a breakthrough on a stalled research program. To mitigate this problem, researchers should hunt for uncertainty, seek to measure it, be explicit about it, avoid overselling a simulation, and ensure that relevant caveats always travel with the model and any conclusions drawn from it.
- Of particular concern to scholars in the humanities and interpretative social sciences, simulations can narrow the evidential base by drawing attention to the evidence that can be incorporated into a simulation and away from evidence that doesn't fit the conceptual shape of the simulation. The mitigating strategy here is for model designers and builders to remember that not all knowledge can be formalized and incorporated into a simulation and to be explicit about the difference this makes in each case. For example, a model that answers an empirical question does not necessarily also answer a related normative question, which may call for different kinds of data and even a new simulation design.

As we have noted, there are mitigating strategies for each of these dangers. We have found that scholars in the humanities and interpretative social sciences are particularly good at identifying when a simulation design and analysis process is approaching danger territory; their training in hermeneutics of suspicion and sensitivity to hidden assumptions are priceless assets. Our recommendation is that they not hide their light under a bushel of resentment about the fate of their disciplinary homes in university cultures but rather step out and make themselves useful, thereby reminding everyone why their skillsets are to be prized.

Artificial Ethics

All computational technologies are surrounded by profound ethical concerns, and CSS is no exception. We need to conduct ethical analysis of the assumptions and limitations built into simulations. For example, leaving out crucial stakeholder perspectives in a simulation-design process is a recipe for encoding bias into the operations of the simulation, which is nothing if not ethically problematic. We also need to be prepared for ethical complexities when considering the implications and applications of social simulations. For example, sometimes social simulations can be used to support ethically questionable actions or lead to failure to acknowledge design limitations. At the same time, as Gilbert et al. (2018) point out, when social issues are so complex and ethically challenging, it would seem unethical *not* to use these tools, given the power they possess to generate useful insights.

Teamwork between stakeholders, designers, and subject-matter experts is a vital asset for managing such ethical challenges. Ethics specialists informed about simulation methodology can also be useful members of simulation teams in both design and deployment phases. Professional codes of ethics offer guidance, including especially the Society for Modeling and Simulation International's Simulationist Code of Ethics (Tolk, 2017). We have also found it helpful to employ a framework for ethical awareness and analysis—a simple yet relatively comprehensive way of thinking about what might be at stake in any effort to design and deploy CSS tools (for more details, see Shults & Wildman, 2019, 2020a).

The ethical framework we present here benefits from existing work in AI ethics. Winfield et al. (2019) divides AI ethics into two branches. The first branch is commonly referred to as "AI ethics" and focuses on ethical issues surrounding the design and use (or misuse) of AI. Some computational simulations can be thought of as AI agents or as networks of AI agents, depending on the type of simulation involved. Here one finds questions such as what are the far-reaching economic disruptions of generative AI? How should individual programmers deploy AI that could be used to manipulate people in marketing? What algorithms should be used to determine the value of the different types of people's lives (e.g., an elderly woman or a little boy in the crosswalk) when programming an autonomous vehicle's behavior in the face of unusual driving situations that require a decision about whom to hit if the vehicle cannot stop quickly enough. As cross-cultural experiments have shown, humans in different contexts and regions make quite different kinds of moral assessments in such situations. How, then, are we to decide the "right" way to program autonomous vehicles to act (Awad et al., 2018)? Anxiety about the ethical use of AI is particularly common when dealing with areas in which humans feel particularly ambivalent about our own moral decisions, such as "making war" and "making love." Military use of AI is already routine and "killer robots" with offensive capabilities that go well beyond military drones are not far away (Lin et al., 2014; Noorman & Johnson, 2014). And AI is already being used commercially to produce "sex robots" with astonishing interpersonal sophistication (Richardson, 2016; Danaher & McArthur, 2017).

A second branch, sometimes called "ethical AI" or "machine ethics" (Anderson & Anderson, 2011), addresses broader issues related to the very possibility of building an AI that can behave "ethically." What would it mean if this were possible, and what is the potential value and risk of trying to construct an ethical machine (Cave, Nyrup, Vold, & Weller, 2018)? For example, in the case mentioned earlier describing autonomous vehicles, should the latter be considered *morally* autonomous, and, if so, is this in a literal or a metaphorical sense? Can a moral machine be programmed that can learn ethics by interacting with an environment and receiving feedback, thereby making its own decisions, rather than being controlled by an exhaustive suite of algorithms conveying moral decisions made by human designers and programmers? Such thought (and computational) experiments bear on debates among philosophers about solving dilemmas such as the infamous "trolley problem." This has led to increased dialogue between philosophers and computer engineers.

> Philosophers are interested in the outcomes of practical machine ethics not least because—if successful—they lend urgency to the moral questions around ethical machines in society. Equally, engineers engaged in designing ethical machines need philosophers to advise on the definition of appropriate ethical rules and values for these machines. (Winfield et al., 2019, p. 510)

Scholars who operate on one (or both) of these branches are increasingly engaging such philosophical questions.

As philosophers we think this is important, but the main point we want to highlight here is that in both branches of this academic field the focus is typically on individual ethics, that is, on *singular* artificial agents who are understood to be more or less intelligent or moral (compared to humans). Here scholars are shaped by the long history of ethical discourse in Western philosophy which has in fact focused primarily on individual human agents. Some computational architectures model moral assumptions derived from deontological ethics, focusing on the rules individual agents should follow, while others model consequentialist assumptions, focusing on the utility functions individual agents should optimize, and still others model the assumptions of virtue ethicists, focusing on the character traits or dispositions individual agents should cultivate (Allen, Varner, & Zinser, 2000; M. Anderson, Anderson, & Armen, 2005; Grau,

2011; Powers, 2006). This is all philosophically interesting, but notice that the emphasis is still on *individual* ethics in each case. While none of these traditional schools of philosophical ethics completely ignore the communal dimension of human life, they do not typically focus on the way in which cultural contexts and norms, as well as familial and other social identity network relations, help to shape, motivate, and justify moral behaviors.

We argue that it is important to complement debates around artificial individual ethics with debates over artificial *social* ethics, particularly as our species faces new challenges in the Anthropocene (Shults et al., 2021). We are not denying the importance of discussion about the possibility or timing of the "singularity" at which point AI becomes as intelligent as (or more intelligent than) human beings. A great deal hangs on the meaning of "intelligence," and generative AI using deep learning on neural nets has established performative intelligence in specialized domains that is stunningly proficient. Whether this can be extended to general artificial intelligence is the question before us now, even as generative AI upends existing economic arrangements. Questions about the eventual moral superiority of machines are perhaps even more complicated because there is even less consensus on what it means to be "moral." Moor defines an "explicit ethical agent" as one that would be capable of representing ethics explicitly and "then operate effectively on the basis of this knowledge" (Moor, 2006, p. 20). Winfield argues that we can already say that some AI agent architectures qualify as "explicit" ethical agents, insofar as they "have either learned or defined ethical rules and the cognitive machinery to take those rules into account when deciding how to act in a given situation" (Winfield et al., 2019, p. 511). At least one machine-reasoning architecture for robot AI utilizes a simulation-based internal model that claims to enable proactive, transparent, and verifiable ethical reasoning (Bremner et al., 2019). We may not yet be at the "moral" singularity where an individual AI can make explicit and justify its ethical reasoning, but we seem to be getting closer.

When it comes to moral artificial *societies*, however, we are indeed already constructing computational social simulations that generate the emergence of macro-level ethical (or unethical) behaviors and social patterns found in real-world societies. State-of-the-art "digital twins" of human societies do have agents (and clusters of agents) capable of representing "moral knowledge" and operating effectively on the basis of this knowledge. It is not uncommon to find models capable of simulating the emergence of ethically salient macro-level societal phenomena from micro-level "moral" interactions, including cultural norms (Conte et al., 2014; Elsenbroich & Gilbert, 2014). As described earlier, our research teams have participated in this process, developing several computational models that simulate behaviors and interactions that are morally charged, such as in-group reactions to threats (Shults, Lane, et al., 2018), the mutual escalation of intergroup conflict (Shults, Gore, et al., 2018), and the reduction of religious beliefs and affiliation in secularizing contexts (Gore et al., 2018). But so much more is possible, and coming quickly.

What is most needed, we believe, is a flexible moral framework that is agile enough to be adaptable to a host of ethical questions that arise now, and may arise in the future, in relation to CSS (Shults, Wildman, et al., 2018; Shults & Wildman, 2019; Diallo et al., 2021). Such an ethical framework can be seen as analogous to what in the AI literature is sometimes called "machine metaethics" (Anderson, 2011). However, we think expanding the individualistic focus of machine metaethics to artificial *social* ethics is crucial. It is important for the field to focus more explicitly on the way in which cultural norms, social networks, and other environmental parameters shape moral behaviors and interactions, and on how that shaping should occur. The following summary of our proposed framework borrows from our discussion in Shults and Wildman, 2019.

The first aspect of our metaethical framework, which is the most abstract, is explicitly *philosophical*. We encourage computer scientists and subject matter experts to make more explicit their definitions of "the good" and "the right" and of the relation between them. Are the intuitions driving the modeling process more reliant on consequentialist, deontological, virtue, or some other approach to ethics? We are not making a normative claim that all modelers *ought* to take one or the other of those approaches. Rather, we are arguing that they should be as clear as possible about the ethical assumptions shaping their modeling activities. In our case, we take a broadly pragmatic consequentialist framing of ethical issues, primarily because both deontological and virtue approaches (whatever their benefits) have traditionally been framed in relation to transcendental ideals or exemplars of the sort that play a role in the ethical systems of religious in-groups. Consequentialist approaches can also be framed in this way, but we think that this approach to ethics is more conducive to the sort of intersubjective and trans-communal discourse about moral goods required by the challenges of the Anthropocene.

The second aspect of our proposed framework is *scientific*. Here the point is to encourage modelers to take account of the bio-cultural sciences that bear on the evolution of our moral instincts, emotions, and reasoning. This general principle has many specific applications. For example, if our goal is to develop social simulations with realistic cognitive architectures and social networks, then we need to take seriously insights from empirical research in evolutionary biology and moral psychology about the evolved tendency of members of our species to follow the social norms of the in-groups in which we are raised. This propensity would have been naturally selected in contexts where the in-group cohesion of small-scale homogeneous societies was necessary for survival, but in contemporary large-scale, diverse, and densely populated societies of the sort that most of us live in today, such a tendency all too quickly mutates into anxiety about and aggression toward out-group members (Wildman, 2009; Shults, 2018).

The final and *practical* aspect of our metaethical framework follows out the pragmatic implications of the first two aspects. Our only hope for avoiding moral confusion when talking to one another about the social-ethical implications of our modeling and simulation efforts is to learn how to surface and explicate the philosophical assumptions and criteria that shape our construction of artificial societies and simulation experiments. Incorporating scientific insights about the evolved mechanisms that shape human ethical behavior within and among groups can also help us avoid moral evasion of the sort that displaces ethical responsibility onto the hidden supernatural agents of a particular religious coalition (e.g., "the ancestors require it of us"). Mitigating conflict and promoting cooperation beyond parochial and national interests as we respond to the impacts of climate change and other global threats will require us to take responsibility for our own actions as individuals and as groups.

The kinds of simulation presented in this book—SDMs—can be thought of as standalone AIs representing the causal dynamics of a complex real-world social system. They are far less morally risky than the AIs powering autonomous vehicles, robot warriors, or even algorithms that decide whether or not you get a bank loan. But they should not thereby be exempted from ethical scrutiny. In terms of the metaethics just sketched, we design and deploy these SDMs within a consequentialist ethical framework (the philosophical dimension), fully responsive to the sciences of cognition and culture that describe human moral instincts, emotions, and reasoning (the scientific dimension). The practical dimension of these SDMs is primarily a matter of generating insights into the deep history of the human species and especially the profound structural transformations of civilization that have occurred along the way.

The most likely ethical danger is rather modest: that people would thoughtlessly accept what these simulations tell us about human history and the dynamics of civilizational change. We mitigate this danger by combining simulation-based analysis with historical and philosophical reflection to weave what we hope is a persuasive narrative supported by multiple considerations, not the simulations alone. A secondary ethical risk is the distortion of the complexity of human life through the simplifications and abstractions required by simulation models. The mitigating consideration here is that we have tried to be thoughtful about what dynamics to include in the models we build and how to abstract from the intricacy of human experience to generate the least distortion and the greatest insight into the causal dynamics of civilizational transformation.

Artificial Ontology and Epistemology

So far we have focused on the ethics aspect of the matrix we introduced at the end of the previous chapter. We have seen that computational simulation has a complex relationship with ethics, both at the level of ethical evaluation of simulations and at the level of simulation of ethics. The same duality is evident in relation to the other two aspects of that matrix: ontology and epistemology (Shults & Wildman, 2020b). Just as simulations can imply or assume moral norms, they can encode ontological and epistemological assumptions, all of which require critical appraisal. And just as computer systems can simulate ethical reasoning and the emergence of moral norms, they can simulate reasoning about ontology and epistemology and the emergence of convictions in these domains.

We mentioned in the preface that this book adopts a methodologically naturalist approach. This conforms to the morality of inquiry prevalent within the modern academy and is uncontroversial within the scientific study of religion, and indeed in the scholarly study of civilizational transformations. But being "normal" is not the same as being normatively harmless. After all, the more naturalist assumptions in epistemology and ontology are employed to explain and narrate elements of human reality, the more such assumptions come to seem warranted, which means that metaphysical naturalism itself is boosted in plausibility while metaphysical supernaturalism suffers plausibility decline.

Alongside the use of methodological naturalism, the very use of computational simulation also tends to support a normative embrace of metaphysical naturalism, in much the way that evolutionary biology does. We shall explore this analogy to explain the vital point about the long-term metaphysical and epistemological implications or effects of using computational simulation.

For most of the time since the advent of the theory of biological evolution, metaphysical supernaturalists have been in despair about their inability to engage in the scientific process to support their perspective. They sensed something wrong with biological evolution, which proposes to explain the emergence of species from a DNA-powered tree of life, because it doesn't take account of supernatural forces that, they believe, were critical causal factors in the creation and emergence of the world as we know it. Yet research programs in biological evolution had all of the progressive momentum and associated prestige. Moreover, the effectiveness of methodological naturalism made metaphysical naturalism seem sufficient to explain aspects of reality that were formerly so mysterious that they positively demanded supernaturalist explanations. Charles Darwin himself grasped this very early, being the canny natural philosopher that he was: once an enthusiastic proponent of William Paley's intelligent design theory, his own evolutionary theory steadily undermined his belief in the need for supernatural causes to explain the biological realm and ultimately dissolved his confidence in the very idea of a personal deity.

While seeking to protect their children from this calamitous outcome by direct action in local school boards, metaphysical supernaturalists also aimed to find a way into scientific debates. In this way, intelligent design was promoted as a perspective capable of scientific testing and evaluation. To detect intelligent design in a framework of methodologically naturalist scientific research, it would be necessary to propose instances of specified complexity—complex biological forms for which there can be no explanation from natural causes—and then stand by as scientists repeatedly fail to explain them away with reference solely to natural causes. This is precisely in line with what appears to have been Paley's expectations: some specific forms of complexity will always resist explanation solely in terms of natural causes.

The tragedy of intelligent design as a scientific research program is that it is perpetually degenerating, especially relative to the overwhelmingly progressive nature of research programs in biological evolution. Moreover, it has made repeated face-saving adjustments to its core hypotheses as scientists have proposed excellent naturalist explanations for every one of their proposed instances of specified complexity that supposedly can never be explained using solely natural causes. In fact, in its ordinary operation, evolutionary biology has been doing precisely this all along: identifying a hard-to-explain puzzle and working to explain it. The metaphysical supernaturalist is indeed forced to stand by and watch, but without the encouragement of celebrations over expected scientific failure to explain instances of specified complexity. On the contrary, they must witness the relentless advance of scientific explanation that demonstrates no need for supernatural causes. From the eye to the flagellum to protein folding, methodological naturalism is getting the explanatory job done, and in the process metaphysical naturalism is being quietly supported and metaphysical supernaturalism quietly undermined.

It may be tempting for the metaphysical supernaturalist to imagine that formally complex systems—including complex social systems—may prove to be resistant to explanation using solely natural causes. Perhaps this is the domain where instances of specified complexity can be identified that will finally prove resistant to the methodologically naturalist scientific juggernaut. Computational simulation has crushed such hopes as decisively as biological evolution crushed the hopes of metaphysically supernaturalist intelligent design theorists. By using an artificial complex system to effectively model a real-world complex system, formally complex physical and social systems have proved to be susceptible to explanation within the limits of methodological naturalism. And the long-term consequence for ontology and epistemology is that metaphysical naturalism becomes more plausible and metaphysical supernaturalism less so.

While promoting metaphysical naturalism in ontology and epistemology is decidedly not the aim of this book, we are aware that the very use of a powerful method such as computational simulation can have that effect in the long run, if it keeps being successful, that is. We think this is as it should be. If the natural and human sciences can operate effectively within the strict limits of methodological naturalism, then metaphysical naturalism deserves a boost in plausibility over metaphysical supernaturalism. For our purposes in most of this book, we bracket metaphysical questions and just operate within the limits of methodological naturalism. In Chapter 7, however, we will return to the fact that Modernity has breathed life into metaphysically naturalist worldviews, creating a situation of stupendous importance for civilizational transformation in the near future.

Next Steps

This chapter has explained simulation technologies and the specific simulation modality employed in this book (SDMs). It has addressed concerns that scholars in the humanities and interpretative social sciences may have with simulation methods and honestly endeavored to expose these methods to ethical scrutiny.

What comes next are three applications and specifications of the basic conversion SDM presented in this chapter. Each must specify the six flow-rate variables—two birthrates, two exposure rates, and two conversion rates—and make use of the fundamental output of the conversion model, which is the ratio of the subpopulations in two states—the old and the new worldviews and lifeways that for a time must coexist in episodes of large-scale civilizational transformation.

Chapter 4 analyzes the Neolithic transition, where the *before* state is hunting and gathering in kin-based groups and the *after* state is living in towns of farmers working with domesticated crops and animals. Chapter 5 addresses the Axial Age transition, where the *before* state is acceptance of a fusion of supernatural deities and political leaders and the *after* state is centralized and differentiated cultures in which a priestly class can contest the power of political leaders. Chapter 6 takes up the Modernity transition, where the *before* state is social norms guided by supernatural agents and authorities and the *after* state features scientific explanations of the natural and social worlds and social norms that do not depend on supernatural agents and authorities.

4

Modeling the Neolithic Transition

Some years ago, we invested several years in studying the archaeological site for the Neolithic town of Çatalhöyük, which flourished between 7400 and 6000 BCE in what is now south-central Turkey. This period, sometimes called the agricultural revolution, involved the first great transition of civilizational form from hunter-gather lifestyles to small-town life, powered by farming domesticated plants and animals. This was a momentous transition for the human species; it led to agriculture becoming increasingly dominant in human cultures, and eventually triggered a cascade of new lifestyles. Even after ten millennia, there are still a few holdouts—humans who prefer hunting and gathering to farming and settled lifestyles—but almost everyone made the leap to the new lifestyle. Çatalhöyük and a few other places like it provide empirical data for studying this transition.

Our computational simulation of the Neolithic revolution incorporates general factors such as technology and capacity to delay gratification, as well as religiously salient factors such as the tendency to infer supernatural causes in the natural world. It also integrates several relevant empirically grounded theories from fields such as archaeology, cognitive science, and evolutionary biology. Most importantly for our purposes in this book, the simulation provides a basis for making sense of the role of religion in the civilizational transition from hunter-gatherers to domesticated agriculturalists—as one of several necessary-but-not-sufficient conditions for that change to occur.

Why Model the Neolithic Transition?

How did we end up modeling Çatalhöyük? LeRon had been a participant in the first two three-year projects at Çatalhöyük supported by the John Templeton Foundation, and he contributed essays to the two volumes that reported on those projects (Shults, 2010a, 2014a). Throughout those six years of multidisciplinary engagement he was repeatedly invited to focus on the empirical material and asked to help illuminate the concrete findings unearthed at the site and in the surrounding area. This is not what philosophers of religion are trained to do!

During long hours interacting with the scientists at Çatalhöyük and combing through concrete findings in the site research reports during Phase I and Phase II, he increasingly got in the habit of trying to tie his philosophical reflections to the hard data. When invited to return for Phase III, he reached out to Wesley, who was already well versed in simulation and modelling, for help and collaboration. We spent our time together at Çatalhöyük reviewing the data, engaging in even longer conversations with the scientists on site, hammering out the causal architecture for the computer simulations we report on below, and exploring ways to calibrate these models by finding tie-downs to the archaeological data and expert opinion on the interpretation of the site.

The title of the project for Phase III of the Templeton project was "The Primary Role of Religion in the Origin of Settled Life: The Evidence from Çatalhöyük and the Middle East." The general hypothesis guiding the project as a whole was that religion played a primary role in the transition to more sedentary forms of human civilization because it led to—or intensified—the production of "historical depth" and "attachment to place." We focused particularly on the question "How did the 'history house' and the 'history town' at Çatalhöyük emerge?" As we explain in more detail below, our goal was to help answer this question by constructing computer simulations of the emergence of high levels of social investment and religious entanglement in the Neolithic. Another part of our assignment was to reflect on the way in which discussions about the role of religion in providing the conditions for historical depth and attachment to place in early sedentary communities might affect our self-understanding *today*—in late modern, pluralistic, globalizing contexts.

Part of our motivation for pursuing this sort of research has to do with our interest in broader questions about the relation between religion and civilizational forms—questions that are of concern to a wider audience. Here we focus on this early shift from hunter-gatherer societies to relatively egalitarian sedentary societies, using empirical findings from and theoretical arguments about Çatalhöyük to verify and validate our model. But why would an archaeologist (or any other scientist interested in Neolithic societies) care about this sort of computer simulation? In fact, the use of simulation techniques has been growing at least as rapidly in this field as in other social sciences.

To provide the background for understanding the uniqueness and potential value of our model, we begin with a brief overview of some other uses of

CSS in archaeology. Nearly two decades before he became the leader of the Çatalhöyük excavations, Ian Hodder edited a volume called *Simulation Studies in Archaeology*, one of the earliest attempts to encourage the application of CSS techniques to archaeology (Hodder, 1978). Although these techniques were still relatively new at the time, the contributors to that book clearly recognized their potential for facilitating conceptual clarity, hypothesis testing, and the development of new theories. In a summary of trends in computer modeling in archaeology written a decade later, James Bell observed that many of the early simulations were imitative, that is, adopted from other fields, and not explicitly designed for the needs of archaeologists (Bell, 1987).

The adaptation and use of simulations within archaeology increased significantly in the 1990s. Perhaps the most well-known were the agent-based models developed as part of the EOS project, which focused on simulating the emergence of complex social forms in the upper Paleolithic (Doran & Palmer, 1995). In the past decade, archaeologists have taken advantage of even more advanced statistical techniques and increases in computer power (e.g., Costopoulos & Lake, 2010, Gerbault et al., 2014). While CSS techniques cannot prove that a particular archaeological theory is true (what technique could?), they can help to resolve long-standing debates by providing warrant for accepting one hypothesis over another. Despite the limitations and difficulties involved in constructing, calibrating, and validating computer simulations, the general consensus seems to be that this is an important and valuable trend in archaeology (Lake, 2014; Crabtree & Kohler, 2012).

CSS techniques have been applied across a variety of archaeological contexts and time frames, both before and after the Neolithic. For example, computer models of the environmental conditions and likely behaviors during the dispersal of hominids "out of Africa" have helped to provide clarity for scholars involved in debates over the timing and extent of that exodus (Mithen & Reed, 2002; Nikitas & Nikita, 2005). Other models have dealt with sites settled and deserted long after Çatalhöyük, such as the Long House Valley region inhabited by the Kayenta Anasazi (Axtell et al., 2002). Another agent-based archaeological model has simulated the emergence, intensification, and eventual dispersion of prehispanic Pueblo societies (Kohler et al., 2012). Examples of systems-dynamics models include Lowe's simulation of the collapse of the Mayan civilization (1985) and Jayyousi and Reynolds's simulation of the ancient urban center of Monte Albán, which integrates micro-, meso- and macro-levels of systemic change (2014).

The Neolithic transition itself has also been the subject of several computer models. Archaeobotanists have long debated whether or not the transition to agriculture (domestication of plants) was relatively rapid, spreading out from a single location based on key cultivated mutations, or occurred slowly, with long periods of pre-domestic cultivation experiments in multiple locations. The genetic analysis of crops supports the rapid hypothesis, but evidence in the ground concerning crop types suggests that the slow hypothesis is correct. Why the disagreement between lines of evidence? Computer modelling techniques have resolved this problem by demonstrating that, over time, the slow, multilocation, messy domestication process can yield a genetic signature thousands of years later that is nearly indistinguishable from the genetic signature of the fast, single-location domestication process. Thus, genetic analysis can easily miss complexities in domestication from thousands of years ago. The slow and messy hypothesis wins because modelling and simulation explains an anomaly in the evidence (Allaby et al., 2010; Fuller et al., 2010).

Another modelling tool that has been utilized by archaeologists interested in the Neolithic is the Global Land Use and technological Evolution Simulator (GLUES). For example, the results of one simulation study of the Neolithic transition in the Indus valley corroborated the hypothesis of an independent South Asian Neolithic, that is, the emergence of agro-pastoralism on the Indian subcontinent independent of developments in the Levant (Lemmen & Khan, 2012). Another study utilizing GLUES attempted to resolve one of the long-standing arguments among archaeologists about the mechanisms of the transition during which farming and herding were introduced to Europe from the Near East and Anatolia. This simulation found that although demic diffusion (by migration) and cultural diffusion (by trade) can both explain the Western European transition equally well, local adopters of agro-pastoralism appear to have contributed to the process far more strongly than migrating farmers (Lemmen et al., 2011).

Several other models have been developed to study the dynamics of the Neolithic and the emergence of early societies. One agent-based model focused on the function of warfare among early complex hierarchically structured polities and demonstrated the importance of wealth, power, well-defined means of succession, and internally specialized control mechanisms in predicting the outcome of conflict (Gavrilets et al., 2014). Another article reported on the construction of a quantitative model of evolution that involved a population distributed in "patches" and that explored the conditions for the transition from egalitarianism to despotic leadership in the Neolithic and beyond. This model predicts that the transition to a despotic system will occur when surplus resources lead to demographic expansion of groups and dispersal costs limit people's ability to escape the system (Powers & Lehmann, 2014).

As we will explain in more detail below, our systems-dynamics model has several distinctive features relative to these precursors, including its attention to the empirical data derived from the excavations at Çatalhöyük and other sites in the region, and its inclusion of "religious" variables (cognitive, moral, ritual, and social) in its causal architecture.

Synthesizing Theories

In Chapter 2 we introduced a typology of theories about the causes and consequences of transformations of civilizational form, understood as implicitly connected to changes in worldviews and lifeways within a human population. The computational architecture of the model of the Neolithic transition, which we outline in detail below, is an implementation of a synthesis of insights from all three types of theory: ideological-political, material-social, and cognitive-coalitional. Before describing that integration and formalization in the following sections, we point to some examples of insights from each type of theory and introduce the concept of "entanglement," which will guide our integrative efforts in this model.

Graeber and Wengrow, leading examples of the *ideological-political* type in Chapter 2, have devoted considerable thought to the Neolithic, including Çatalhöyük. In *The Dawn of Everything*, they offer an intriguing interpretation of the evidence from this early human town. They see it less as a practical solution to the challenge of supplying more food for a growing population and more as a

> playful or even subversive process ... Seen this way, the 'origins of farming' start to look less like an economic transition and more like a media revolution ... and while we can't know exactly who was doing what in this brave new world, it's abundantly clear that women's work and knowledge were central to its creation; that the whole process was a fairly leisurely, even playful one. (Graeber & Wengrow, 2021, p. 241)

As Jacques Cauvin points out in *The Birth of the Gods and the Origins of Agriculture* (Cauvin, 2000), up until the late twentieth century most archaeologists emphasized the emergence of physical techniques in the means of subsistence as the dominant driver of the Neolithic Revolution, taking what he critiques as a "narrowly economic view" (p. 220). In that book the ideological and religious innovations at Çatalhöyük are critical aspects of his argument that the "interior aspects" of this major civilizational transformation have been overlooked. He concludes that "the Neolithic Revolution is the clear demonstration of the fact that man could not completely transform the way he exploited his natural environment, his own settlements as much as his means of subsistence, without showing at the same time a different conception of the world and of himself in that world" (p. 220).

Such arguments are explicitly aimed against scholars who prefer more or less exclusively *material-social* theories about the causes of civilizational transformation, which as noted above have dominated archaeological theory until relatively recently. Such theories are still popular in many circles and, indeed, still have much to contribute to our overall understanding of this major shift in civilizational form. One of our main examples of this type of theory in Chapter 2 was Ian Morris, who also deals with Çatalhöyük in several of his books including *Why the West Rules—For Now: The Patterns of History, and What They Reveal About the Future* (Morris, 2011). Morris briefly explores cultural aspects of Çatalhöyük, such as the dominant presence of aurochs and the burial of the dead in the floors of the houses, but his focus is on agriculture and sedentation. The shift in civilizational form is less about careful reflection and ideological innovation than about figuring out easier and safer ways to do things, especially capturing energy. Çatalhöyük, then, illustrates what he calls the Morris Theorem: "Change is caused by lazy, greedy, frightened people looking for easier, more profitable, and safer ways to do things" (p. 28).

Harvey Whitehouse, whom we used to illustrate the *cognitive-coalitional* type of theory in Chapter 2, was also part of the JTF project at Çatalhöyük and has engaged the empirical data emerging from the site in order to test his modes of religiosity theory. In the volume that came out of the first phase of the project, Whitehouse worked with Ian Hodder to explore the hypothesis that a shift in ritual mode was a key element of the change that occurred at Çatalhöyük during its millennium and a half of existence. They took the shift from the dominance of feasting (and other) themes in the lower (earlier) levels of the site toward the emergence of homogenization and recurrent themes in the upper (later) levels as supportive of this hypothesis. "It is the relationship between divergent modalities and frequencies of ritual transmission that provides the impetus for increasingly complex social morphology" (Whitehouse & Hodder, 2010, p. 142). His contribution to the second volume tested the theory further, but with far more engagement with the empirical material. There he and his coauthors identified trends that suggest doctrinal religious rituals were linked to variables such as increasing agricultural intensity, population density, and community size (Whitehouse et al., 2014).

We see value and data-grounded plausibility in all three types of theory. In fact, we see the debates over which type of theory best explains what archaeologists find in the ground as slightly misplaced. Consider an analogy. When we run a multiple-regression analysis, we are trying to determine which of several independent factors are responsible for explaining variance in some output measure, Variable X. Say we discover that Factor A explains 30 percent, Factor B 20 percent, and Factor C 10 percent, while the remaining 40 percent of the variance is not explained by the three factors we consider. We'd probably be inclined to conclude that Factor A does most of the work, as much as the other two factors combined, and we'd hope that the linear association points to an underlying causal relationship, so that we can infer something about real-world causal dynamics related to output Variable X.

Social scientists are used to thinking in this way, and it promotes the idea of competition between independent causal factors. But it is all too easy to minimize the importance of the key assumption that the three factors need to be significantly *independent* of one another for the regression analysis to work. What happens when the three factors are strongly dependent on one another? Then looking for a clean victor in a competition among independent causal factors doesn't make sense. In nonlinear dynamical systems, it is common for contributing causal factors to be locked in resonant or dampening loops with one another, which forces a shift in thinking. We no longer look for the factor that explains the most variance in Variable X; instead, we seek a causal architecture that shows how a variety of individually necessary-but-not-sufficient conditions combine to create the conditions under which an interesting phenomenon emerges, the phenomenon we measure with Variable X.

This is what we see happening in the Neolithic transition: ideological-political, material-social, and cognitive-coalitional factors are locked in nonlinear relationships of looping dependence. So how can we integrate insights from all of them? Here we will use religious "entanglement" as a key concept for synthesizing theories—that is, we think of entanglement as an emergent feature of Neolithic social life. The intensity of entanglement is the "Variable X" that defies explanation using competitive, linear-modeling approaches and calls instead for nonlinear modeling techniques using complex causal architectures.

In this context our use of the term "entanglement" follows that of Ian Hodder, for whom it refers to the co-evolutionary reciprocal dynamics between humans and (other) things whereby they are increasingly bound together through complex dynamics of (mutual) production, enablement, constraint, and limitation. Hodder spells out the philosophical sense of this term in most detail in *Entangled: An Archaeology of the Relationships between Humans and Things* (2012), but he has been using it to describe the evolutionary codependence of human beings and other material things for many years. In discussing the Neolithic engagement of "spirits" (animal spirits or ancestor ghosts) in *Çatalhöyük: The Leopard's Tale*, for example, Hodder suggests that "as people, society and crafted materials increasingly became entangled and codependent, so the codependent material agents were further enlisted and engaged in a social world in which spirits were involved" (Hodder, 2006, p. 195) —a classic example of looping nonlinearity.

Leading up to and throughout the life cycle of Çatalhöyük, human beings became increasingly entangled with the natural objects of their world, including plants, animals, and building materials, as well as with their own social productions, including agricultural technologies, figurines, and houses. Hodder's use of the term "entanglement" has been adapted and adopted by several other scholars associated with the Çatalhöyük project in their attempts to interpret various aspects of the Neolithic. For example, in several places Dorian Fuller and colleagues have explored the way in which humans and plants were entangled or mutually entrapped in the long pathway to domestication (Fuller et al., 2012).

Our simulation includes variables related to the domestication of plants and animals, but our primary interest is in teasing out the way in which things (and processes) deemed religious became entangled in the human-thing codependent evolutionary nexus during the Neolithic. Hodder emphasized the role of religion in the introduction to the volume reporting on Phase II of the project. He noted that religion, as an integral part of life at Çatalhöyük, played varying roles in instigating and producing transformative change throughout the site sequence from 7400 to 6000 BCE. Religion was central to the complex world of the community, which was constituted by sodalities akin to mystery cults, and dominated by symbols such as the leopard and the bear. As Hodder pointed out, however, it was the ancestors and the wild bull that served as the primary foci around which social groups formed and developed relations with each other (2014, p. 3).

In their reflections on the "magical" relation to material artifacts at Çatalhöyük in the same volume, Nakamura and Pels also stressed the importance of religion in the ever complexifying web of people-thing relations. They noted that "various archaeological accounts of the site point to a fairly distinctive symbolic sphere at Çatalhöyük that was deeply entangled in the daily lives of people and the beings (both living and dead) with whom they shared their world." Nakamura and Pels refer to this sphere of interaction as "the transcendent nonhuman world of Çatalhöyük" (2014, p. 195).

As we noted in Chapter 1, the term "religion" is highly contested, and not only in archaeology. Even—or especially—in departments of religious studies it is hard to find a consensus on its meaning. For our purposes here, we will use the term in the way it commonly functions in the discourse among scholars interested in studying religion from a cognitive-science perspective. In this context, "religion" is used in a broad sense to designate modes of shared imaginative engagement with the supernatural agents culturally postulated by an in-group, which promote cooperation, commitment, and cohesion in the face of out-group threats and environmental challenges (see Shults, 2014b). With reference to Çatalhöyük, this means ritual interaction with culturally postulated, putatively disembodied, intentional forces such as auroch-spirits and ancestor-ghosts.

It is important to emphasize that what we are calling "religion" is itself an always evolving nexus of entangled variable forces (cognitive, moral, ritual, social, etc.). This is why describing it well requires the integration of multiple disciplinary perspectives. The model we present below is in fact based on an *entanglement of theories*, a causal architecture that integrates insights from a wide variety of fields, including cognitive science, psychology, sociology, political theory, and economics—as well as the scientific study of religion.

In the conclusion to the volume reporting on Phase I of the JTF project, Hodder cited an offhand comment by LeRon who had teasingly admitted his initial annoyance and impatience with scientists' obsession with details about "petrified poop" and relative inattention to the far more interesting philosophical implications of the site (2010, p. 351). In the conclusion to the volume on Phase II of the project, Hodder noted the danger that interdisciplinary scholars might bring their pet theories and impose them on Çatalhöyük. He wondered whether the "big data" from the site really caused theorists to change their minds (2014, p. 346). In the wake of Phase III of the project, both of us authors can confirm that the whole process has led us to a new appreciation of the importance of big theory *and* of the intricacies of archaeological data—as well as a new tool for linking them tightly together.

NSIM: The Neolithic Social Investment Model

The Neolithic Social Investment Model (NSIM) is built on the conversion framework explained in Chapter 3. Figure 3.8 lays out the conversion model in as much detail as the abstraction from particular times and places permits. Figure 4.1 is a revised version of that diagram, specific to the Neolithic context in which the *before* state (State A) is called "low investment" (LI) and the *after* state (State B) is called "high investment" (HI). The stocks and flows are renamed appropriately, as are the six flow rates. As in Figure 3.8, so in Figure 4.1, the next stage is all about designing a causal architecture capable of specifying the six flow rates and responding to the output variable "HI_Prop," which expresses the proportion of the HI subpopulation within the entire population. The notation is also slightly simplified: parameters are designated as circles having wedges (only one is shown), variables are designated as circles without wedges, stocks are designated as squares, flows are thick arrows, and flow rate adjustment factors are thin arrows. As always, mathematics lurks behind the scenes: simple calculus defines the relations between stocks and flows, while intuitive algebraic formulas explain precisely how parameters and variables combine to determine flow rates and other variables.

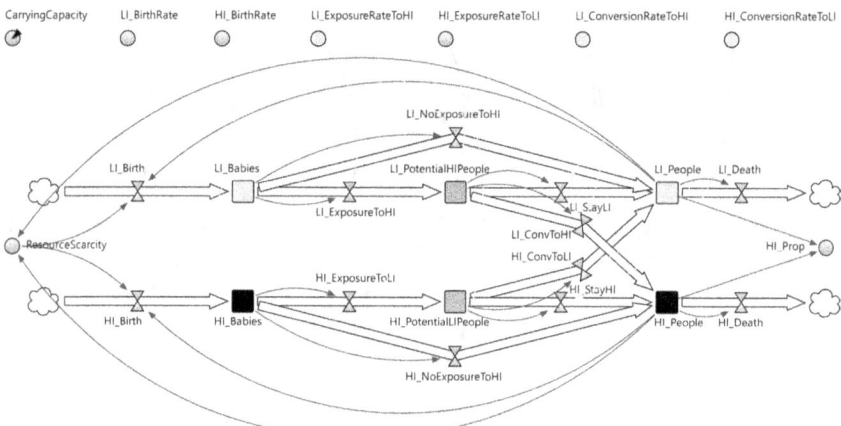

Figure 4.1 Stock-and-flow diagram for conversion model between low-investment (LI) and high-investment (HI) lifestyles.

This specification of the conversion model invites a narrative explanation. The conceptual framework for NSIM is *lifestyle conversion* within a constrained geographical area (such as the Konya Plain, where Çatalhöyük is located). Here "lifestyle" is shorthand for "worldview and lifeway." The LI lifestyle encompasses hunter-gatherer groups and people who used farming techniques without embracing the intensification of sociality and human-thing entanglement that we see in Çatalhöyük. They could plan for the future and delay gratification to some extent but were not as intensely entangled with people, places, and things.

For example, people in LI lifestyles lacked permanent healthy storage facilities for grain, which limited the scale and intensity of crop cultivation. The HI lifestyle involves agricultural settlements with higher levels of entanglement with the vital forces of their environment, including people, animals, plants, objects, and culturally postulated spirits. For example, people in HI lifestyles were far less likely to move around than people in LI lifestyles because of this difference in entanglement with people and place; they built houses and incorporated healthy storage facilities for grain within them, so they could do a lot more with crop cultivation.

These two lifestyles (and related worldviews) are treated as alternatives with transition paths between them. The six variables needed to determine how the population flows through the conversion model, and thereby the ratio of HI to LI people, are birthrates for each type, rates of exposure to the other type of lifestyle, and rates of conversion to the alternative lifestyle.

The model presents babies being born into LI (top left) and HI (bottom left) lifestyles according to the corresponding birthrates (LI_BirthRate and HI_BirthRate). The LI people are exposed to the HI lifestyle alternative at the rate dictated by the matching variable (LI_ExposureRateToHI). The LI people who are so exposed then may convert to the HI lifestyle at a rate depending on the conversion variable (LI_ConversionRateToHI). A parallel conversion path exists to move from the HI lifestyle over to the LI lifestyle (with variables HI_ExposureRateToLI and HI_ConversionRateToLI). Of course, everyone dies in the end. The model also includes a CarryingCapacity parameter that contributes, with total population size, to resource scarcity, which in turn modifies birth rates. Figure 4.1 suppresses other parameters that influence the two birthrates.

The links indicate causal connections between elements of the diagram. For example, the ResourceScarcity variable is defined intuitively in mathematical terms by (*LI_People + HI_People*) */ CarryingCapacity*. The stocks (boxes) are defined by first-order differential equations. For instance, the HI_PotentialConvertsToLI stock is defined by *d(HI_PotentialConvertsToLI)/dt = HI_ExposireToLI − HI_ConvertToLI − HI_StayHI* (the right-hand side is just inputs minus outputs). The flows (broad arrows) are defined by simple mathematical formulas for flow rates (represented by the double triangle in the center of each flow arrow). For instance, the LI_ConvertToHI flow rate is defined as follows: *LI_ConversionRateToHI × HI_PotentialConvertsToLI*. These formulas are natural and, we believe, non-controversial.

To apply this conversion model to the Neolithic transition, we need a theoretically persuasive way to produce the six key variables (the two birth rates, two exposure rates, and two conversion rates). Think of this "theoretically persuasive way" vaguely for now, and call it a "Causal Nexus." We will define this Causal Nexus, which is a collection of fully specified and carefully clustered mechanisms, in more detail shortly, but it needs to have several characteristics. (1) We need the Causal Nexus to be responsive to the HI_Prop variable, which expresses the proportion of HI people in the entire population in the geographical area of interest. (2) We also need the Causal Nexus to produce six variables as output. And (3) we need the Causal Nexus to have a range of parameters as inputs, along with the HI_Prop variable input, so that we can explore the model's behavior in a variety of ecologically meaningful conditions. So, what's in the Causal Nexus?

The theoretical core of the Causal Nexus is presented in Figure 4.2. This is the heart of what we consider to be the causal architecture of the Neolithic transition, at least within the limitations of the Neolithic Social Intensity Model (NSIM). The five input parameters on the left side of the diagram define the beginnings of a parameter space whose characteristics we will describe later. The HI_Prop variable (the proportion of high-intensity people in the population, derived from the conversion model) is presented as an input on the right side of the diagram. The remaining variables and the connections between them express the theoretical elements of the causal architecture. After explaining this architecture, we'll show how we extract from it the six input variables (i.e., the two birthrates, two exposure rates, and two conversion rates) needed to drive the conversion model.

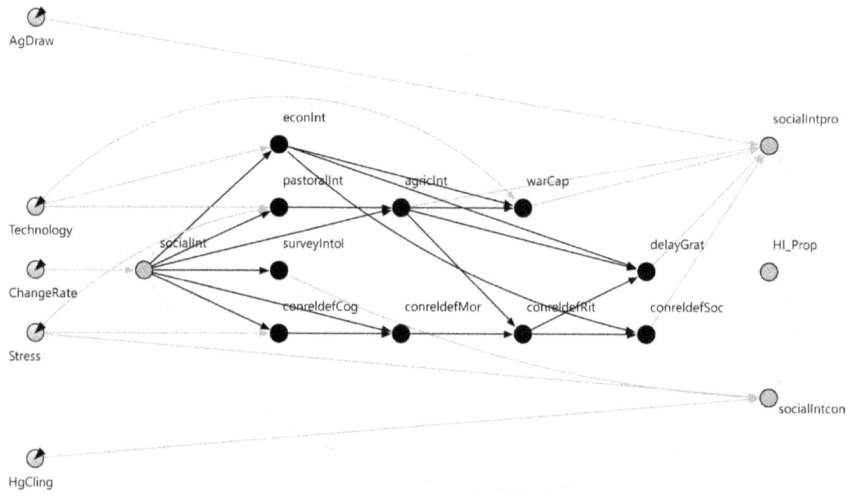

Figure 4.2 The core of the Causal Nexus for the Neolithic transition.

This causal architecture is consistent with Hodder's entanglement hypothesis. However, it also incorporates insights from several other theories derived from empirical research during the past couple of decades within the cognitive science of religion and related disciplines (for a detailed survey, see Shults, 2014b).

The Social Intensity variable (socialInt) toward the left side of the diagram is a quantitative proxy for the social aspects of the degree of entanglement present in the region in question. As social relationships become more complex and people's connections to objects, animals, plants, places, and processes become richer, the Social Intensity variable increases, which in turn influences a variety of theoretically motivated intervening variables.

Note that the Social Intensity variable (socialInt) and the proportion of HI people (HI_Prop) are different conceptual constructs. On the one hand, the contrast between HI and LI lifestyles reflects the degree of entanglement between people and the animals, plants, places, objects, and invisible forces of their environment, and high HI_Prop means that more people have chosen the HI lifestyle. High social intensity, on the other hand, is a narrower concept—it represents a key component of the HI lifestyle but is not equivalent to it. While we expect these two variables to rise and fall in the same direction, it is conceivable that they could change at quite different rates. For instance, HI_Prop might begin to increase early and change slowly, while socialInt might increase quickly but only after the model has been running for a while; or the opposite might occur. We designed the causal architecture of NSIM to reflect the possibility that the aspect of the HI lifestyle we call social intensity, which is particularly relevant to understanding religion, might develop partially independently of the embrace of HI lifestyles. Yet we also expect that HI_Prop could only reach the highest levels if socialInt were also high.

Jumping to the right side of the diagram, we can see that some of these intermediate variables tend to increase Social Intensity (the degree of increase represented by the socialIntpro variable) while others tend to decrease Social Intensity (the degree of decrease represented by the socialIntcon variable). These two variables on the far right increment and decrement (respectively) the Social Intensity variable, with their effects weighted by the proportion of HI people and the proportion of LI people (respectively). The ChangeRate parameter determines how quickly both incremental variables change the Social Intensity variable, thereby speeding up or slowing down the transition described within the model. The loop established in this way means that Social Intensity both impacts and is impacted by all intermediate variables.

Within this fundamental feedback loop, the theoretical action takes place in the interactions between the intervening variables and between those variables and the four parameters that influence them (AgDraw, Technology, Stress, and HgCling). We'll explain these variables one by one in what follows, spelling out the theoretical underpinnings of the causal architecture along the way. Table 4.1 lists these parameters and variables with their abbreviations and definitions.

First, we will describe the five parameters that function as inputs to the Causal Nexus (note that the names of these parameters begin with upper-case letters to distinguish them from variable names). Parameters are fixed for any given run of the model and define a parameter space that spans all of the possible dynamics of NSIM.

Agricultural Draw (AgDraw parameter) is the tendency to want to embrace the HI lifestyle associated with settled agriculture, domesticated animals, and town life. AgDraw impacts socialIntpro: an increased tendency in the population to embrace the HI lifestyle will ratchet up HI growth.

Technology (Technology parameter) is the level (complexity, quantity, quality, entanglement) of technological advancement within the regional population. Technology includes farming know-how, tool design and manufacture, knowledge of medicinal plants, house-building techniques, and so on. Technology impacts:

- warCap: Increased technological advancement raises the capacity of a population to wage war.
- econInt: Increased technological advancement improves a population's capacity for managing more complex economic exchange and increases the diversity and value of traded products.
- pastoralInt: Increased technological advancement improves a population's capacity to maintain and breed its domesticated animals.

Change Rate (ChangeRate parameter) sets the rate at which socialIntpro increments and socialIntcon decrements the socialInt variable.

Stress (Stress parameter) is the level of anxiety-producing or survival-threatening conditions in the natural environment of the population. Stress impacts other variables in the Causal Nexus in an inverted parabolic way, as the formula $4 \times \text{Stress} \times (1 - \text{Stress})$ indicates. This means that the greatest impact occurs when Stress is middling, and that both low and high Stress have less impact. Stress affects:

- pastoralInt: Moderate stress puts pressure on individuals to grow crops and domesticate animals, if they know how. If conditions are less stressful, the LI hunting-and-gathering lifestyle is easier, decreasing pastoralInt. If conditions are more stressful, crops won't grow and domesticated animals die, decreasing pastoralInt.

Table 4.1 Causal Nexus parameters and variables constituting the causal architecture of the model

Abbreviation	Name	Definition
Parameters		
AgDraw	Agricultural Draw	Varies between 0.01 and 1.00
Technology	Technology	Varies between 0.00 and 1.00
ChangeRate	Change Rate	Varies between 0.01 and 1.00
Stress	Stress	Varies between 0.00 and 1.00
HgCling	Hunter-Gatherer Cling	Varies between 0.01 and 1.00
Variables that covary with Social Intensity		
econInt	Economic Intensity	(socialInt + Technology)/2
pastoralInt	Pastoral Intensity	Technology × socialInt × (4 × Stress × (1 − Stress))
agricInt	Agricultural Intensity	(pastoralInt + socialInt)/2
warCap	Warmaking Capacity	(Technology + agricInt + econInt)/3
surveyIntol	Surveyance Intolerance	socialInt
delayGrat	Delay of Gratification	(econInt + agricInt + conreldefRit)/3
Variables related to contesting evolutionarily stabilized religion-relevant defaults		
conreldefCog	Contest Religious Defaults: Cognitive	socialInt × 4 × Stress × (1 − Stress)
conreldefMor	Contest Religious Defaults: Moral	(socialInt + conreldefCog)/2
conreldefRit	Contest Religious Defaults: Ritual	(agricInt + conreldefMor)/2
conreldefSoc	Contest Religious Defaults: Social	(conreldefRit + econInt)/2
Variables structuring the major feedback loop		
socialIntpro	Social Intensity Pro	((econInt + agricInt + warCap + delayGrat + conreldefSoc)/5) × AgDraw × HI_Prop
socialIntcon	Social Intensity Con	((surveyIntol + (1 − 4 × Stress × (1 − Stress)))/2) × HgCling × (1 − HI_Prop)
socialInt	Social Intensity	min(max(socialInt + ChangeRate × (socialIntpro − socialIntcon),0.01),0.99)

- conreldefCog: Moderate stress puts pressure on individuals to contest their religious-cognitive defaults (e.g., they resist their tribal tendencies and begin to explore new ways to cooperate and share resources with people beyond their immediate kith/kin group). High levels of stress reinstate religious cognitive defaults (as terror management theory suggests), while low levels of stress do not induce people to challenge those defaults.
- socialIntcon: High stress puts too much pressure on individuals, overriding their capacity to contest defaults or delay gratification, tempting them to adopt LI lifestyles. Low stress yields no incentive to cooperate or increase social intensity. Moderate stress produces the least resistance to social intensity. Note that, in this case only, the formula regarding stress takes the form *(1 – 4 × Stress × (1 – Stress))* rather than *4 × Stress × (1 – Stress)*, inverting the parabola.

Hunter-Gatherer Cling (HGcling parameter) is the tendency to want to conserve the LI lifestyle associated with hunter-gatherers. Hgcling impacts socialIntcon because an increased tendency in the population to want to conserve the LI lifestyle will ratchet down HI growth and thus Social Intensity.

Second, let's consider the intermediate variables that the Social Intensity variable directly or indirectly impacts.

Economic Intensity (econInt variable) is the level (complexity, quantity) of economic exchange within and across groups. Economic intensity increases with both social intensity and technology. The econInt variable impacts:

- socialIntpro: Increased economic exchange ratchets up the need to keep investing in a HI sedentary-domestication lifestyle.
- warCap: Increased economic exchange improves social networking and cooperation skills and imports technology and know-how, which raise the capacity to wage war.
- delayGrat: Increased economic exchange contributes to social entrainment of individuals such that they learn to delay gratification.
- conreldefSoc: Increased economic exchange contributes to social entrainment of individuals such that they learn to be less vigilant of non-kith/kin, reciprocators, and cultural others.

Pastoral Intensity (pastoralInt variable) is the level (complexity, extent) of entanglement between a group of humans and the animals they (at least partially) domesticate. Pastoral intensity increases with both the social intensity required to cooperate and the technology required for domesticating animals, and both elements are important simultaneously (this is why the formula uses multiplication rather than averaging). The pastoralInt variable impacts agricInt in the same way because increased pastoral (animal) entanglement requires increased agricultural (plant) entanglement to feed the animals.

Agricultural Intensity (agricInt variable) is the level (complexity, extent) of entanglement between a group of humans and the plants they (at least partially) domesticate. Agricultural intensity rises as pastoral and social intensity rise; both factors are equally important. Of course, agricultural intensity also drives pastoral intensity, a subordinate causal link expressed through the mediation of the socialIntpro variable. The agricInt variable impacts:

- socialIntpro: As more of the population becomes agriculturally entangled, the general willingness to invest in HI lifestyles increases.
- warCap: The capacity to wage war is improved when agricultural entanglement increases because of the way in which the latter improves general social cooperation skills and makes it easier to provide regular food for training and utilizing troops.
- delayGrat: As more of the population becomes agriculturally entangled, it becomes easier to trust the farming process and delay one's need to gratify desires quickly.
- conreldefRit: As more of the population becomes agriculturally entangled, participation in imagistic, high-impact rituals declines in favor of low-impact oft-repeated rituals that bind people more closely together in socially stable and religiously reinforced configurations.

Warmaking Capacity (warCap variable) is the overall capacity of groups to wage war on other groups. The capacity and willingness to wage war increases with technological sophistication, economic intensity, and agricultural intensity. The warCap variable impacts socialIntpro: increased capacity to wage war ratchets up the general tendency toward investing in HI lifestyles.

Surveyance Intolerance (surveyIntol variable) is the level of annoyance at being watched by others. The more intense sociality becomes, the more everyone knows your business and the more tension there is around surveyance. The surveyIntol variable impacts socialIntcon: annoyance at being watched can have a ratcheting-down effect, leading to a higher percentage of the population resisting the HI lifestyle. (Note that this variable mirrors Social Intensity [socialInt], and this adds nothing new; it is included only to help explain this dimension of increased intensity of social life.)

Delay of Gratification (delayGrat variable) is the willingness to delay immediate gratification of desires. Experimental studies suggest that religion can increase the ability (Rounding et al., 2012), or at least the motivation (Harrison & McKay, 2013), to delay gratification, which lends warrant to the idea that it may have played some adaptive role by enhancing self-control and in-group cooperation. The ability to delay gratification is increased, to about the same degree, by economic intensity, agricultural intensity, and the willingness to contest religious ritual defaults. The delayGrat variable impacts socialIntpro: the willingness to invest in HI sedentary-domestication lifestyles is ratcheted up by an increase in the population's willingness and ability to delay gratification.

Third, we come to the variables pertaining to contesting evolutionarily stabilized cognitive defaults that are more directly relevant to religion.

Contest Religious Defaults: Cognitive (conreldefCog variable) is the extent to which the evolved religious cognitive defaults (terror-management-motivated engagement with narratively immediate, small-scale idiosyncratic spirits) are contested. The willingness to contest religious-cognitive defaults increases so long as two other factors both increase (thus multiplication rather than averaging appears in the underlying mathematics): when social intensity increases and when moderate stress forces people to become more aware of cognitive defaults. Extremely low or extremely high stress has the opposite effect. The conreldefCog variable impacts conreldefMor: preference for and willingness to think outside the scope of a small group calls for contesting default moral intuitions that support small-group lifestyles.

Contest Religious Defaults: Moral (conreldefMor variable) is the extent to which evolved religious moral defaults (e.g., high concern for purity, parochial care for in-group) are contested. The willingness to contest religious moral defaults increases as social intensity increases and when some capacity to contest cognitive defaults is in place. The conreldefMor variable impacts conreldefRit: preference for and willingness to engage in less imagistic, divine agent rituals increases as freedom from small-group moral defaults increases.

Contest Religious Defaults: Ritual (conreldefRit variable) is the extent to which the evolved religious ritual defaults (high-intensity, infrequent, "imagistic" rituals engaging active spirit-agents) are contested and transformed in favor of low-intensity, more frequent, social-bonding, "doctrinal" rituals that imaginatively engage supernatural agents relevant to larger groups (McCauley & Lawson, 2002; Whitehouse, 2004). The willingness to contest religious-ritual defaults in this way increases with agricultural intensity and rising willingness to contest moral defaults. The conreldefRit variable impacts:

- delayGrat: Increased openness and willingness to engage in non-imagistic rituals improves one's ability and willingness to delay gratification because the engaged spirits are concerned with the larger group's welfare.
- conreldefSoc: Increased openness and willingness to engage in non-imagistic rituals makes one accustomed to being around and trusting non-kith/kin, reciprocators, and cultural others.

Contest Religious Defaults: Social (conreldefSoc variable) is the extent to which the evolved religious social defaults (vigilance toward non-kith/kin, reciprocators, and cultural others) are contested and transformed in favor of openness to outsiders, to trading goods, and to learning about strangers. The willingness to contest religious social defaults is driven up by increasing willingness to contest religious ritual defaults and by economic intensity that forces mixing with strangers. The conreldefSoc variable impacts socialIntpro: willingness to invest in sedentary-domestication lifestyles is ratcheted up by an increase in the population's trust in non-kith/kin, reciprocators, and cultural others.

Fourth, what about the variables defining the fundamental feedback mechanism of the Causal Nexus?

Social Intensity Pro (socialIntpro variable) is an incrementing mechanism by which socialInt is increased. Five factors contribute to the increase of social intensity: economic intensity, agricultural intensity, war-making capacity, the willingness to delay gratification, and the willingness to contest religious social defaults. This effect is amplified by both the proportion of HI people and the AgDraw parameter.

Social Intensity Con (socialIntcon variable) is a decrementing mechanism by which socialInt is decreased. Two factors contribute to the decrease of social intensity: allergy to surveyance and either low or high stress (but not moderate stress). This effect is amplified both by the tendency to cling to LI hunter-gatherer lifestyles and by the proportion of LI people (i.e., 1–HI_prop).

Social Intensity (socialInt variable) has been discussed already as an important component of entanglement in HI lifestyles. The socialInt variable increments (via socialIntpro) or decrements (via socialIntcon) its own old value. All of the model's reinforcing loops involve the link from socialIntpro to socialInt (+) and all balancing loops involve the link from socialIntcon to socialInt (–). The socialInt variable impacts six intermediate variables as follows:

- econInt: Economic exchange within and across groups will become more complex as willingness to invest in a HI sedentary-domestication lifestyle grows.
- pastoralInt: Pastoral entanglement will become stronger as people become more willing to invest in HI sedentary-domestication lifestyles.
- agricInt: Agricultural entanglement will become stronger as people become more willing to invest in HI sedentary-domestication lifestyles.
- surveyIntol: The more people live close to each other in the same place, doing the same things repeatedly, the higher the susceptibility to being annoyed by having people watching them.
- conreldefCog: Participation in a HI sedentary-domestication lifestyle forces the contestation of defaults toward focusing on narratively immediate, terror-managing engagement with small-scale idiosyncratic spirits.
- conreldefMor: Participation in a HI sedentary-domestication lifestyle forces the contestation of defaults toward overriding purity concerns related to in-group care.

The Causal Nexus has a lot of moving parts! Importantly, the explanation of its parameters, variables, and mathematical relationships in the foregoing makes clear that all three kinds of theoretical factors—ideological-political, material-social, and cognitive-coalitional—are richly represented. Thus, in an important sense, the design of the Causal Nexus expresses the hypothesis that all three types of theoretical factors are *individually* necessary but not sufficient conditions for explaining the Neolithic transition, yet *collectively* a sufficient explanation for the emergence of high-intensity lifestyles in farming communities with domesticated plants and animals.

The final challenge on the way to a complete causal architecture is to make the Causal Nexus we have described generate the six key output variables that function as inputs to the conversion model. To reiterate, those output variables are two birthrates (LI_BirthRate and HI_BirthRate), two exposure rates (LI_ExposureRateToHI and HI_ExposureRateToLI), and two conversion rates (LI_ConversionRateToHI and HI_ConversionRateToLI).

Figure 4.3 depicts the links between the various components of the Causal Nexus and these six output variables. Note that we have suppressed the display of links already discussed to clarify the diagram. Also, we now display three more parameters; these are important for generating some of the output variables but do not impact variables within the Causal Nexus itself. All three are biologically and environmentally determined aspects of human beings: the minimum

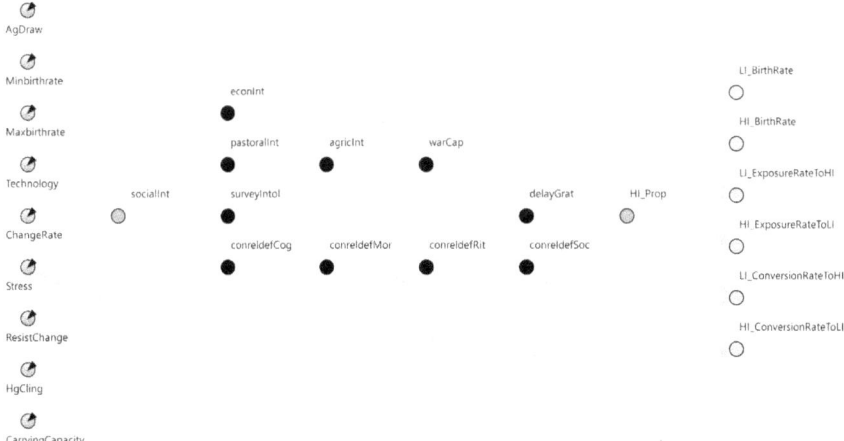

Figure 4.3 Six outputs from the Causal Nexus.

birthrate, the maximum birthrate, and the average psychological tendency to resist change.

Table 4.2 lists those parameters along with the definitions of the six output variables.

We now explain the mathematical formulas for the six *output* variables.

LI_BirthRate: In LI societies, increasing stress drives birth rates down from the maximum toward the minimum. Note that there is a linear rather than a parabolic effect of the Stress parameter here.

HI_BirthRate: In HI societies, either increasing agricultural intensity or decreasing stress (thus: $min((agricInt+(1-stress)),1)$) will drive birth rates upward from the minimum to the maximum.

LI_ExposureRateToHI: In LI societies, exposure to HI alternatives occurs through either trade or war, amplified by the prevalence of HI people and the overall level of technology.

HI_ExposureRateToLI: In HI societies, exposure to LI alternatives depends on both low technology and the prevalence of LI people ($1-HI\_prop$).

LI_ConversionRateToHI: In LI societies, conversion to HI alternatives becomes more frequent when economic intensity, war-making capacity, and the willingness to contest religious-cognitive defaults rise. Middling stress increases this conversion rate while low stress or high stress inhibit it. All factors are roughly equal in importance, and their average effect is moderated by resistance to change.

HI_ConversionRateToLI: In HI societies, conversion to LI alternatives occurs under four roughly equally weighted conditions. Surveyance intolerance

Table 4.2 Additional parameters impacting output variables but not Causal Nexus variables

Abbreviation	Name	Definition
Parameters		
Minbirthrate	Minimum Birth Rate	Varies between 0.50 and 2.00 (children per person)
Maxbirthrate	Maximum Birth Rate	Varies between 1.00 and 5.00 (children per person)
ResistChange	Resistance to Change	Varies between 0.00 and 1.00
Six output variables from the Causal Nexus that function as inputs to the conversion model		
LI_BirthRate	LI Birth Rate	$Minbirthrate + (Maxbirthrate - Minbirthrate) \times (1 - Stress)$
HI_BirthRate	HI Birth Rate	$Minbirthrate + (Maxbirthrate - Minbirthrate) \times min((agricInt + (1 - stress)), 1)$
LI_ExposureRateToHI	LI Exposure Rate to HI	$((econInt + warCap)/2) \times Technology \times HI\_prop$
HI_ExposureRateToLI	HI Exposure Rate to LI	$(1 - Technology) \times (1 - HI\_prop)$
LI_ConversionRateToHI	LI Conversion Rate to HI	$((econInt+warCap+conreldefCog+(4\times Stress\times(1-Stress)))/4)\times ResistChange$
HI_ConversionRateToLI	HI Conversion Rate to LI	$((surveyIntol + HI\_prop + max(0, 2 \times warCap - 1) + (1 - conreldefCog) + (1 - (4 \times Stress \times (1 - Stress))))/5) \times ResistChange$

drives up this conversion rate. So does war-making capacity, but only when it becomes extreme so that it interferes with the benefits of township life (thus the formula *max(0, 2 × warCap − 1)*). The willingness to contest religious-cognitive defaults has the opposite effect, driving this conversion rate down. And either low stress or high stress makes this type of conversion more likely, while middling stress makes it less likely. All factors are roughly equal in importance, and their average effect is moderated by resistance to change.

All computational simulations need to specify how model time versus real-world time works. We needed to explore the NSIM dynamics before we could be sure about what real-world time to associate with one cycle of the model. After running a few experiments, we concluded that we could interpret *one cycle of the model as one year of real-world time*.

Simulation Experiments

The system-dynamics model we have described above is connected to the data from Çatalhöyük in two important ways. On the one hand, as we'll make clear in a moment, NSIM has been able to model the growth of the percentage of high-investment people in a Neolithic population in a way that conforms to widely accepted interpretations of the archaeological evidence from the site and surrounding areas. At the very least, we have constructed a theoretically grounded causal architecture that simulates the emergence of a population pattern that plausibly represents the growth of Çatalhöyük during the first millennium of its existence.

On the other hand, the primary virtue of theory-centric models like NSIM is the way in which they facilitate the construction and clarification of causal architectures that are based on scientific hypotheses rooted in empirical data and provide a means for experimentally exploring the validity and implications of more general theories about, for example, the transformation of civilizational forms. Although the quantitative aspects of the model are not explicitly testable in the traditional scientific sense, they were deeply informed by the data from Çatalhöyük and contribute to the confirmation of several important theories. The most prominent among these is Hodder's theory of entanglement, which is grounded in a mass of archeological data. However, NSIM also helps to validate and explore the consequences of a host of theoretical developments within the cognitive science of religion and related fields, all of which are rooted in current-day experimental data (Wildman, 2009). The cognitive-science theories are relevant to Çatalhöyük on the almost universally accepted assumption that intervening genetic changes do not materially impact the relevant aspects of human cognition.

The first step in exploring a model such as this one is to validate it in a variety of ways. At the theoretical level, validation consists in evaluating the plausibility of the various mathematical formulas and the decisions about where the major causal links belong. The mathematical formulas themselves are rather straightforward, given the causal reasoning they reflect. Given that all variables directly or indirectly affect all other variables, the leading theoretical-validation issue is which links (thin grey arrows) in Figure 4.2 should be thought of as expressions of the strongest lines of causation. In the model development process, we debated the most important causal links in great detail.

At a technical level, an important validation question is whether NSIM yields stable equilibrium states between the extremes of 0 and 1 for the proportion of HI people in the wider population (HI_prop variable). It turns out that the model does produce relatively stable equilibria intermediate between extremes, which suggests that the Neolithic transition is not an all-or-nothing process. It is also a sign that NSIM contains interesting behavior worth analyzing in more detail. Another technical validation question is whether the evolution of the simulation within a single run produces an interpretable model of life at Çatalhöyük and within the surrounding Konya Plain. Most of our analysis was dedicated to this kind of validation, as we now explain.

The challenge in analyzing this model's parameter space is to understand how the model represents the transition pathways from a high percentage of LI people to a high percentage of HI people. For the sake of concrete analysis and manageable communication, we stipulated a specific transition pathway and asked about the conditions under which the model's development approximates that pathway. The pathway we specified had the percentage of HI people (HI_prop) increasing from zero steadily up to 50 percent at the rate of 10 percent per century, staying around that 50 percent mark for about 200 model cycles (about two centuries), then jumping up to 80 percent in a single century, and then climbing to 100 percent at the rate of 10 percent per century. We think this is a plausible approximation of the growth of Çatalhöyük over the first millennium of its existence: growing steadily, perhaps with a few slowdowns and leaps, and eventually drawing in most of the people from the Konya Plain.

We call this pathway the Target transition pathway in view of the fact that we asked our model to approximate it. Figure 4.4 plots NSIM's best solution along with the Target transition pathway. Table 4.3 displays the parameter settings producing this best approximation to the stipulated ideal.

Taking this best approximation to the Target transition pathway as a starting point, we varied parameters around the solution to evaluate the behavior of the model. We were particularly interested in the Stress and Technology parameters, which reflect ecological conditions and accumulating theoretical knowledge and practical know-how. While we were focused on the HI_prop variable, we also kept track of the Social Intensity variable (socialInt), because this furnishes a convenient way to judge the extent to which changing model dynamics depend on Social Intensity understood as a key component of HI lifestyles. The results of our investigation can be expressed as answers to a series of questions.

First, what happens to Social Intensity (socialInt) as the model moves through the pathway that best approximates the stipulated Target transition

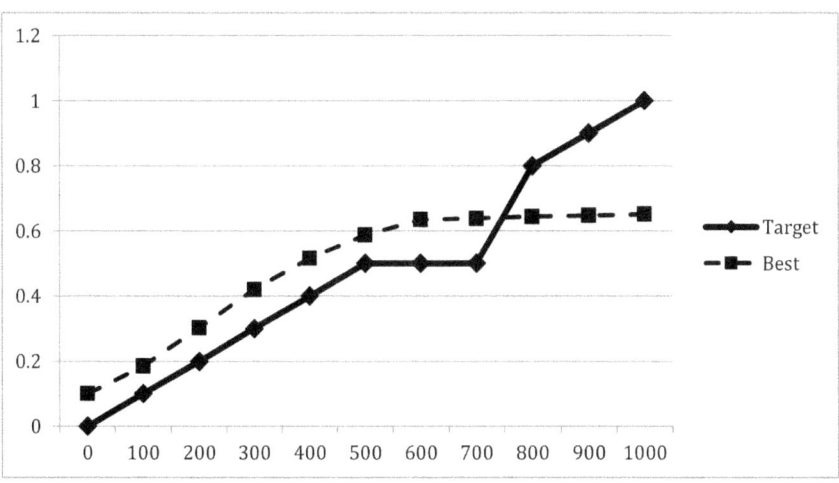

Figure 4.4 Closest solution to the Target transition pathway for the growing population of Çatalhöyük.

Table 4.3 Parameter settings yielding the closest approximation to the target transition pathway through the model's parameter space from a low to a high proportion of HI people

Parameter	Setting
carryingCapacity	10,000
Changerate	0.051
Technology	0.679
Resistchange	0.99
Maxbirthrate	2.5
Minbirthrate	0.5
Stress	0.34
Hgcling	1.0
Civdraw	0.34

pathway? Figure 4.5 gives the answer. As HI_prop increases relatively smoothly, socialInt stays low, moves through a period of rapid changes, stabilizes at a high value, and finally cycles close to its high-value equilibrium. We had tentatively hypothesized that socialInt would increase smoothly, like the HI_prop variable does, though perhaps at a different rate. Instead, the model describes a phase transition between low and high Social Intensity, with the transition involving a lot of ups and downs over the course of about a century. Upon reflection, that pattern probably does make more sense as a description of the rocky process

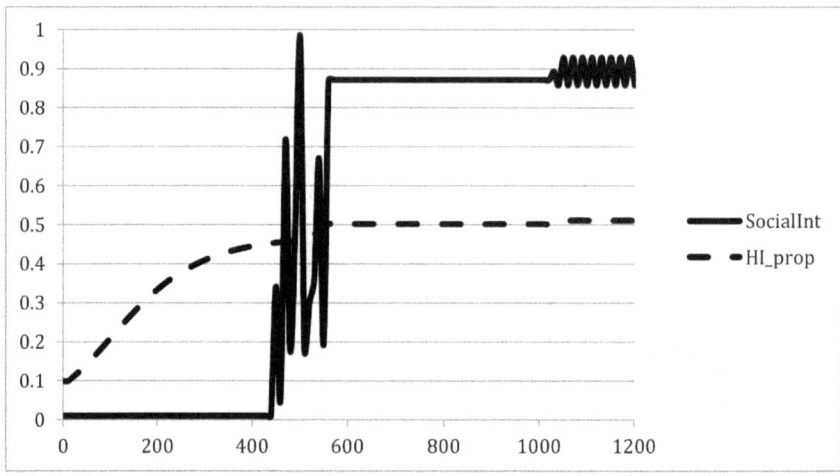

Figure 4.5 The behavior of Social Intensity (socialInt) as the simulation runs through the best approximation to the Target transition pathway.

of civilizational transformation. The cyclical behavior of socialInt in the last 150 years of the model's timespan is intriguing. It suggests periodic upheavals in the social order, but of a relatively minor sort, and without much overall effect on the achieved equilibrium.

Second, what is the impact on HI_prop of varying the Stress parameter while holding other parameters at the values they have in the best approximation to the Target transition pathway? Figure 4.6 tells us that, under low stress, relatively opportunistic agricultural and pastoral labor (mixed with whatever hunting and gathering remained in the Konya Plain at the start of the Çatalhöyük settlement) is relatively easy and the delayed gratification of HI lifestyles is unnecessary and less appealing than it might otherwise be; HI_prop does not reach its maximum value under these circumstances. Under medium stress, food production and energy capture are difficult enough to induce people to invest in cooperative agricultural and pastoral lifestyles; this is when HI_prop attains its maximum value. Under high stress, the crops won't grow and the domesticated animals die so the civilizational transformation to HI settled farming lifestyles is thwarted; HI_prop stays low in such conditions.

Third, what is the impact on HI_prop of varying the Technology parameter while holding other parameters at the values they have in the best approximation to the Target transition pathway? Unsurprisingly, Figure 4.7 indicates that there is a close link between Technology and the proportion of high-investment people. You can't run a farming settlement unless you have enough know-how to handle

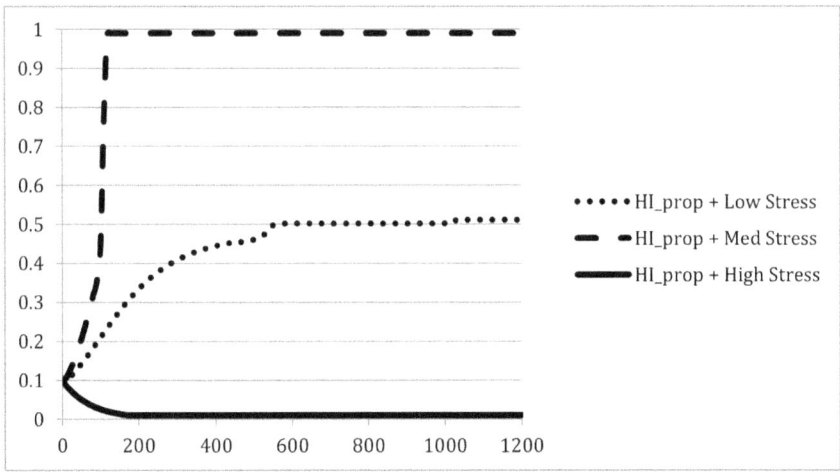

Figure 4.6 The impact on HI_prop of varying the Stress parameter while holding other parameters at the values they have in the best approximation to the Target transition pathway. Low Stress = 0.34; Medium Stress = 0.50; High Stress = 0.90.

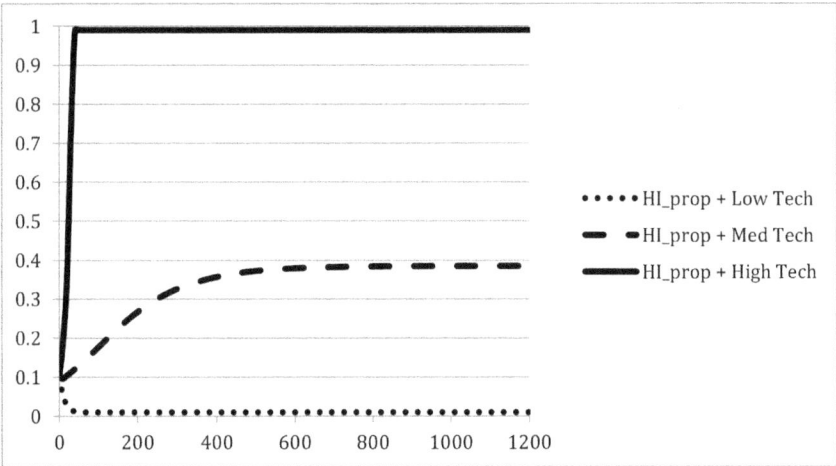

Figure 4.7 The impact on HI_prop of varying the Technology parameter while holding other parameters at the values they have in the best approximation to the Target transition pathway. Low Technology = 0.34; Medium Technology = 0.68; High Technology = 0.90.

domesticated crops and animals and to defend yourself from opportunistic marauders.

Fourth, how often do we get particular ranges of values of socialInt when parameters are varied around their values in the solution to the calibration experiment? From answers to the previous two questions, we know that Stress is particularly sensitive in the interval between 0.3 and 0.4, and that Technology is particularly sensitive in the interval between 0.6 and 0.7. We ran a Monte Carlo experiment varying Stress and Technology within those limits in steps of 0.001, making enough runs to be 95 percent confident that socialInt would be within 5 percent of the reported number. This yielded 10,100 distinct runs with various combinations of parameter settings, from which we generated a probability distribution function and a cumulative distribution function for Social Intensity (the socialInt variable; see Figure 4.8).

The graph in Figure 4.8 expresses the stochastic character of NSIM. There are some parameter settings that produce very high values for socialInt, but less than 13 percent of parameter combinations yield more than 80 percent of people in the population adopting the high degree of social intensity that appears to have been present in Çatalhöyük, which is probably what happened in the Konya Plain (these cases are represented in the last two bins on the right side of Figure 4.8).

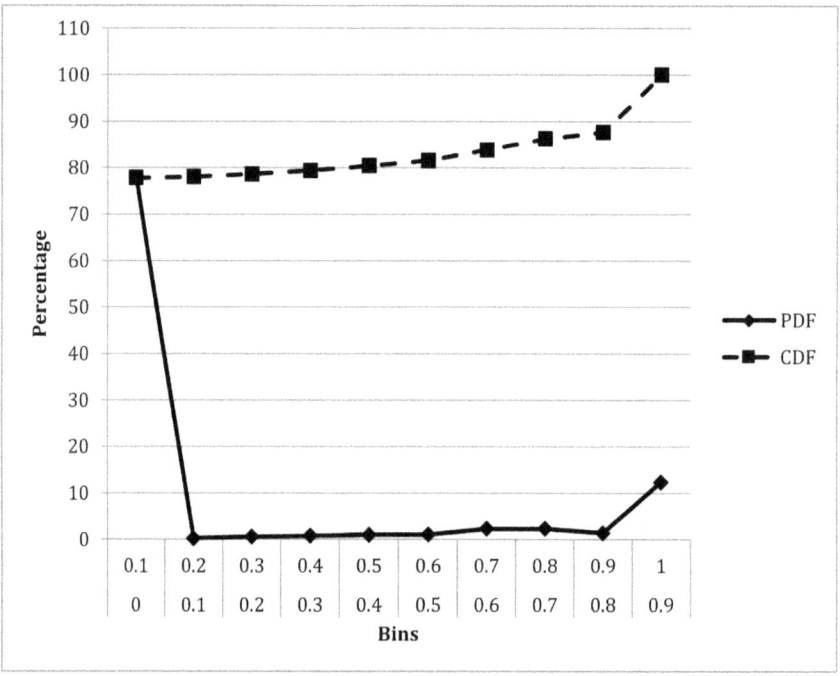

Figure 4.8 Probability distribution function (PDF) and cumulative distribution function (CDF) for the proportion of people adopting high-intensity lifestyles (HI_prop variable).

Other parameter settings lead nowhere or yield a smaller proportion of the population in HI lifestyles than occurred at Çatalhöyük. By the standards of this model, therefore, Çatalhöyük was a special place and a lot had to go right to make its phenomenal growth possible.

How Religion Mattered in the Neolithic

How does NSIM shed light on the question of whether, or the extent to which, religion mattered in the Neolithic transition? The incorporation of religious variables is perhaps the most important contribution of NSIM to understanding the rise of HI lifestyles in the Konya Plain, and possibly elsewhere as well. NSIM articulates a version of the entanglement hypothesis that explicitly incorporates *religious* beliefs and practices as part of the environment within which human beings are entangled as the civilizational form shifts slowly (then suddenly) from primarily hunter-gatherer to primarily sedentary-agricultural worldviews and lifeways. We don't need to choose between ideological-political, material-social, or cognitive-coalitional explanations for this revolution, and indeed we ought not choose. By recreating the Neolithic transition (including religion) *in silico*, using a causal architecture that treats all three types of factors as individually necessary but not sufficient, and as collectively sufficient, conditions, we have demonstrated the plausibility of the claim that religion matters, just as politics and energy capture matter.

So much for generalities; the details are fascinating. Referring back to NSIM's causal architecture in Figure 4.2, for a given value of the ecological Stress parameter, Social Intensity (socialInt) drives the willingness to contest the evolutionarily stabilized cognitive defaults underlying religious belief and practice. This is a plausible causal hypothesis grounded on empirically validated, cross-cultural theories within the bio-cultural study of religion. As a human group became larger and more entangled with its environment, a stronger type of social glue was required to motivate people to cooperate with and commit to individuals beyond the limits of their kith and kin. Shared imaginative engagement with morally relevant (and potentially punitive) invisible beings that were interested in the behavior of larger groups would have helped. The way the people of Çatalhöyük revered animal and ancestor spirits is evident in archaeological remains and suggests that this is how they generated the necessary social glue.

The fundamental connection between Social Intensity and the willingness to contest religious cognitive defaults impacts the rest of the causal architecture, driving Social Intensity higher in a reinforcing cycle of social complexity and religious entanglement. NSIM suggests that this process would have had several ripple effects. Default moral approaches to outsiders, laced with religiously loaded intuitions about purity, would be supplanted by a wider moral vision, in which all moral actors, insiders and outsiders, are monitored by supernatural watchers. Ritually, people would contest default tendencies to high-arousal, infrequent ritual acts and embrace more regular rituals that bind larger groups more closely together. Socially, clannish in-group-out-group monitoring would yield to acceptance of a larger social identity with a wider conception of the in-group.

These socially broadening effects of increased Social Intensity would have led to larger groups and more intricate ways of organizing the social field. The archaeological evidence reveals that earlier (lower) levels have houses as sites for the narration of history and formation of corporate identity, while the later (upper) levels give signs of complexifying culture with special-expertise groups (sodalities) active in the Çatalhöyük settlement. Increasing Social Intensity probably played a key role in the shift from primarily house-based to primarily sodality-based modes of "history-making," as described by Hodder and Pels (Hodder & Pels, 2010).

In these ways, NSIM suggests that Social Intensity is a necessary condition for the dominance of HI lifestyles. As we saw in Figure 4.5, and as seems to have occurred in the Konya Plain, HI lifestyles can grow in prominence as people consolidate agricultural and pastoral know-how. At a certain point in the embrace of HI lifestyles, however, Social Intensity becomes a major factor in leveraging a new kind of religiously potentiated entanglement, an increasingly intense form of sociality, and greater numbers of people with shared civilizational projects and imaginative worlds. NSIM suggests that this is what may have happened in Çatalhöyük.

Let's spell this out in relation to the matrix we introduced in Chapter 2. From the perspective of each of the three major types of theory discussed in that chapter, how can we think about the changes in worldviews and lifeways that would have occurred during the Neolithic transition, as illustrated in Çatalhöyük? More specifically, how can we think about the shifts in ontology, epistemology, and ethics in light of these theories and the simulation results of the computational model that integrated them into a single causal architecture? Table 4.4 provides an overview for the following discussion.

Modeling the Neolithic Transition 97

Table 4.4 Matrix for neolithic transition

	Ontology	Epistemology	Ethics
Ideological-political	Shift from animal spirits and active ancestors being mercurial and unpredictable to having specific pro-social interests	Shift to internalizing ideals fitted to larger group, shamanic navigating of supernatural powers	Surrendering freedom and privacy in exchange for large-group benefits; complying with large-group-identity story
Material-social	Increasing causal naturalism due to exercising skillful control in agriculture, technology, art, and social organization	Shift to greater knowledge of natural environment, passing knowledge and skills through sodalities, from agriculture to war	Promoting corporate well-being through agriculture, food storage, and trade; complying with town rules and expectations
Cognitive-coalitional	Sedimentation and cultivation of broader in-group identity; likely belief in manipulability of the cosmological environment	Shift to greater delay of gratification, planning over longer time-frames, differentiating self as having distinctive identity and roles	Overriding purity concerns; tolerating middens, strangers, and constant scrutiny; shift toward doctrinal ritual

Beginning with the first row, what insights from *ideological-political* theories can inform our understanding of shifts in ontology, epistemology, and ethics? Insofar as such theories emphasize the role of ideas, symbols, and concepts in shaping polity, or the mode of social organization and cohesion in a population, they draw our attention to the key role of belief in supernatural agents. Invisible beings are richly present in the ontological inventories of human worldviews and lifeways on both sides of the Neolithic transition. However, the nature of those agents, as well as the roles they play in knowledge claims and social norms, changes significantly. Variables such as "delayed gratification" and "surveyance intolerance" are particularly relevant. As the population increasingly believed in and ritually engaged with animal spirits and ancestors in a more homogenous and pro-social way, they vested ideals of the larger group in their supernatural agents and then used those supernaturalist beliefs to internalize those ideals, which helped them to conform to unfamiliar group-identity stories and new behavioral norms. These included planning over longer time frames, giving up valuable freedoms, and adapting to more consistent and intrusive types of political and religious elites.

What about *material-social* theories? How do they shed light on the changing ontologies, epistemologies, and ethics of human populations as they shifted from primarily hunter-gatherer to primarily agricultural-sedentary civilizational forms and worldviews-lifeways? As humans gained more control of the world around them, especially through domestication technologies, supernaturalism would have slowly and minutely lost some of its hold on the imagination, supplanted by the persuasiveness of naturalistic understandings of causal forces. Religion still plays a dominant role but the techniques for managing reality, and for protecting the town from out-group invaders, were learned through sodalities (shepherds, planters, shamans, warriors) rather than more immediately or within smaller, idiosyncratic groups with more flexible and opportunistic epistemologies. Ethically, the emphasis would have shifted from naturally occurring moral intuitions grounded in biological evolution toward more socially constructed norms that were oriented to promoting the well-being of a larger corporate structure. Practically, this would mean limiting one's freedom and complying with town rules and expectations in a way that hunter-gatherers would have initially found deeply problematic and probably extremely annoying. But they did it to gain the advantages that come with agricultural townships, and their religious beliefs helped them make the transition.

The variables most relevant for *cognitive-coalitional* theories are those on the bottom of the causal architecture in the figures above.

- conreldefCog: Participation in a HI sedentary-domestication lifestyle forces the contestation of defaults toward focusing on narratively immediate, terror-managing engagement with small-scale idiosyncratic spirits.
- conreldefMor: Participation in a HI sedentary-domestication lifestyle forces the contestation of defaults toward overriding purity concerns related to in-group care.
- conreldefSoc: Increased openness and willingness to engage in non-imagistic rituals makes one accustomed to being around and trusting non-kith/kin, reciprocators, and cultural others.

- conreldefRit: As more of the population becomes agriculturally entangled, participation in imagistic, high-impact rituals declines in favor of low-impact oft-repeated rituals that bind people more closely together in socially stable and religiously reinforced configurations.

The main insight here is that as these naturally evolved cognitive defaults were increasingly contested and the correlated coalitional strategies emerged and reinforced one another, worldviews-lifeways shifted to cultivate new ways of identifying with the group, manipulating the cosmological environment, differentiating the self, and overriding purity concerns as doctrinal modes of ritual slowly gained dominance, reinforcing group self-understandings and behavioral norms.

The main limitation of NSIM is one it shares with other computer simulations: it cannot "prove" the correctness of an archaeological (or any other) theory. It only provides added warrant for accepting the plausibility of Hodder's entanglement hypothesis by demonstrating that a social transition of the sort that did actually occur at Çatalhöyük can emerge based on the interactions among the variables included within its causal architecture. Like all systems-dynamics models, NSIM is also limited by the coherence and constraints of the theoretical integration behind this architecture. Perhaps better—or at least different—theoretical integration and algorithms could be constructed. This is where critics might offer their alternative analyses.

Another important limitation of this model is that there are fewer explicit links to hard data than we would have liked. Our calibration efforts were based on our review of the empirical literature and long discussions with experts at Çatalhöyük, but the nature of the system-dynamics CSS technique employed here precluded us from getting down to the level of "petrified poop." It is important to note that NSIM is also limited to the emergence and sustenance of the civilizational form that characterized Çatalhöyük. It does not help us understand why the site was eventually deserted—at least not directly. One might tease out hypotheses about its desertion from the causal architecture by asking questions such as Might the abandonment of the site have been related to the disappearance (or weakening) of one or more of the causal links embedded within the Causal Nexus?

Despite these limitations, we believe that NSIM helpfully shows the plausibility of the religious entanglement theory widely embraced by Çatalhöyük experts. It also serves the function of pressing scientists toward conceptual clarity in their formulations and critiques of theory. Other scholars may not like our general proposal to synthesize ideological-political, material-social, and cognitive-coalitional theoretical elements, or may disagree with particular aspects of it, but by setting out our assumptions about the relevant factors in such detail, and outlining our theoretical integration so openly, we hope to have made it easier for them to criticize us and generate or reformulate their own proposals with at least the same level of detail.

As we mentioned in the introduction to this chapter, our efforts here are to contribute to a better understanding not only of the transitional dynamics of the Neolithic but also to the forces of civilizational transformation at work in the contemporary world. Before jumping to Modernity, however, let's model the Axial Age.

5

Modeling the Axial Age Transition

As we have seen, computational modeling offers a new way of dealing with competing concepts and theories, as well as new insights into meta-theoretical questions that are important to scholars from all of the relevant fields of inquiry. Our Multiple Axialities Model (MAxiM), whose construction and validation we describe in this chapter, takes full advantage of developments in computational modeling and simulation techniques. One of the advantages of computer modeling is that it forces us toward *conceptual* clarity. Every variable must be explicitly defined and operationalized. This process helps us discover when and where scholars are talking past each other or utilizing concepts that are too broad (or too narrow) for the purpose at hand. Computer modeling also forces us to make explicit relevant interconnections among competing *theories*. Rather than merely narrating a possible interdisciplinary synthesis, our computational model has clear algorithms that determine every postulated theoretical integration, enabling more concrete arguments about the hypothesized causal interactions.

The causal architecture for MAxiM is based on the reconstruction and integration of the three most popular types of theories about the causes and consequences of the massive shift in civilizational form that occurred during this period in west, south, and east Asia. MAxiM shows that the most significant and empirically well-documented mechanisms from the relevant sciences (such as cognitive science, anthropology, archaeology, sociology, and history) can be articulated and implemented within a single system-dynamics model (SDM). The plausibility of the model is supported by the capacity of simulation experiments to "grow" the shift in an artificial population where the majority adopts Axial ideologies and social forms (worldviews and lifeways).

Why Model the Axial Age Transition?

Although many other important transitions occurred in the intervening millennia between the Neolithic and Modernity, including the invention of writing and the creation of military cultures, we think the most profound and impactful was the so-called Axial Age (*c.* 800–200 BCE). During this period, human populations grew in size and density across fertile areas in west, south, and east Asia. In each case, new complex forms of social organization were required. As we have seen, scholars debate which factors played a dominant role in this shift. Was it political ideas, energy capture, or critical reflection on human nature and its environment? In this chapter we provide a model that shows how all of these can be integrated in a single causal architecture, clarifying the role that religion played alongside other causal factors within the wider process of political, social, and worldview-lifeway change. Each of these factors is necessary but not sufficient for the Axial Age to occur, and only together, deeply coordinated, do they render that transition in civilizational form inevitable as well as surprising.

Where did the idea of an "Axial Age" come from and why is it important? Karl Jaspers's *The Origin and Goal of History* was published in German shortly after the end of the Second World War. His historical overview of the *origin* of the "axis of history [which] is to be found in the period around 500 B.C., in the spiritual process that occurred between 800 and 200 B.C." took up less than a tenth of the book. Jaspers devoted most of his energy to emphasizing the universal *goal* of human history. At the beginning of the book, he announces that "man, as we know him today, came into being" during this "most deepcut dividing line in history" (Jaspers, 1953, p. 1). By the end of the book, however, it has become clear that "what really matters" is not "historical knowledge" but our "ultimate knowledge" of the supra-historical, our "consciousness of Being" or the appearance of the eternal in time (1953, p. 276).

It is not difficult to understand Jaspers's motivation. Like many scholars in the middle of the last century, he was searching for a way to resist the fanaticism and violence that are all too often associated with exclusivist claims to absolute truth. Jaspers believed that such claims, which have led to division and devastation, especially in the modern West, "can be vanquished by the very fact that God has manifested himself historically in several fashions and has opened up many ways toward Himself. It is as though the deity were issuing a warning, through the language of universal history, against the claim to exclusiveness in the possession of truth" (1953, p. 20).

Today, however, most social scientists are wary of meta-narratives about "universal history" (Hegelian or otherwise) and tend to resist both anthropological analyses based on theological assumptions and political proposals based on divine revelation. Moreover, the genealogy of the concept of an "Axial Age" (Joas, 2012) as well as its religious and hegemonic use in modern, Western discourse have come under severe criticism (Boy and Torpey, 2013). Nevertheless, academic interest in the link between the societal transformations that led to the emergence of Axial and Modern civilizational forms has grown rapidly in recent years (Thomassen, 2010; Smith and Vaidyanathan, 2010; Bowman, 2015; Boy, 2015; Casanova, 2012).

The phrase "multiple modernities" was introduced by Shmuel Eisenstadt, perhaps the leading figure in the revival of interest in—and revisioning of—Jaspers's thesis about the Axial Age (Eisenstadt, 1999, 2001, 2002, 2011). His goal was explicitly to counter what he construed as the totalizing approaches associated with the catch phrases "the end of history" (Fukuyama, 2006) and "the clash of civilizations" (Huntington, 2011). Eisenstadt believed that more careful attention to the complexities of the Axial Age could shed light on the complexities of the Modern Age. For example, he argued that the tensions among a range of "transcendent visions," inherent to the Axial civilizations, later became "most fully articulated" in the "Great Revolutions" of Modernity, such as the transformations wrought by the French and American revolutions (Eisenstadt, 2005b, p. 73). In his own writings about the Axial Age, to which we will return, Eisenstadt did occasionally use the phrase "multiple axialities" (e.g., 2005a, p. 561), but he never spelled out the idea in any detail.

Here we want to emphasize the concept of *multiple axialities* for two reasons. First, we want to draw attention to the *multiplicity of concepts* swirling within and around controversies over the Axial "Age." While most scholars acknowledge that a significantly new form of human civilization emerged during this period, there are substantial disagreements over which causal processes play the most important role in the transition as well as the concept of "axiality" itself. Second, we also want to draw attention to the *multiplicity of theories* that compete as explanations of this major social transformation. Our model synthesizes the most empirically validated causal claims of three major types of theory and integrates their most relevant conceptual variables within a single computational architecture: a complex adaptive system involving multiple axialities.

In Chapter 4, we outlined our computational model of the Neolithic transition from hunter-gatherers to domesticated agriculturalists, and in Chapter 6 we will explain our simulation of the slow rise of non-supernaturalist worldviews and lifeways during the modern age. Both of those models focus on the critical role of (and critical reflection on) religion in those major societal phase transitions. Variables related to religiosity are also important in the model described in this chapter. Faced with all this conceptual complexity within and across disciplinary boundaries, how might we begin searching for a more coherent and comprehensive explanation of the Axial Age?

Synthesizing Theories

The concepts and theories most relevant for MAxiM concern the processes that led to the emergence of the first millennium BCE civilizations commonly referred to as "Axial." In what follows, we reconstruct and integrate three major types of theories that have attempted to trace the causal factors at work en route to the Axial Age. The first type of theory is *ideological-political*. This is the approach taken by Jaspers who emphasizes the role of reflective thought in orienting new political visions, and it is frequently championed by scholars from disciplines such as sociology and history. Proponents of *material-social* theories insist that Jaspers's approach puts the ideological cart before the materialist horse. The real driver of cultural change, they claim, was energy capture, which in turn led to new forms of social organization. Defenders of *cognitive-coalitional* theories argue that shifts in the expression of evolved cognitive and coalitional biases were the key factors behind the beliefs and behaviors that emerged in the large-scale societies of the Axial Age.

Another advantage of the methodology behind MAxiM is that it opens up new ways to address meta-theoretical questions, such as the seemingly interminable debates about the relative value of *verstehen* (understanding) and *erklären* (explanation). For Jaspers, it was almost a matter of pride that the Axial Period could be partially understood but never fully explained. He was aware of the many sociological conditions behind the phenomena that so impressed him, but he insisted that those conditions do not provide a sufficient explanation. "No one can adequately comprehend what occurred here and became the axis of world history! ... (it) grows more mysterious the more closely we examine it." The manifestation of similar Axial forms in diverse geographical areas "is in the nature of a miracle, in so far as no really adequate explanation is possible within the limits of our present knowledge" (1953, p. 18).

Most supporters of the material-social and cognitive-coalitional pathways to the Axial Age favor approaches that rely on quantitative evidence from fields such as archaeology or cognitive science. They are often more interested in explanation than understanding, in Jaspers's sense of those words. Eisenstadt, like many scholars who have focused primarily on the first pathway, was more interested than Jaspers in finding explanations for the emergence of these new civilizational forms. Over sixty years after the publication of *The Origin and Goal of History*, however, he concluded that "the *conditions* under which such groups could arise have *not yet been adequately addressed or systematically analyzed* in the social sciences" (Eisenstadt, 2011, p. 209, emphasis added).

The methodological approach behind the conceptual and theoretical integration represented in MAxiM enables us to take advantage of both the careful, hermeneutical work of scholars with expertise in ideographic interpretations of particular civilizations and the precise, hypothetical-deductive work of scholars focused on nomological explanations. Our computational model does intend to offer an explanation for the emergence of the Axial Age by showing how such complex civilizations emerge from basic interactions and causal processes. As we demonstrate further on, MAxiM simulates the rise of Axial civilizations in an artificial society. However, its explanatory power is only as good as its integration of the theoretical and empirical literature concerning the onset of the Axial Age.

Each of the three hypothesized pathways to axiality outlined later is our own reconstruction; no single scholar has articulated any one of them in precisely this way. The figures are graphic representations of theoretical frameworks broadly shared by groups of scholars within (and occasionally across) academic disciplines. As we will see, intellectual travelers who prefer one pathway may occasionally refer to points of interest on a road less traveled, so the paths sometimes intersect. In what follows, we explicate these hypothesized pathways to axiality. We will then show how they can be integrated within a single conceptual model and implemented within a computational architecture. We argue that all of these pathways are needed to produce Axial civilizations—all of them operating together, simultaneously. As with our analysis of the Neolithic transition, the three major theories about causal pathways are individually necessary but not sufficient, yet collectively sufficient, to produce Axial civilizations.

The ideological-political pathway to axiality, which was initially popularized by Jaspers, is depicted in Figure 5.1. In later sections, we more rigorously define the concepts in the boxes and the formulas behind the lines that connect them. At this stage the goal is simply to present the distinctive character and internal coherence of each pathway.

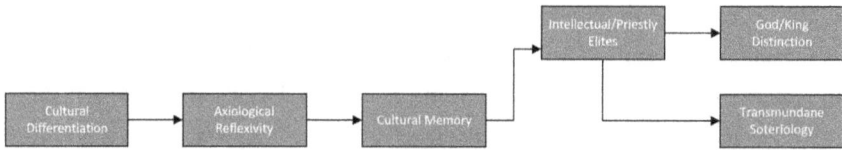

Figure 5.1 The ideological-political pathway.

In *The Origin and Goal of History*, Jaspers focused mostly on the concepts we refer to here as axiological reflexivity and trans-mundane soteriology. Philosophical reflection on the conditions for the human experience of value led to a vision of the social field and the cosmos as oriented toward a salutary end by an ultimate or trans-mundane reality.

Jaspers mentioned most of the other shaded constructs in Figure 5.1 as well, but in his view they played only a secondary role in the story of the Axial Period. "What is new about this age, in all three areas of the world, is that man becomes conscious of Being as a whole, of himself and his limitations" (1953, p. 2). What is new exactly? "In some way or other man becomes certain of transcendence." What conditions this certainty? Jaspers proposes that "the Godhead is origin and goal, it is peace of mind. There is security" (1953, p. 219). There are still some scholars who continue to focus primarily on these factors (e.g., Armstrong, 2007), but they tend to be religious apologists. Eisenstadt and most of those who (at least partially) followed in Jaspers's footsteps have been far more attentive to the "principled intolerance" that arose during this period and the potentially destructive aspects of Axial civilizations (Eisenstadt, 1986, p. 12; see also Eisentstadt, 2011).

Most later followers of this trajectory have attended more carefully than Jaspers did to the role of other factors, such as the increasing differentiation within the cultures that eventually became "axialized." As Eisenstadt put it, one "common denominator" of Axial civilizations was "the opening up of a range of possible institutional formations" and their transformation "into relatively autonomous spheres of society, regulated according to autonomous criteria" (2011, p. 279). The crystallization of such civilizations was marked by a "pattern of decoupling of the various structural and cosmological dimensions of social order, and of development of noncongruent societies" (2005a, p. 537), and the "disembedment" of many aspects of human life, which led to "more complex social systems with 'free' resources that could be organized or mobilized in different directions" (2009, p. 114).

Eisenstadt also argued that the rise of competing intellectual and priestly elites was a crucial factor in the rise of Axial civilizations. These "autonomous articulators" of "transcendental conceptions" actively pursued the instantiation or institutionalization of a new, this-worldly order based on their transmundane visions (Eisenstadt, 1986, p. 4–5). Competing groups of priestly and cultural elites were the "carriers" or "transmitters" of axiality; as such, they were "a distinct sociocultural mutation ... that differed greatly from the ritual, magical, or sacral specialist in pre-Axial civilizations" (2011, p. 284–5). These carriers, who played a key role in the emergence of axiality in east, south, and west Asia, have been referred to as "righteous rebels" (Runciman, 2012). Of course, it would not have been possible to have such "scholarly" carriers of Axial visions without the invention of external mnemonic technologies facilitating efficient methods of communication (papyrus, parchment, books) that provide new ways of transmitting cultural memory (Assmann, 2012; Bellah, 2011, Bellah and Joas, 2012).

It is important to note that Eisenstadt and others *do* emphasize the two variables originally stressed by Jaspers. What distinguishes Axial from pre-Axial civilizations is the emergence of "a new type of reflexivity rooted in 'theory,' and of new criteria of justification and legitimation of the social and political order" (Eisenstadt, 2011, p. 280). Other scholars have used different terms to describe this new mode of reflectivity, such as "second-order thinking" (Elkana, 1986). There were significant differences among the regions in which Axial civilizations emerged, including ancient Israel, Greece, China, India, and Iran. However, each of these involved a "qualitative increase in *reflexivity, historicality and agentiality*" that led to a "reasoned distinction between political order and religious-cultural order," a distinction whose possibility can never be "unthought" (Wittrock, 2005, p. 78, emphasis added).

One key outcome of this reflectivity among priestly and intellectual elites that emerged during this era was "the perception of a sharp disjunction between the mundane and transmundane worlds" (Eisenstadt, 1986, p. 3). In other words, the central driver of the "revolutionary breakthroughs" of Axial civilizations was "the emergence and institutionalization of new basic ontological metaphysical conceptions of a chasm between transcendental and mundane orders" (Eisenstadt, 2000, p. 4).

Among proponents of this path, another common way to describe the distinctive outcome of Axial transformation is the distinction between god and king. Robert Bellah, for example, argues that the "very hallmark of the axial transformation" is raising "the critical question of the relation between god and king" (Bellah, 2005, p. 83). Unlike archaic civilizations, in which the place of god-kings (despots, pharaohs, emperors) in the cosmological order was rarely questioned, Axial civilizations were characterized by groups of competing priestly-intellectual elites who strongly distinguished between a transcendent God (or ultimate Reality) and worldly "kings." The latter came to be construed as a "secular" ruler, who still might embody sacred attributes, but who was accountable, at least in principle, to a higher divine authority or transcendental law. This Axial Age distinction, argues Bellah, was "the entering wedge" that, two millennia later, would make the modern idea of the separation between church and state thinkable (2011, p. 323).

Scholars who defend this route to axiality tend to be sociologists or historians, and their arguments typically revolve around the extent to which (or the order in which) the factors in the shaded boxes of Figure 5.1 contributed to the emergence of the Axial Age (for a review of other literature in support of this pathway, see Wittrock, 2012). Our own hypotheses about the relationships among these variables, and their relation to key variables in other pathways, are clarified further on. For Jaspers, the origin and goal of history is "the One of transcendence ... thus this deepest unity is elevated to an invisible religion, to the realm of spirits, the secret realm of the manifestation of Being in the concord of souls" (1953, p. 265).

Proponents of *material-social* theories of civilizational transformation will have none of this idealism. They prefer materialist explanations of the development of more complex social forms, emphasizing factors such as energy capture, war-making capacity, information technology, and city size. At root here are strategies for survival and flourishing. Baumard and colleagues argue that the changes that really matter in the history of religions are not doctrinal but motivational. The most important change in the Axial Age was a shift from reliance on short-term or "fast" strategies for acquiring material needs to long-term or "slow" strategies that require delayed gratification far beyond what was required even for agriculture with domesticated plants and animals (Baumard et al. 2014; Baumard and Chevallier, 2015, Baumard et al., 2015).

For some scholars who follow this general trajectory, social complexification is best explained by developments in warfare technologies and subsistence technologies. The latter are emphasized by Peoples and Marlowe, who identify "a causal direction through which social and ecological forces led to the evolution and spread of belief in High Gods" (Peoples & Marlowe, 2012, p. 255). Peter Turchin emphasizes the former: "Warfare is the chief selective force for increased society size" (2010, p. 13). Larger societies have a better chance of successful defense (or predation) because they can mobilize greater resources to support bigger armies. "Something about the Axial Age must have brought a shift in the social environment, tilting the field to favor the message of the prophets and philosophers. But what? The answer lies to the north of the civilizations of the Ancient World—with the plains of Eurasia." What lies there? New military technology (2015, p. 193). Turchin is not shy about proposing a grand unified theory for the (relative) decrease in violence in human history. All of the relevant forces in this decline "do indeed share a single cause. The key process ... has been the increase in the scale of human cooperation," which was driven by improved effectiveness in military and crime-suppressing institutions (2015, p. 218).

The partially shaded boxes and the dashed lines that connect them in Figure 5.2 depict the material-social pathway. Our reconstruction of this theoretical framework relies most heavily on the work of Ian Morris who, as we noted in Chapter 2, comes down "strongly on the materialist side" in the debate over the role of material and cultural forces in shaping history (2013, p. 253). Morris identifies the transition from "low-end" toward "high-end" states as the defining characteristic of the Axial Age. But what made this transition possible? He argues that such a shift was driven primarily by new and more efficient modes of capturing energy, which itself was driven by factors such as advances in war-making capacity, information technology, and social organization. The influence of Axial "thought"—or what proponents of the third pathway described further on call "theoretic culture" (the non-shaded box on the far-right side of Figure 5.2)—only came later in the process, after large, more differentiated governmental systems learned how "tame" such ideas and put them to work for their own social agendas (Morris, 2011, p. 262).

In other words, for Morris, "Axial thought was just one of the things that happened when people created high-end states, and disenchanted the world" (2011, p. 263). The ideological "peculiarities" of the Axial Age were not causes of this civilizational transformation but rather consequences of prior (and primary) material and social forces. The same can be said of the Modernity transition, which we will examine in the next Chapter. Morris insists that "an explosion in

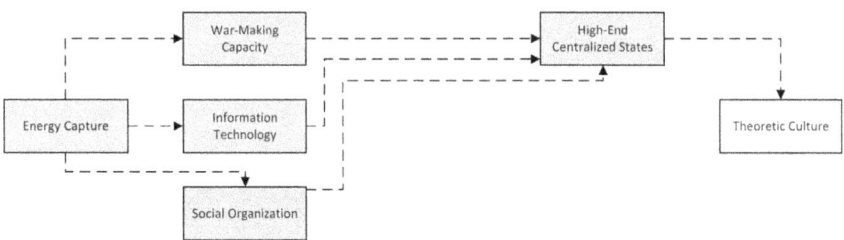

Figure 5.2 The material-social pathway.

energy capture, provided by an industrial revolution tapping into the power of fossil fuels, followed by the application of energy to new walks of life" (p. 258) was the one and only path to Modernity.

According to the Morris principle, all significant social changes since the last Ice Age have been driven by the same motor: "Lazy, greedy, and frightened people found easier, more profitable, and safer ways to do things, in the process building stronger states, trading farther afield, and settling in greater cities" (2011, 263). This applies to the Axial Age no less than the other major shifts in civilizational form. As we noted in Chapter 2, he makes this even more explicit in his later book *Foragers, Farmers and Fossil Fuels*, where he bluntly states that "Changes in energy capture drive changes in human values" (Morris et al., 2015, p. 223). For Morris, "energy capture *determines* values" and "culture, religion, and moral philosophy play only rather *small causal roles* in the story of human values" (Morris et al., 2015, p. 5, 10, emphasis added).

Most proponents of the third type of theory operate within academic disciplines such as cognitive science, psychology, and anthropology. We call this path cognitive-coalitional because its supporters claim that the most significant factors in the Axial transformation had to do with the interaction among (and adaptation of) cognitive and coalitional tendencies that had evolved during the early Holocene. Here the endpoint—or primary indicator—of Axial civilizations is not transmundane soteriology, the god/king distinction, or high-end centralized states, but a complex cultural coalescing made possible (and held together) by a shift in a human population toward greater reliance on a certain kind of cognitive capacity in the organization of human life. Merlin Donald has called this the shift from "mythic culture" to "theoretic culture" (1993).

The most distinctive variables in this pathway are the non-shaded boxes depicted in Figure 5.3. Two boxes from the other pathways also appear as stepping stones on this postulated road to axiality (represented by dotted arrows). As in the earlier diagrams, this is our reconstruction of a plausible pathway that can be derived from the empirical evidence and theoretical developments presented by scholars in the relevant fields. The focus here is less on the ideological and

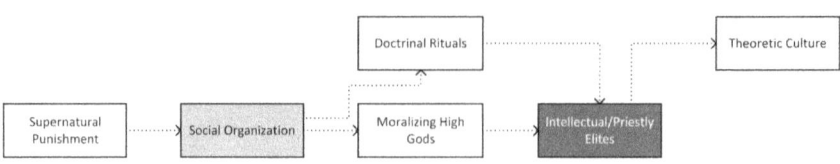

Figure 5.3 The cognitive-coalitional pathway.

material conditions for axiality and more on the evolution of new modes of cultural cohesion made possible by new expressions of cognitive capacities.

Widespread belief in the existence of disembodied intentional forces that could be watching (ready to punish norm violators) decreased the number of cheaters and freeloaders in early ancestral environments and increased the social cohesion of human groups. This is the basic claim of the broad supernatural punishment hypothesis (Johnson, 2015; Watts et al., 2015). Such beliefs would have enhanced the capacity of individuals to cooperate with one another as well as their capacity to compete with out-groups for resources. Some scholars argue that it was belief in bigger, smarter, and more punitive moralizing gods that drove the transformation of civilizational forms that led to the Axial Age (Shariff & Norenzayan, 2011; Gervais & Norenzayan, 2012; McNamara et al., 2014). Populations with high levels of belief in this sort of "high god" would have fed the growth of competing groups of priestly elites.

The ritual modes theory (Whitehouse, 2004) also plays an important role in this pathway. Evidence suggests that rituals typically come in one of two forms. First, "imagistic" rituals, which are high arousal and low frequency, facilitate the initiation of individuals into relatively egalitarian small-scale societies. "Doctrinal" rituals, on the other hand, which are low arousal and high frequency, are characteristic of larger-scale societies and require more complex hierarchies to maintain orthodoxy and orthopraxis. Imagistic rituals create intense bonds in local communities while doctrinal rituals foster identification with larger and more extended social groups. Whitehouse argues that the shift from imagistic to doctrinal modes of ritual engagement played a central role in the emergence of more complex religious hierarchies and the expansion of theoretic cultures (Atkinson & Whitehouse, 2011; Whitehouse & Hodder, 2010).

Figure 5.3 represents our reconstruction of a plausible cognitive-coalitional pathway to Axial civilizations based on our assessment of the empirical data and theoretical arguments in the literature. Part of the beauty of the methodology behind MAxiM is that those who disagree with us are free to alter the causal architecture and test their own alternative proposals. Computational models encourage scholars to render their concepts more explicit and surface their assumptions about the connections among them. It also provides a new way to explore the possible links between one's favorite theories and theories from other disciplines. Further on we will explain how our model is implemented and report on the results of our simulation experiments. First, however, we need to show how (and why) we integrate these theories within a single postulated system that can help explain the emergence of the Axial Age.

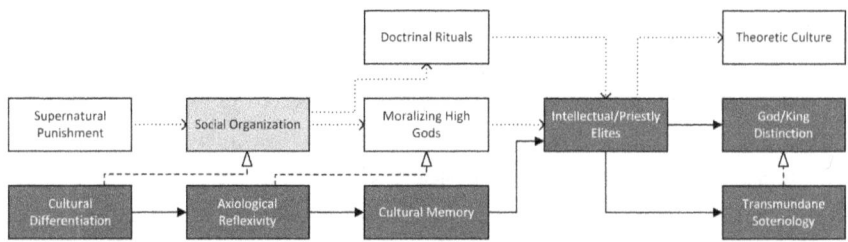

Figure 5.4 Integrating the ideological-political and the cognitive-coalitional paths.

As we saw in Chapter 2's discussion of the desirability of theoretical synthesis, many scholars of the Axial Age are somewhat open to the possibility that the engine behind this civilizational transformation was a complex adaptive system with a multiplicity of variables that can be clarified by a multiplicity of theories from different disciplines. MAxiM attempts to weave these pathways together into one causal architecture.

We begin by integrating the ideological-political and cognitive-coalitional pathways (Figure 5.4). Notice that this synthesis involves three new postulated causal connections (indicated by lines with white arrowheads). More complex forms of social organization are fostered by cultural differentiation. Belief in and ritual engagement with moralizing high gods are dependent on increased axiological reflexivity. And, finally, we argue that cosmological and soteriological visions of a trans-mundane reality ground political distinctions of the god/king type. The details of each part of this synthesis are clarified further on, in the computational translation of this theoretical synthesis.

The last step in the construction of our integrative conceptual model is to merge the material-social pathway into the other two. Figure 5.5 depicts the final synthesis of all three theoretical frameworks, which is the Causal Nexus of MAxiM.

Four new lines (with white arrowheads) are added in this final stage of constructing the causal architecture. The first is a new line from "information technology" to "cultural memory." The tools that supported the transmission of cultural memory through writing and accounting would have been fostered by increased emphasis on the development of technologies that facilitated the transfer of information. The second is the line from "high-end centralized states" to the "God/King distinction." The distinction between god and king would have been supported not only by priestly elites but also by the bureaucratic structures reinforcing highly centralized states. The third new line is from "supernatural punishment" to "war-making capacity." Increased

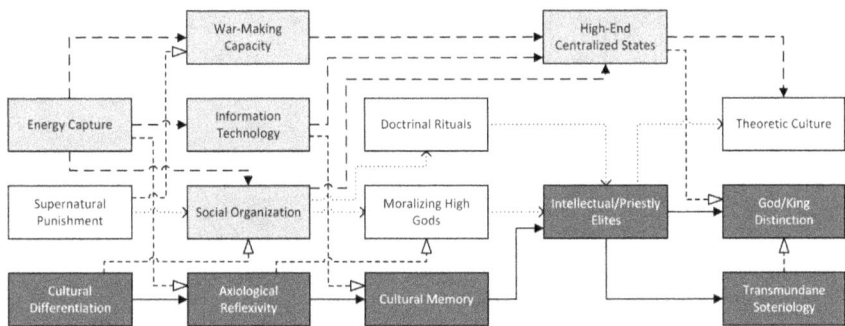

Figure 5.5 Conceptual integration of three theories about the emergence of Axial Age civilizations.

belief in punitive, norm-enforcing gods would enhance, for example, willingness to follow social authorities. The fourth and final new line is from "energy capture" to "axiological reflexivity." The leisure time needed to reflect on abstract issues such as axiology would be provided by sufficiently high levels of energy capture.

MAxiM: A Computational Simulation of the "Axial Age"

With the theoretical synthesis of Figure 5.5 in hand, we are now ready to implement MAxiM within a SDM and test the plausibility of its computational architecture through a series of simulation experiments. Recall that a SDM expresses the "flow" of some quantity between "stocks" where the flow is governed by "flow rates." Differential equations define the relationship between stocks and flow rates. MAxiM simulates the flow of people, from birth, through exposure to Axial and pre-Axial (or "traditional") ways of thinking, shifts from one way of thinking and behaving to the other, until death. As with NSIM (Chapter 4), MAxiM is a kind of two-way conversion model, as described in Chapter 3; boxes represent stocks (of people), arrows are flows (of people), and double triangles are flow rates. The Causal Nexus of both NSIM and MAxiM is a computational expression of the corresponding theoretical synthesis that yields the key flow rates and in turn is affected by the ratio of people in the two worldview-lifeway states (see Figure 3.8).

Figure 5.6 depicts the conversion model with the variables named to suit its application to the Axial transition. In this case, the six critical flow rates are two birthrates for traditional (trad_BirthRate) and Axial (axial_BirthRate) people, two exposure rates of one type to the ways of thinking of the other (trad_ExposureRateToAxial and axial_ExposureRateToTrad), and two conversion rates for those exposed (trad_ConversionRateToAxial and axial_ConversionRateToTrad). The proportion of people in Axial worldviews-lifeways is recorded in the variable axialProp.

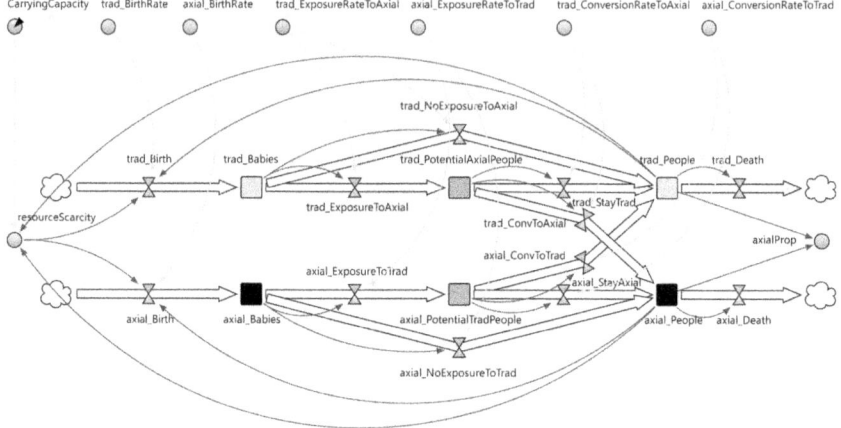

Figure 5.6 The conversion component of the model, showing the role of six key variables related to birth rates of people with the two kinds of worldview-lifeways (traditional and Axial), rates of exposure to people of the other kind, and rates of conversion for those exposed.

Figure 5.7 presents MAxiM's Causal Nexus, which is the theoretical synthesis described in the foregoing (Figure 5.5) converted into computational form. We shall explain the components of Figure 5.7 in three stages.

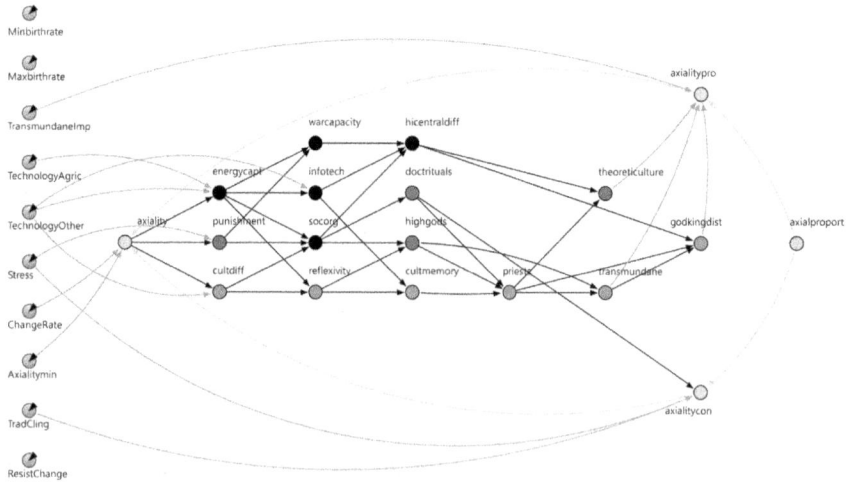

Figure 5.7 The Causal Nexus of MAxiM, which expresses the theoretical synthesis.

First, as with NSIM, MAxiM captures feedback-loop dynamics using four additional variables besides those identified in the theoretical synthesis described above. These are represented by the light gray circles in Figure 5.7.

- axiality: expresses the degree to which a society embraces in its institutional form a highly centralized, differentiated, "theoretic" culture characterized by a distinction between the king and god (or ultimate reality) and a global vision of a religious utopia. A high value for the axiality variable would indicate an Axial civilization and a low-value would indicate a traditional (pre-Axial) civilizational form.
- axialitypro: an incrementing mechanism by which axiality is increased in the population; it combines the impact of all variables capable of increasing axiality.
- axialitycon: a decrementing mechanism by which axiality is decreased in the population; it combines the impact of all variables capable of decreasing axiality.
- axialproport: the percentage of the population with Axial worldviews (supplied from the conversion part of the model, see Figure 5.8 further on). The effects of the variables axialitypro and axialitycon are amplified or suppressed by the proportion of people of both types (i.e., traditional and Axial worldviews), captured in the variable axialproport.

Second, Figure 5.7 shows the control parameters of MAxiM, depicted as grey circles with black notches. Table 5.1 summarizes those parameters, which are used to express different conditions under which an Axial transition may or may not occur. Collectively, they define a multidimensional space that we can analyze to discover the model's behavior. These parameters inform model behavior by tuning the Causal Nexus, which yield the six rates for birth, exposure, and conversion that drive the conversion component of the model, which in turn produces the proportion of people in Axial worldviews-lifeways, which affects the Causal Nexus—one very large looping dynamic structure in which all variables update all other variables.

Third, Table 5.2 presents the variables in the theoretical synthesis of Figure 5.7, together with the way they are related to one another, to the parameters, and the output variables (flow rates).

Fourth and finally, the theoretical integration depicted in Figure 5.7 also yields the six key flow rate variables that drive the conversion model. Figure 5.8 presents the links, and the corresponding formulas are in Table 5.3.

Table 5.1 Parameters for MAxiM

Parameter	Name in Model	Description
Minimum birthrate	Minbirthrate	The minimum birthrate for the population [0.50 to 2.00 (children per person)]
Maximum birthrate	Maxbirthrate	The maximum birthrate for the population [1.00 to 5.00 (children per person)]
Importance of trans-mundane	TransmundaneImp	The extent to which people value a higher transcendental moral or metaphysical order beyond any given reality, and which impinges on this-worldly organization shaped by a global vision of a religious utopia. This parameter expresses the fact that some civilizations weigh trans-mundane soteriology more highly than others [0,1]
Agricultural technology	TechnologyAgric	The population's level (complexity, quantity, quality, entanglement) of agricultural advancement [0,1]
Other technology	TechnologyOther	The population's level (complexity, quantity, quality, entanglement) of technological advancement that is nonagricultural [0,1]
Stress	Stress	The level of anxiety-producing or survival-threatening change in the population's natural environment [0,1]
Change rate	ChangeRate	The rate at which axialitypro increments and axialitycon decrements axiality [0,1]
Axiality minimum	Axialitymin	Expresses the irreversibility of some degree of axialization [0,0.1]
Cling to tradition	TradCling	The tendency to prefer the familiar, traditional worldview rather than the new Axial way of thinking [0,1]
Resistance to change	ResistChange	The extent to which the members of the population are resistant to change [0,1]

Simulation Experiments

The model's parameter space has regions of stable behavior: an equilibrium regime for a traditional society and an equilibrium regime for an Axial society. For many combinations of parameter settings, both equilibrium regimes are present in the model, and for such cases we identified transition pathways from one equilibrium regime to the other. We first present our analysis of the pathways that the model produced along with which societies transition from traditional to Axial. Then we offer an analysis of the conditions under which the Axial transition does and does not occur.

Table 5.2 Variables in MAxiM, together with attached links from other variables, parameters, and output variables

Variable	Link	Formula and Description
Axiality	From axiality, Axialitymin, ChangeRate, axialitypro, axialitycon	$axiality = min(max(Axialitymin, axiality + ChangeRate \times (axialitypro - axialitycon)), 0.99)$ Axiality increments (via axialitypro) or decrements (via axialitycon) its own old value. All the model's reinforcing loops involve the link from axialitypro to axiality, and all balancing loops involve the link from axialitycon to axiality.
	To energycapt	As people become more willing to participate in Axial lifestyles, they will be more willing and motivated to participate in more complex forms of energy capture.
	To punishment	As people become more willing to participate in Axial lifestyles, they will be confronted with and become more open to accepting a plurality of beliefs in punitive supernatural agents, imaginative engagement with whom facilitates their inclusion in more competitive (cooperative, committed) groups.
	To cultdiff	As people become more willing to participate in Axial lifestyles, they will be confronted by and become more open to accepting the differentiated structures of the larger society.
Punishment	From axiality, Stress	$punishment = (axiality + Stress) / 2$ The tendency of a population to broaden its belief in and shared imaginative engagement with a wide range of punitive supernatural agents increases with the adoption of Axial lifestyles and the presence of stressful circumstances.
	To warcapacity	Belief in more punitive supernatural agents increases the capacity to wage war because, for example, it reinforces people's willingness to follow social authorities in defending the society and attacking others.
	To socorg	Belief in a broad range of punitive gods increases the capacity of a society to organize the energy it captures in more complex ways because it implicitly motivates cooperation and commitment within larger groups

(*Continued*)

Table 5.2 (Continued)

Variable	Link	Formula and Description
Cultdiff	From axiality, TechnologyOther	$cultdiff = (axiality + TechnologyOther) / 2$ The extent to which a society is characterized by distinct and relatively stable sodalities, guilds, ethnic groups, or classes increases with the adoption of Axial lifestyles
	To socorg	The extent to which a society is characterized by distinct and relatively stable sodalities, guilds, ethnic groups, or classes increases the capacity of the population to develop more complex forms of social organization.
	To reflexivity	The extent to which a society is characterized by distinct and relatively stable sodalities, guilds, ethnic groups, or classes increases the extent to which members of the population critically reflect on the accepted norms and values of their in-group.
Energycapt	From TechnologyAgric, TechnologyOther, axiality	$energycapt = (TechnologyAgric + TechnologyOther + axiality) / 3$ Energy capture increases with both the increase in axiality and the increase in technology, to about the same degree.
	To warcapacity	Increased level of energy capture improves social networking and cooperation skills and imports technology and know-how, which raise the capacity to wage war.
	To infotech	Increased level of energy capture improves the ability of the population to develop more complex forms of managing information.
	To socorg	Increased level of energy capture improves the capacity of the population to develop more complex forms of social organization.
	To reflexivity	Increased level of energy capture increases the extent to which members of the population critically reflect on the accepted norms and values of their in-group.

	To trad_ConversionRateToAxial	Increased level of energy capture makes Axial lifestyles seem more tempting, increasing conversion.
Warcapacity	From energycapt, punishment	$warcapacity = (energycapt + punishment) / 2$ The capacity and willingness to wage war increases with improvements in energy capture.
	To trad_ExposureRateToAxial	Increased capacity to wage war increases the chances that traditional people would encounter the war-making Axial people.
	To hicentraldiff	Increased capacity to wage war stabilizes and intensifies highly centralized states.
Infotech	From energycapt, TechnologyOther	$warcapacity = (energycapt + TechnologyOther) / 2$ The level of information technology increases with improvements in energy capture.
	To cultmemory	Increased capacity to manage/disseminate information improves a state's ability to develop tools that support the transmission of cultural memory through writing and accounting.
	To hicentraldiff	Increased capacity to manage/disseminate information improves a state's ability to maintain and strengthen its highly centralized organizational structure.
Socorg	From energycapt, punishment, cultdiff	$socorg = (energycapt + punishment + cultdiff) / 3$ Social organization increases so long as energy capture and (broadening supernatural) punishment increase.
	To hicentraldiff	The capacity of a society to organize the energy it captures improves its ability to maintain and strengthen a highly centralized organizational structure.

(Continued)

Table 5.2 (*Continued*)

Variable	Link	Formula and Description
	To axial_ExposureRateToTrad	The capacity of a society to organize the energy it captures improves the chances that it will attract traditional peoples or provide its own members opportunities for encountering them.
	To doctrituals	At high levels of complexity, the capacity of a society to organize the energy it captures drives the population toward doctrinal rituals.
	To highgods	At high levels of complexity, the capacity of a society to organize the energy it captures drives the population toward belief in bigger (smarter, stronger) gods.
Reflexivity	From energycapt, cultdiff	*reflexivity = (energycapt + cultdiff) / 2* The extent to which a society is characterized by distinct and relatively stable sodalities, guilds, ethnic groups, or classes increases the tendency of its population to critically reflect on the accepted norms and values of their in-group.
	To highgods	The tendency of a population to critically reflect on the accepted norms and values of their in-group drives it toward belief in bigger (smarter, stronger) gods.
	To cultmemory	The tendency of a population to critically reflect on the accepted norms and values of their in-group increases the chances it will develop tools that support the transmission of cultural memory through writing and accounting.
	To trad_ConversionRateToAxial	The tendency of a population to critically reflect on the accepted norms and values of their in-group increases the chances that traditional people will convert to Axial worldviews and lifeways.

Hicentraldiff	From warcapacity, infotech, socorg	*hicentraldiff = (warcapacity + infotech + socorg) / 3* The ability of a state to construct, maintain, and strengthen a highly centralized and differentiated organizational structure increases with its capacity to wage war, organize and disseminate information, and organize the energy it captures, each to similar degrees.
	To axial_BirthRate	The ability of a state to construct, maintain, and strengthen a highly centralized and differentiated organizational structure increases the birthrate of its population.
	To theoreticulture	The ability of a state to construct, maintain, and strengthen a highly centralized and differentiated organizational structure increases the tendency in the population to give up "mythical" modes and rely more heavily on "theoretical" modes of memory and social governance.
	To godkingdist	The ability of a state to construct, maintain, and strengthen a highly centralized and differentiated organizational structure increases the extent to which people accept a distinction between the highest God and the leader (despot) of the state; that is, the ruler is ultimately accountable to God or a divine law.
Doctrituals	From socorg	*docrituals = socorg = (energycapt + punishment + cultdiff) / 3* The tendency of a population to prefer and engage in doctrinal rituals increases with the tendency of a society to organize the energy it captures in more complex and differentiated ways. (Note that docrituals is identical to socorg, and they are distinguished for the purpose of explanation.)
	To axialitycon	If doctrinal rituals become too tedious, that is, if they are not balanced with some imagistic-like religious experiences, some members of the population will convert from Axial to traditional.

(Continued)

Table 5.2 (Continued)

Variable	Link	Formula and Description
	To priests	As more of the population becomes accustomed to doctrinal rituals, this ratchets up the general willingness to support competing priestly/intellectual elites.
Highgods	From socorg, reflexivity	$highgods = (socorg + reflexivity) / 2$ The tendency of a population to believe in bigger (smarter, stronger) punitive gods increases with the tendency of a society to organize the energy it captures in more complex and differentiated ways.
	To priests	The tendency of a population to believe in bigger (smarter, stronger) punitive gods ratchets up the general willingness to support competing priestly/intellectual elites.
	To transmundane	The tendency of a population to believe in bigger (smarter, stronger) punitive gods increases the extent to which people believe in a higher transcendental moral or metaphysical order that is beyond any given this- or other-worldly reality.
Cultmemory	From infotech, reflexivity	$cultmemory = (infotech + reflexivity) / 2$ The extent to which a society comes to rely on external systems of notation, such as writing, for communicating memories across generations increases the level of its information technology.
	To priests	Higher reliance on external systems of notation and memory storage increases the relevance and need for competing coalitions of intellectual/priestly elites.

Priests	From cultmemory, highgods, doctrituals	*priests = (cultmemory + highgods + doctrituals) / 3* The extent to which a society is characterized or influenced by competing coalitions of priestly-intellectual elites distinct from political elites increases with axiological reflexivity, doctrinal rituals, high gods, and cultural memory about to the same degree.
	To theoreticulture	The growth of competing coalitions of priestly-intellectual elites increases the extent to which the population within a culture relies less on mimetic or "mythical" modes of memory and social governance and more on "theoretic" modes.
	To godkingdist	The growth of competing coalitions of priestly-intellectual elites increases the extent to which people accept a distinction between the highest God and the leader (despot) of the state; that is, the ruler is ultimately accountable to God or a divine law.
	To transmundane	The growth of competing coalitions of priestly-intellectual elites increases the extent to which people believe in a higher transcendental moral or metaphysical order that is beyond any given this- or other-worldly reality.
	To trad_ExposureRateToAxial	The growth of competing coalitions of priestly-intellectual elites increases the extent to which traditional people will be exposed to Axial people because, for example, it promotes proselytizing.
Theoreticulture	From priests, highcentraldiff	*theoreticulture = (hicentraldiff + priests) / 2* The growth of competing coalitions of priestly-intellectual elites increases the extent to which the population within a culture relies less on mimetic or "mythical" modes of memory and social governance and more on "theoretic" modes

(*Continued*)

Table 5.2 (Continued)

Variable	Link	Formula and Description
	To axialitypro	The success of societies that rely more on "theoretic" modes of analysis/organization, that are built on the symbolic use of external graphic memory devices, and that foster analysis and more principled reflection, promotes axiality in the population.
	To trad_ConversionRateToAxial	The success of societies that rely more on "theoretic" modes of analysis/organization, that are built on the symbolic use of external graphic memory devices, and that foster analysis and more principled reflection, makes them more attractive to traditional people.
Transmundane	From priests, highgods	$transmundane = (highgods + priests) / 2$ The more a society relies on and supports competing coalitions of intellectual and priestly elites, the more its population will believe in a higher transcendental moral or metaphysical order that is beyond any given this- or other-worldly reality.
	To axialitypro	Increased belief in a higher transcendental moral or metaphysical order that is beyond any given this- or other-worldly reality promotes axiality in the population.
	To godkingdist	Increased belief in a higher transcendental moral or metaphysical order that is beyond any given this- or other-worldly reality ratchets up people's willingness to accept a distinction between the highest God and the leader (despot) of the state; that is, the ruler is ultimately accountable to God or a divine law.

	To axial_ConversionRateToTrad	The more a population believes in a higher transcendental moral or metaphysical order that is beyond any given this- or other-worldly reality, the more likely some Axial people will convert to traditional worldviews and lifeways because, for example, such beliefs can seem too counterintuitive or irrelevant.
axialitycon	From TradCling, Stress, doctrituals, axialproport	$axialitycon = ((doctrituals − 0.6) \wedge 2 / 0.36 + (1 − 4 \times stress \times (1 − stress)) + tradcling) \times 1/3 \times (1 − axialproport)$ Two factors contribute to the decrease of axiality: extremely high levels of tedious doctrinal rituals and either extremely low or extremely high stress. Their combined effect is amplified by the tendency to cling to pre-Axial lifestyles. This effect rises quickly as the proportion of traditional individuals grows and then maxes out as traditional people become dominant.
	To axiality	This increments the axiality variable.
axialitypro	From theoreticulture, godkingdist, transmundaneImp, transmundane, axialproport	$axialitypro = ((theoreticulture + godkingdist + transmundaneImp \times transmundane) \times axialproport) / (2 + transmundane)$ Three factors contribute to the increase of axiality: theoretic culture, the god-king distinction, and trans-mundane soteriology. This effect rises quickly as the proportion of Axial individuals grows and then maxes out as Axial people become dominant.
	To axiality	This decrements the axiality variable.
axialproport	From axialProp	$axialproport = axialProp = axialPeople / (axialPeople + tradPeople)$ This is taken directly from the conversion model; it is the proportion of the population living in Axial social arrangements.
	To trad_ExposureRateToAxial	The higher the percentage of the population is Axial, the more likely members of the two groups will be exposed to one another.

(Continued)

Table 5.2 (*Continued*)

Variable	Link	Formula and Description
	To axial_ExposureRateToTrad	The higher the percentage of the population is Axial, the more likely members of the two groups will be exposed to one another.
	To axialitycon	The higher the percentage of the population is involved in traditional lifestyles, the quicker axiality drops.
	To axialitypro	The higher the percentage of the population is involved in Axial lifestyles, the quicker axiality itself is ratcheted up.

Table 5.3 Flowrate definitions in MAxiM

Parameter	Description
trad_BirthRate	minbirthrate + (maxbirthrate − minbirthrate) × (1 − stress)
axial_BirthRate	minbirthrate + ((maxbirthrate − minbirthrate) × (hicentraldiff + (1 − stress)) / 2)
Trad_ExposureRateToAxial	((warcapacity + priests) / 2) × axialproport
Axial_ExposureRateToTrad	socorg × tradcling × (1 − axialproport)
Trad_ConversionRateToAxial	((theoreticulture + reflexivity + energycapt) / 3) × resistchange
Axial_ConversionRateToTrad	((2×max(0, (−1 + 2 × stress)) + max(0, (−1 + 2 × transmundane))) / 3) × resistchange

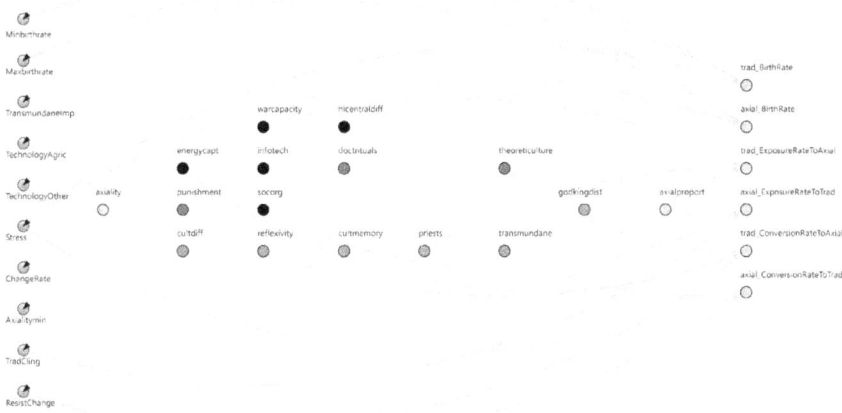

Figure 5.8 The Causal Nexus of MAxiM, illustrating the way it produces the six flow rates that feed into the conversion component of the model. Extraneous information is suppressed for clarity.

Because MAxiM's Causal Nexus expresses an integration of theoretical frameworks, some of which focus on worldviews (and related lifeways) and others on institutional form, the model allows the number of people holding Axial worldviews-lifeways (the *axialproport* variable) to change independently from the degree to which the civilization is Axial in social and institutional form (the *axiality* variable). This enables us to explore how these two variables behave during the transition from a traditional equilibrium regime to an Axial equilibrium regime, when that transition occurs.

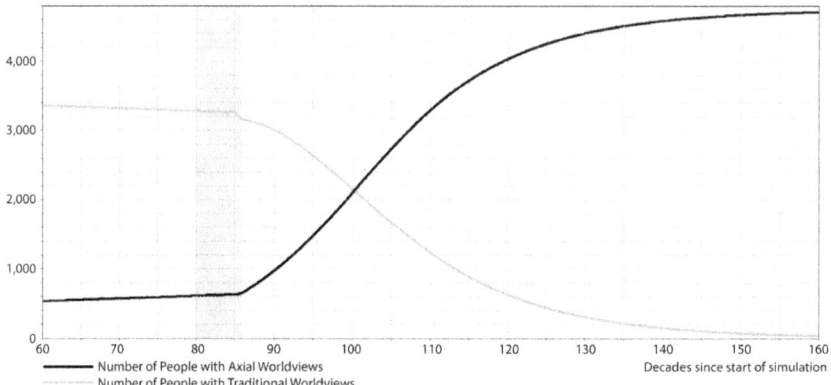

Figure 5.9 The number of people with traditional and Axial worldview-lifeways over time. The horizontal axis counts decades in model time. The shaded section is the time period focused on in Figure 5.10.

It turns out that the Axial transition does not always occur but that it occurs in more or less the same way whenever it does occur. Figures 5.9 and 5.10 display the recurring pattern of the transition. In Figure 5.9, the black line is the number of people with Axial worldviews and the gray line the number of people with traditional worldviews, out of a maximum potential population of 10,000 (the actual population is typically lower due to resource constraints).

The number of Axial people slowly increases from close to zero at time zero until it reaches a transition about eighty decades in, after which Axial people rapidly increase in number and come to dominate the population, reaching near saturation around 600 years after the transition begins. The parameter settings for this particular run are:

- Minbirthrate = 0.9 [per person]
- Maxbirthrate = 2.5 [per person]
- TransmundaneImp = 0.99 [range: 0–1]
- TechnologyAgric = 0.55 [range: 0–1]
- TechnologyOther = 0.8 [range: 0–1]
- Stress = 0.54 [range: 0–1]
- ChangeRate = 0.01 [range: 0–1]
- Axialitymin = 0.01 [range: 0–0.1]
- TradCling = 0.1 [range: 0–1]

- ResistChange = 0.1 [range: 0–1]
- CarryingCapacity = 10,000

For other parameter settings, the Axial transition may occur much earlier, and take a different length of time to complete, but it always has this structure when it does occur. The shaded section in Figure 5.9 indicates the start of the transition.

How does the axiality variable (the degree to which a society embraces in its institutional form a highly centralized, differentiated, "theoretic" culture characterized by a distinction between the king and god—or ultimate reality—and a "global" vision of a religious utopia) change during this transition? Our investigations of the parameter space of the model showed that, in contrast to the slow transition of the proportion of people with Axial worldviews, the axiality variable changes rapidly, in the space of about two generations.

Figure 5.10 displays the beginning of this transition period, greatly magnified, with the black line representing the proportion of people with Axial worldviews (*axialProp* = *axialproport*) and the gray line representing axiality, which starts becoming unstable around eighty simulated decades into a simulation run and, with a few fits and starts, completes a comprehensive transition within five decades. Once the institutional transformation is complete, there is a relatively rapid increase of the proportion of people with Axial worldviews, followed by an asymptotic approach to 100 percent (refer back to Figure 5.9, which displays a much longer timespan).

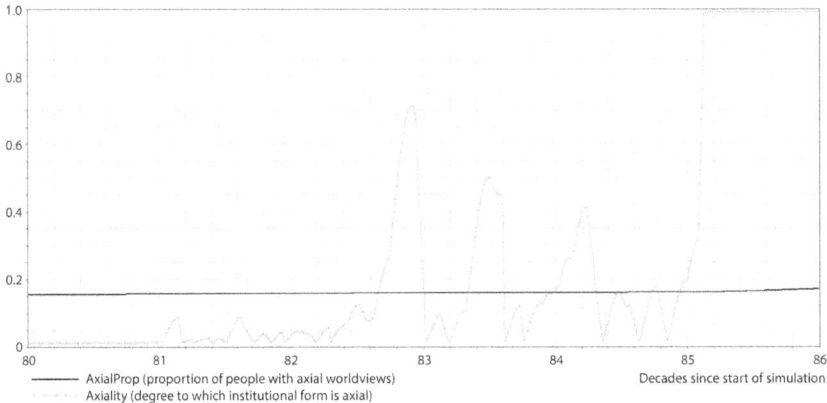

Figure 5.10 Key transition period during the Axial transition: slow increase in Axial worldviews-lifeways punctuated by a rapid change in civilizational form. This is followed by a rapid increase in the proportion of people holding Axial worldviews-lifeways, as illustrated in Figure 5.9.

This suggests that the number of people holding Axial worldviews-lifeways must reach a threshold before an Axial civilizational transformation can occur. The threshold varies with model parameters, but there is always a threshold. This means that ideas and ideation matter, to some degree. But this result also suggests that Axial ideas require an Axial civilizational transformation before they can become widespread and dominant. At this point, ideology and cognition are secondary to social and material circumstances, to some degree. Jointly, these insights affirm the core convictions of the three types of theories we integrated in the causal architecture of MAxiM, while also challenging the idea that any one of those theories provides a comprehensive explanation.

All of the variables in MaXiM are highly correlated with each other so, to explore the model's behavior in detail, we need to turn to specialized methods of analysis, beginning with a parameter sweep. Because the model has no stochastic elements, we ran each combination of parameter settings only once. The variation of these parameters resulted in a total of 1,152,000 unique simulation runs. Each simulation run corresponds to a single artificial society with distinctive parameter settings, its data collected after enough time to allow an equilibrium to emerge in almost all cases. We used the resulting dataset to determine the conditions under which the axiality transition occurs and to run sensitivity analyses on parameters and key variables.

Collinearity among MaXiM variables is often too high to run meaningful linear regressions on all variables, but multiple regression is feasible for three key variables—energy capture, cultural differentiation, and supernatural punishment, representing the material-social, ideological-political, and cognitive-coalitional types of theories, respectively. Note that this is not a traditional linear-regression model, with input variables predicting an output variable, because all variables affect all others in an SDM; nevertheless, a linear regression can still tell us about meaningful relationships.

With energy capture, cultural differentiation, and supernatural punishment as independent variables and the degree to which institutions have cultural form (axiality) as a dependent variable, the regression has adjusted $R^2 = 0.955$, the ANOVA yields significance below 0.001 (F = 8,154,825), and the coefficients are all highly significant (see Model 1 in Table 5.4). With the same independent variables, but the proportion of people having Axial worldviews-lifeways (axialproport) as the dependent variable, the result is almost the same ($R^2 = 0.955$, F = 8,161,409, $p < 0.001$; see Model 2 in Table 5.4).

These regressions show that there is an intensely close association between each of the two dependent variables and all three predictor variables, considered

Table 5.4 Multiple regressions examining the association between three key variables—energy capture, cultural differentiation, and supernatural punishment, representing the material-social, ideological-political, and cognitive-coalitional types of theories, respectively—and the degree to which institutions have cultural form (axiality; model 1) and the proportion of people having axial worldview-lifeways (axialproport; model 2)

	Unstandardized Coefficients		Standardized Coefficients	
Model	B	Std. Error	Beta	T
Model 1: dependent variable is degree to which institutions have cultural form (*axiality*)				
(Constant)	−.197	.000		−952.914
Energycapt	.185	.001	.101	226.940
Punishment	.865	.000	.714	2281.029
Cultdiff	.318	.001	.222	438.902
Model 2: dependent variable is proportion of people having Axial worldview-lifeways (*axialproport*)				
(Constant)	−.253	.000		−1161.439
Energycapt	.201	.001	.104	233.142
Punishment	.919	.000	.719	2296.587
Cultdiff	.324	.001	.214	424.079

separately and together. This confirms that each of the material-social, ideological-political, and cognitive-coalitional types of theories tell us something important about the Axial transition, which is valuable information. But this analysis is coarse, especially considering how many artificial societies there are in this MaXiM-generated dataset. We will learn more if we delve into details.

Figure 5.11 depicts a plot of all simulation runs from the parameter sweep. The vertical axis is axialproport (the proportion of people with Axial worldviews) and the horizontal axis is axiality (the degree to which the civilization and its institutions are Axial in form); these are the output variables. Shading corresponds to energy capture (energycapt) with darker shades indicating relatively low energy capture and lighter shades indicating relatively high energy capture; this is the input variable, but we'll set that aside for a moment. To see points more clearly, a small amount (3 percent) of random jitter has been added to the plot and the points have been made quite transparent. The random jitter spreads points very close together a small way apart to improve readability and understanding of the underlying data.

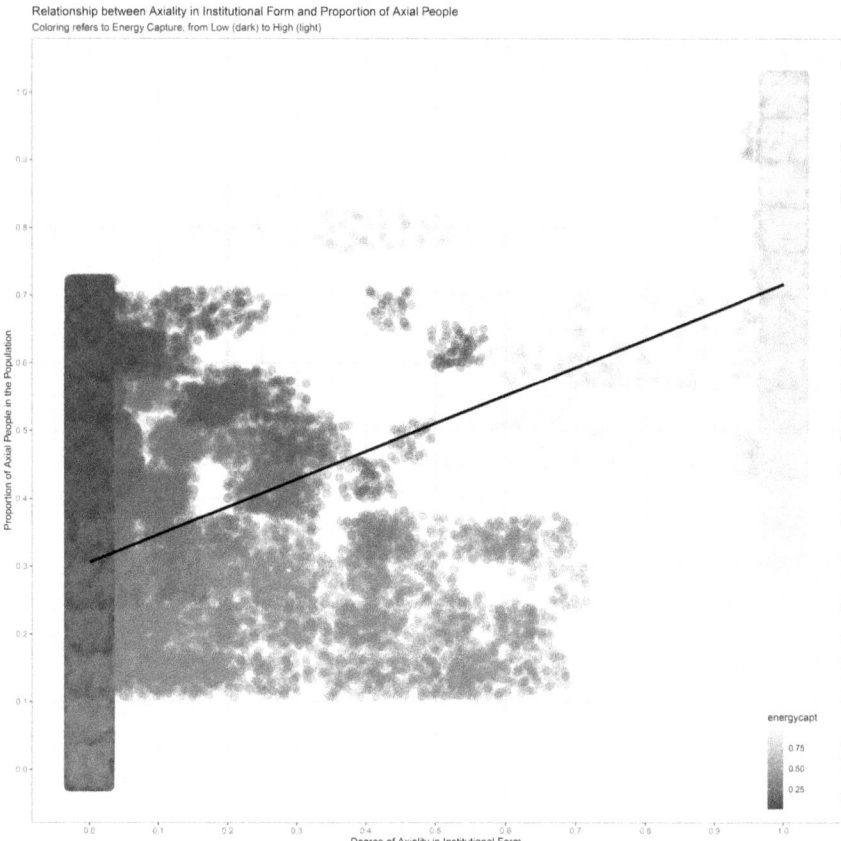

Figure 5.11 Many virtual societies (represented by a dot) pictured in terms of their equilibrium state with energy capture (shading) as the input variable and both proportion of Axial people (vertical axis) and degree of axiality in institutional form (horizontal axis) as the two output variables. Random jitter (3 percent) has been added to improve readability.

To begin with, only about 44 percent of the societies make it all the way to full axiality in their institutional form; most of the rest stay pre-Axial, save for a few that transition part way. Graphically, this appears in Figure 5.11 as large bars of points at the left and right edges of the plot (remember the jitter, which prevents these bars from being a line of stacked dots). Only about 2 percent of the artificial societies are scattered between the two horizontal extremes. Similarly, the vast majority of societies stabilize around equilibria with most people pre-Axial (54 percent) or Axial (44 percent) and the rest scattered in between vertically (less than 2 percent). The black regression line in Figure 5.11 shows a strong association between the degree of axiality in institutional form and the number of people who ultimately adopt Axial worldview-lifeways, meaning that typically both aspects of axiality occur together, or fail to occur together. It is not a perfect correlation, though, since there are exceptions to this trend, with either institutional form resistant to the population trends or the population's worldview-lifeways heading a different direction than the institutional trends.

Continuing to ignore shading (i.e., energy capture), Figure 5.11 also offers important information about how the Axial transition occurs, when it does. No movement in the direction of an Axial society occurs unless Axial worldviews-lifeways have taken hold in at least 13 percent of the population (the jitter introduced to improve readability moves points about 3 percent in a random direction so what looks like a minimum of 10 percent is really a minimum 13 percent). No society makes it all the way to Axial form in its institutions unless one-third of the population embraces Axial worldviews-lifeways, and no society with more than two-thirds of people holding Axial worldviews-lifeways can prevent the Axial transition from occurring at least to some extent, and almost all of them go all the way to fully Axial form. When Axial worldviews-lifeways have penetrated the population to a middling degree, many intermediate equilibria appear (though, if we ran the simulation longer, some of those might drift more toward the extremes).

Now, let us add energy capture into the analysis. Figure 5.11 uses shading to depict energy capture: societies with higher energy capture have lighter tones. The points (corresponding to societies) are quite transparent, so shading can blend to some degree, but there are very clear indications about how important energy capture is. The societies that do not complete the Axial transition tend to have relatively low energy capture, though there are some that have relatively higher levels of energy capture. Societies that do transition tend to have relatively high energy capture. Importantly, the right side of Figure 5.11, which displays the societies that fully transition, shows lighter tones at the bottom of the column and slightly darker tones at the top. This means that the highest levels of energy capture are needed to make the Axial transition when relatively few people have embraced Axial worldview-lifeways. Meanwhile, when a large majority of people have adopted Axial worldview-lifeways, there is more flexibility around the degree of energy capture needed to make the transition in institutional forms.

This is a good illustration of what we have come to expect from all three models presented in this book. A factor such as energy capture is very important in the Axial transition, but by itself doesn't force the transition to occur. Even when energy capture is not very high, the Axial transition can still occur if other factors are suitable. In other words, at least a moderately high degree of energy capture is necessary but not sufficient to drive the Axial transition. This supports material-social theories but also checks any claims to their sufficiency or all-importance.

We can modify Figure 5.11 by introducing faceting. Figure 5.12 displays the same information with energy capture used to define four facets. The societies with lowest energy capture are displayed in the top-left facet; none of those societies make the Axial transition all the way, though some get started. Societies with highest energy capture are displayed in the

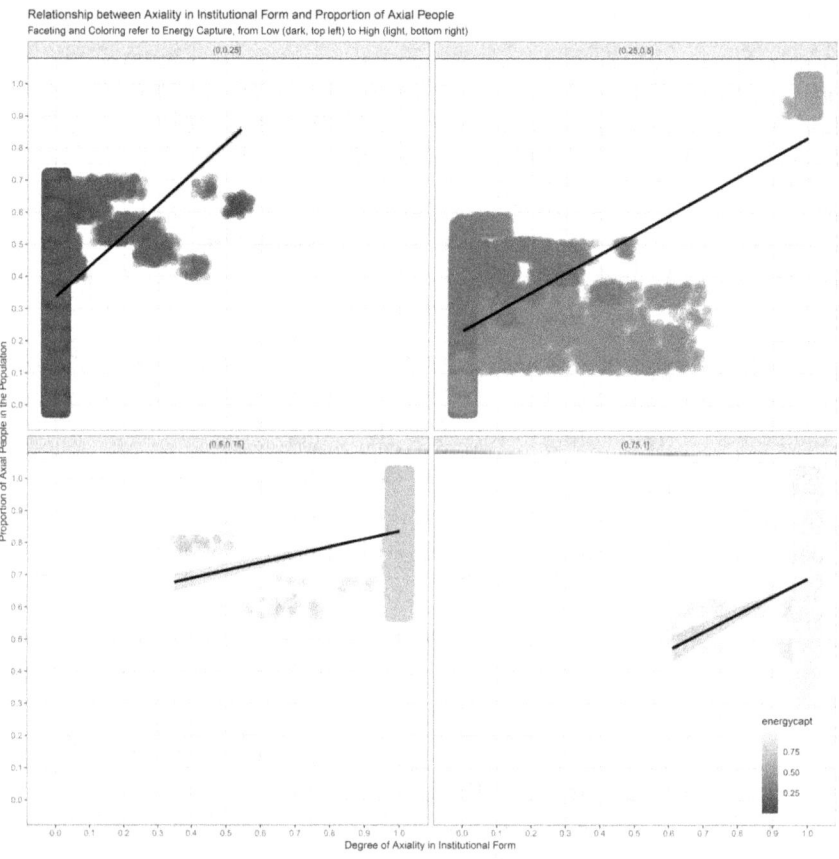

Figure 5.12 Many virtual societies (represented by dots) pictured in terms of their equilibrium state with energy capture (shading) as the input variable and both proportion of Axial people (vertical axis) and degree of axiality in institutional form (horizontal axis) as the two output variables. Energy capture is also used to create the facets of the diagram, with societies having the lowest levels of energy capture in the top-left facet and societies with the highest levels of energy capture in the bottom-right facet.

bottom-right facet, and most of them go all the way, with the very highest able to drag into Axial form even societies having relatively few people with Axial worldviews-lifeways.

Moving on to ideological-political factors, Figure 5.13 displays much the same information as Figure 5.11, except with cultural differentiation (cultdiff) instead of energy capture represented in the shading of the dots. As with energy capture, so here: cultural differentiation appears to be a necessary but not sufficient condition for the transition to a fully Axial society to occur.

For cognitive-coalitional factors, Figure 5.14 delivers a similar message. In this case, the shading expresses the extent of belief in supernatural punishment within each society (punishment). Here again we see all the signs that this

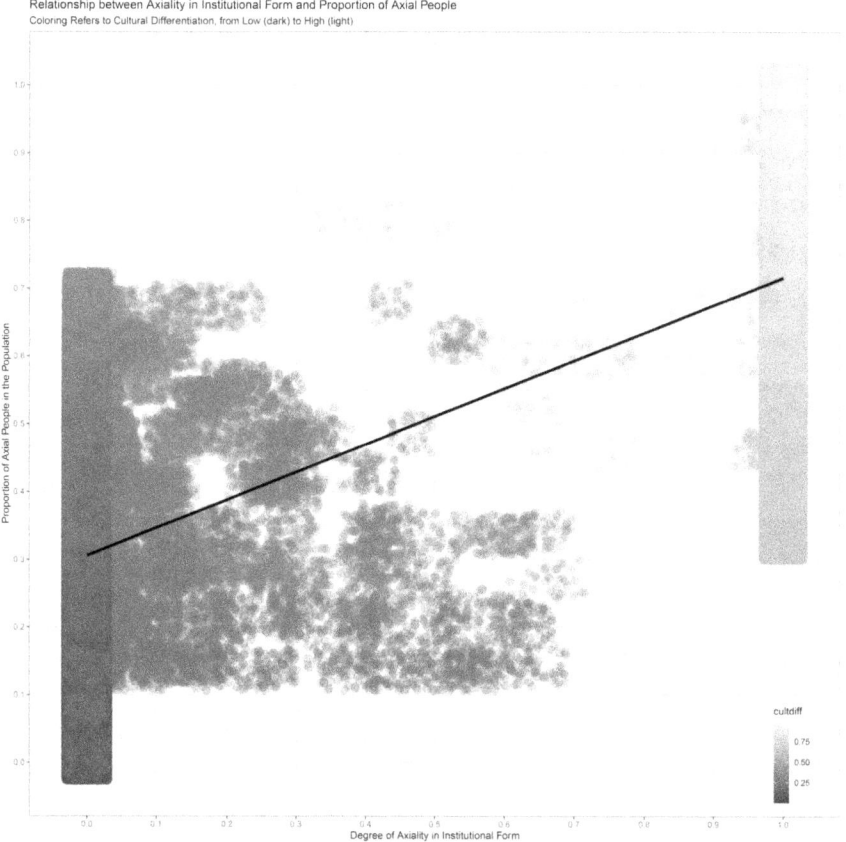

Figure 5.13 Many virtual societies (represented by dots) pictured in terms of their equilibrium state with cultural differentiation (shading) as the input variable and both proportion of Axial people (vertical axis) and degree of axiality in institutional form (horizontal axis) as the two output variables.

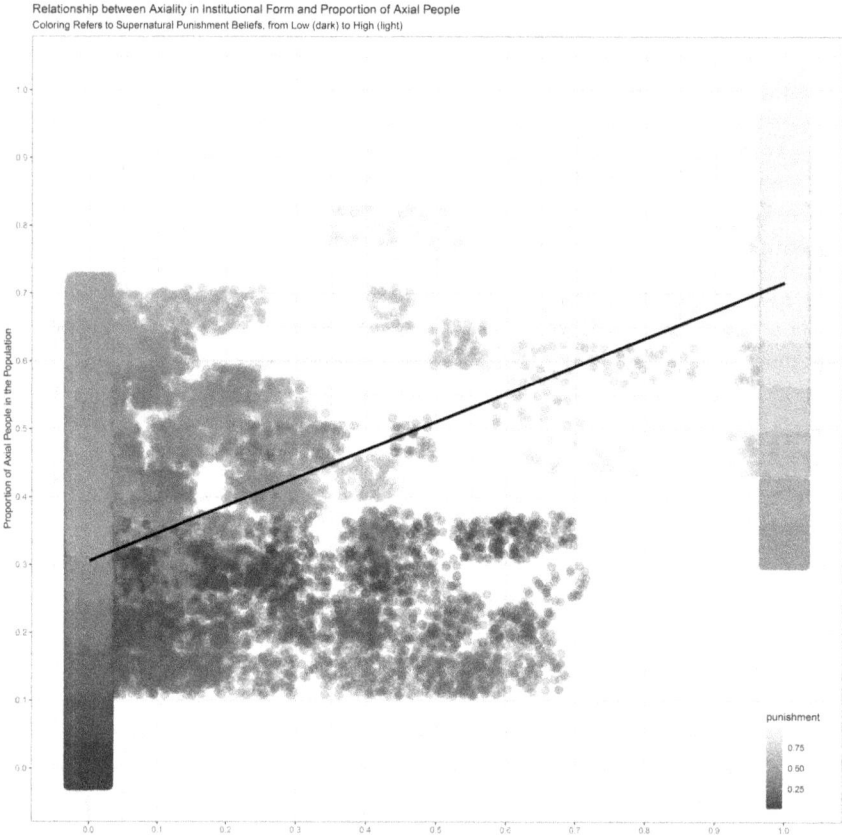

Figure 5.14 Many virtual societies (represented by dots) pictured in terms of their equilibrium state with supernatural punishment (shading) as the input variable and both proportion of Axial people (vertical axis) and degree of axiality in institutional form (horizontal axis) as the two output variables.

kind of belief, which is much talked about within the cognitive science of religion as a powerful form of social glue that fosters collaboration and trust, is a necessary but not sufficient condition for the Axial transition to occur. In particular, for societies that begin but do not complete the Axial transition, with the prevalence of Axial worldviews-lifeways remaining under the one-third threshold; note the presence of dark shading, indicating the lowest levels of belief in supernatural punishment. Other factors can drive a society part of the way to Axial form in its institutions but supernatural punishment beliefs are needed to go all the way.

We find the same when we move to other theoretically important variables, such as belief in moralizing high gods (highgods), axiological reflexivity

(reflexivity), and the dominance of doctrinal-style rituals (doctrituals): these need to arise for the axial transition to occur, further supporting the ideological-political and the cognitive-coalitional pathways, but they can't drive a society into an axial form by themselves. In particular, material-social conditions such as energy capture and the capacity to wage war are also important.

Finally, it is worth considering whether content biases (such as belief in supernatural punishment by morally invested gods) or context biases (such as the doctrinal form of rituals or the importance of priestly elites) are more important in the Axial transition. Figure 5.15 presents a plot showing how both the degree of axiality in institutional form and the proportion of people having axial worldviews-lifeways related to the importance of priestly elites. That can be compared to Figure 5.14, where belief in supernatural

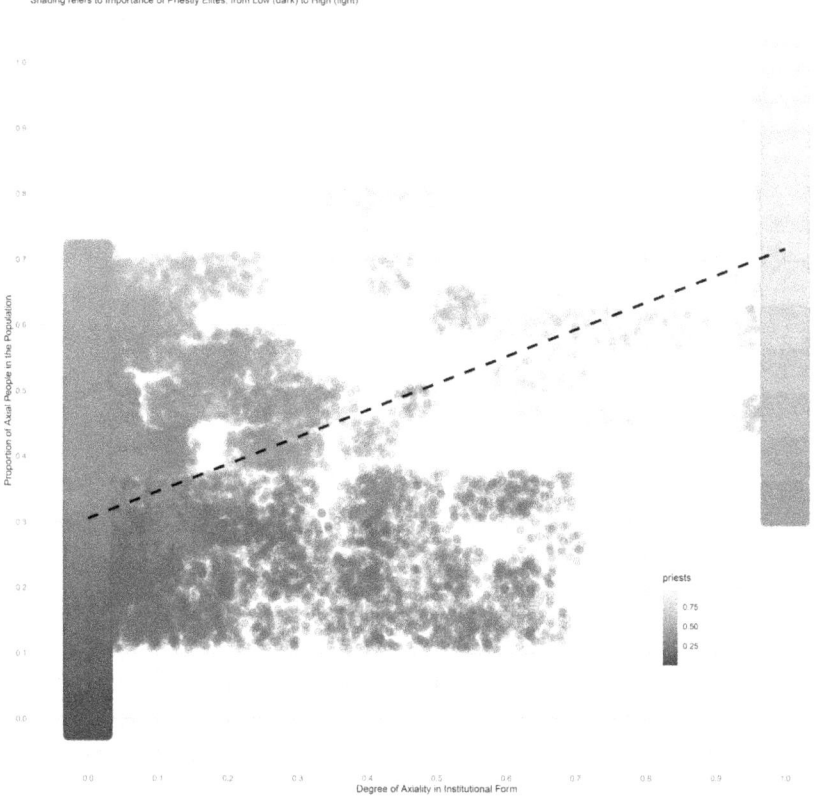

Figure 5.15 Many virtual societies (represented by dots) pictured in terms of their equilibrium state with the importance of priestly elites (shading) as the input variable and both proportion of Axial people (vertical axis) and degree of axiality in institutional form (horizontal axis) as the two output variables.

punishment determines the shading of points instead of priestly elites. The plots show a similar distribution of light and dark, and a similar result applied when examining the extent to which ritual practices are doctrinal in form. This indicates that, in MAxiM at least, content biases and context biases are roughly equally important in the Axial transition. This finding is food for scholarly thought in the ongoing debates among cognitive and evolutionary scientists of religion about the relative importance of these biases in the emergence and maintenance of early ancestral as well as contemporary religious beliefs and behaviors (Guthrie, 1993; Gervais & Henrich, 2010; Van Elk & Zwaan, 2016; Langston et al., 2018).

This exploration of MAxiM's parameter space offers additional support for the plausibility of our theoretical integration of the three main hypothesized pathways and reinforces concerns about claims that any one theory can provide a comprehensive explanation of the Axial transition.

How Religion Mattered in the Axial Age

Materially, this chapter contributes to our understanding of the Axial Age by providing an overarching integration of multiple theories about the causal factors involved in this change in civilizational form. Methodologically, it adds to the growing body of literature demonstrating the value of computer modeling and simulation as a tool for theorizing about the complex interactions among cognitive and cultural developments in human history. As with NSIM, some scholars may not like our general proposal or may disagree with particular aspects of it, but by exposing our assumptions about the relevant factors in such detail and outlining our theoretical integration openly, we hope to have made it easier for them to criticize us and generate or reformulate their own proposals.

Ian Morris—our primary representative of the material-social pathway—refers to *foragers, farmers,* and *fossil fuels* as a shorthand way of expressing the key stages along the evolution of the organization of human social life from hunter-gathering, sedentary-agricultural lifestyles, to the modern world. Proponents of the ideological-political pathway might prefer to speak of *pagans, priests,* and *pluralists.* Supporters of the cognitive-coalitional pathway, on the other hand, might speak of the shift from territoriality, to axiality, and finally to Modernity by referring to beliefs in *ghosts, gods,* and *governments.* Our computational model suggests that the core insights of each of these theoretical frameworks can be integrated within a single architecture that upholds their key causal claims while pushing back against overreaching exclusivistic assertions that one causal pathway can explain the entire process of emerging axiality. On our account, the three causal pathways are entangled as individually necessary but not sufficient and as jointly sufficient to explain the Axial transition.

At this stage of analysis, MAxiM can be face-validated by comparing the results of the simulation experiments to what we know historically about the emergence of the Axial Age. For example, our findings are consistent with another quantitative comparative historical analysis of 414 societies over the past 10,000 years, which found a common pattern in the "tempo" of evolutionary change in human social systems (Turchin et al., 2017). The analysis revealed that many historical trajectories "exhibit long periods of stasis or gradual, slow change interspersed with sudden large increases in the measure of social complexity over a relatively short time span." The authors concluded that the evolution of stable larger polities requires "a relatively rapid change in sociopolitical organization, including the development of new governing institutions and social roles" (2017, p. 7).

Our experiments on MAxiM, which were performed before the publication of the study just cited, indicate that the emergence of Axial Age civilizations would indeed have needed to follow this sort of "punctuated equilibrium" pattern (see Figures 5.9 and 5.10). Unlike previous models, however, MAxiM is also able to account for the role of ideological-political and cognitive-coalitional mechanisms in the generation of the Axial Age.

How then, concretely, did religion matter in the Axial Age? It mattered in the way it played a role in the shifts in worldviews-lifeways that occurred as pre-Axial populations were replaced by Axial populations. This involved ontological, epistemological, and ethical changes, all of which can be illuminated in various ways by the three major types of theory about the causes of civilizational transformation. Table 5.5 summarizes some of the key elements of the following discussion.

As in Chapter 4, let's explore this heuristic matrix beginning with the top row. As we have seen, *ideological-political* theories emphasize the role of ideation and creative political organization as the key driver in civilizational transformation. During the Axial Age, the supernatural agents that populated the ontological inventories of the population became bigger, more rational, less mercurial, morally relevant gods. Cosmologies became more comprehensive as cultures became more "theoretic." As priests took over from shamans, appeals to supernatural authority became more rigid, homogenous, and institutionally

Table 5.5 Axial Age matrix

	Ontology	**Epistemology**	**Ethics**
Ideological-political	Change to bigger and morally relevant gods, universal cosmologies that purport to interpret all human beings, and comprehensive anthropologies that treat the human being as the ultimate political animal	Accepting knowledge from priestly elites as authoritative and vesting institutions and their priestly representatives as supernaturally authorized bearers of divinely revealed truth	Linking divine command ethics with a cosmological and rational vision of the good; expected compliance with abstract national or state identity narratives; emergence of more privacy of opinion
Material-social	Change to greater naturalism due to increased control of energy capture and the social field and to interpreting human beings as *Homo economicus*	More specialized knowledge and organizing society around conveying specialized techniques, in education, technology, and war	Expectation that members of a mega-state have a moral duty to comply with state's behavioral expectations and fulfill moral duties to state
Cognitive-coalitional	Change to humans having greater control over the natural and social environment, expressing the providential aims of the gods, and inspiring the idea that human beings are created in the divine image	Depending on reading, writing, communities of debate, and other tools to extend human reasoning and memory, which inspires greater self-differentiation, reflective contemplation, and self-awareness of life meaning	More doctrinal rituals to reinforce state identity narratives, reinforce cosmological concepts of the good, and challenge default in-group morality in favor of visions of universal human community

reinforced. Divine command ethics emerged, along with a cosmological (rather than local) notion of the good and the right, with correspondingly universal moral interpretations of all human beings. Compliance was now with ideals authorized and maintained within large-scale societies (e.g., city-state or empire), which were more abstract than small-scale social norms reinforced by particular animal-spirits and the ghosts of the ancestors of the living members of the group.

Material-social theories tend to highlight the material (especially economic) conditions driving such change and the specific social arrangements that make possible new technologies for energy capture and social management. The Axial transition would have led to even more naturalism insofar as humans gained greater control over their lives and their natural environment, in large part as a result of the invention of writing, money, and more advanced machines. Understanding the world and learning to assess claims to truth would have required even more specialized techniques and more war making than in the civilizational forms that came before. Ethical responsibilities would increasingly be tied to larger social organizations such as states, and individuals would have been forced to comply with wider legal expectations.

Cognitive-coalitional theories emphasize the way in which new cultural coalitional forms are evoked and sustained by distinctive modifications (e.g., contestations) of naturally evolved cognitive capacities and tendencies. Ontologically, humans were seen as more linked to the divine in a specific way (e.g., as the image of a god). Belief in "big gods" or at least morally interested supernatural agents who could track larger populations contributed to pro-social behaviors that could help hold together large-scale societies. With the invention of reading, writing, and communities of debate, there were new tools to extend cognition, making "theoretic" culture possible and helping it grow and expand more rapidly. As noted earlier, the doctrinal mode of religiosity plays a far greater role in Axial cultures, taking advantage of semantic memory and reinforcing the identity narratives of large-scale states. The downside of doctrinal approaches to ritual is that they are less fun than the ecstatic, high emotional arousal experienced in imagistic modes. All cognitive defaults mentioned in Chapter 4 on the Neolithic transition must be further contested in the Axial transition.

Our goal in this chapter has been to provide a model of the Axial Age that incorporates key elements of all three types of theories and includes crucial variables influencing and being influenced by the shifts in worldviews-lifeways that characterized the dawn of the Axial Age. We turn next to our final model, which leaps ahead two millennia to the early modern period and provides insights into possible futures for transformations of civilizational form that involve substantial changes in religion.

6

Modeling the Modernity Transition

Many scholars have pointed to the connection between the shifts in the Axial Age and shifts occurring in the modern age, in which secularization plays a central role. Several competing theories, especially among sociologists, purport to explain what factors lead to the demise of supernaturalist religious worldviews in human populations, the very worldviews that the Axial Age had birthed. We provide a theoretical framework that incorporates the main insights of the six empirically most robust hypotheses about the path from supernaturalist religious worldviews to secular cultural imaginaries, while also taking account of the spectacular changes in energy capture, technology, communication, travel, and medicine. This model traces the conditions under which twin transformations related to religion occur after 1700 CE. One is the secularization of societies, institutions, and individuals. The other is the decreasing plausibility of supernaturalist worldviews. The transitions are related but distinct, and both emerge within Modernity through intricately entangled mechanisms. This approach supports both modeling the past and simulating alternative futures, including one in which the majority of human beings no longer believe in invisible supernatural agents and one in which human societies revert to widespread embrace of supernatural beings.

We refer to the computer simulation presented here as FOReST, an acronym for the "future of religious and secular transitions." FOReST indicates that the conditions for producing widespread rejection of supernaturalist religion are highly specific, hard to produce, and difficult to sustain because they are individually necessary. When those necessary conditions combine, which is historically rare, there emerges a stable social equilibrium within which most people can contest what Robert McCauley (2013) calls "maturationally natural" cognitive tendencies to embrace supernaturalist thinking and behaving. Because it requires steady inputs of substantial energy to resist maturationally natural cognition and behavior, this post-supernaturalist social equilibrium may be easier to destabilize than more common social equilibria that take advantage of maturationally natural cognitive tendencies toward supernaturalist beliefs and practices.

Why Model the Modernity Transition?

Despite the resurgence of supernaturalist religion in many parts of the world, some subcultures reliably produce people who deny the existence of supernatural entities. This social phenomenon has evoked competing explanations, many of which enjoy empirical support. We synthesize six of the most influential social science explanations, demonstrating that they provide complementary perspectives within a complex causal architecture. We incorporate this theoretical synthesis into FOReST, a computer simulation that identifies conditions under which the predominant attitude toward supernaturalist religion in a population shifts from acceptance to rejection (and vice versa).

In Scandinavian and Northern European nations today, as well as most coastal regions of the United States and many parts of Australia and New Zealand, a growing number of individuals do not believe in supernatural entities and reject religion—religious beliefs, practices, and institutions—in general. However, surveys show that supernaturalist beliefs remain strong in many parts of the world, and the Axial Age religions are powerful forces in Africa, Asia, and most of the Americas (Pew Research Center, 2015). Why is widespread rejection of supernaturalist worldviews so rare, historically speaking? And what is so unusual about the social contexts within which post-supernaturalism becomes widespread?

Several social theories have attempted to describe pathways through which a culture can shift away from supernaturalist religiosity and toward post-supernaturalist secularity, many of which enjoy significant empirical support. After an exhaustive literature review, we identified the following six as being (1) the most influential, (2) the most relevant to interpreting the emergence and stabilization of post-supernaturalist cultures, and (3) the most empirically well supported.

- The Existential Security Path (e.g., Inglehart, Norris)
- The Cultural Particularity Path (e.g., Putnam, Campbell)
- The Human Development Path (e.g., Norris, Inglehart)
- The Meaning Maintenance Path (e.g., Berger)

- The Subjectivization Path (e.g., Heelas, Woodhead)
- The Supply-Side Path (e.g., Stark, Finke, Iannaccone)

Although some champions of these theories view them as inherently competitive or even mutually exclusive, we argue (as we also did for NSIM in Chapter 4 and MAxiM in Chapter 5) that these mainstream theories offer partial perspectives on a more complex architecture of causal factors, driving changes in the religiosity and secularity of human populations. We are not the first to try to integrate aspects of two or more of these approaches. Ruiter and van Tubergen, for example, have attempted to show how (what we are calling) the existential security and supply-side paths can be "taken together" to "provide insights into differences in initial conditions, path dependency, and the reason why religious trends are sometimes reversed" (2009, p. 889).

Probably the most ambitious attempt so far to produce a unified theoretical model is Stolz (2009), where correlations between aspects of some of these theories (and some others) are explored using multilevel multiple regression modeling, though Stolz doesn't take account of post-supernaturalism as a dependent variable, and the method of analysis doesn't support robust causal inference. Such integrative attempts are rare, and none developed to date illustrates concretely how the causal elements of all these theories can function together. It is important to note that we selected these six theories before trying to integrate them. We needed to experiment to determine whether integration would be possible and whether the meaning of the resulting synthesis would tell us anything interesting about transitions between supernaturalist religion and post-supernaturalist secularity.

We synthesize the core elements of these six theories into a consistent conceptual architecture and implement the resulting model in a system-dynamics computer simulation. This allows us, first, to demonstrate the coherence of the synthesis, because implementing it in a computational simulation imposes demanding requirements of conceptual clarity and consistency. The simulation experiments also enable us to identify plausible conditions under which a population with a majority of individuals embracing supernaturalist beliefs (we will use *supernaturalist religious* to refer to this posture, which explicitly excludes naturalist forms of religion) changes to a population in which most individuals have learned to contest inbuilt cognitive tendencies toward supernaturalism, thereby becoming "post-supernaturalists" (we will call this posture *post-supernaturalist secular*, referring both to personal views and to a corresponding form of sociopolitical organization where beliefs in and practices related to supernatural agents play no role; the unwieldy name is warranted to avoid confusion with low-frequency cross cases involving post-supernaturalist religiosity). The same simulation also indicates plausible conditions under which a society moves in the *opposite direction* (i.e., from post-supernaturalist secular to supernaturalist religious).

This computational model also provides insight into the means by which supernaturalist religious coalitions and secular post-supernatural coalitions might inhibit or catalyze social transformation in either direction. As suggested in Chapter 3, computational modeling and simulation is a fruitful substitute for experimentation when (as with many social issues) experiments are impossible or unethical, the periods concerned are too long, or datasets spanning many decades are not available. Conceptually, computer simulation is not so different from demographic projection: both model a set of hypothetical scenarios by working out the implications of specific assumptions. This means that FOReST also has the ability to support population projections, though in qualitative form rather than demographic detail.

Synthesizing Theories

As a simulation built upon empirically well-grounded theories, FOReST provides a plausible model of the complex causal processes that underlie transitions from religious to secular and vice versa in actual human societies. Each theory synthesized represents a different path in our model (however, this model is a systems-dynamic model, *not* a structural equation or path model, as previously used in the secularization literature). These paths—represented by different arrows of causation in Figures 6.1–6.7—are explained below. Inglehart et al. (2008) used "path" to refer to lines of society-level change in the direction of human development, inspired by the "paths" in the underlying structural-equation model that is incorporated into FOReST. We mean something similar, though with a different target: the six paths are lines of society-level change in the direction of decreasing or increasing prevalence of supernaturalism within a population.

Let's begin with the two theories that fit best into what we have been calling the *ideological-political* type. The first is the *Meaning Maintenance Path* (Figure 6.1), which is more directly informed by psychology than most sociological theories. Peter Berger's sociology of knowledge, for example, incorporates psychological concepts such as the need to relieve the discomfort of cognitive dissonance and the drive to create meaning (Berger, 1969, 1973). Similar approaches can be

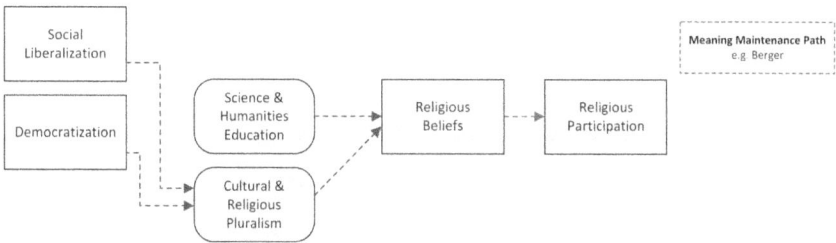

Figure 6.1 Conceptual model of the Meaning Maintenance Path.

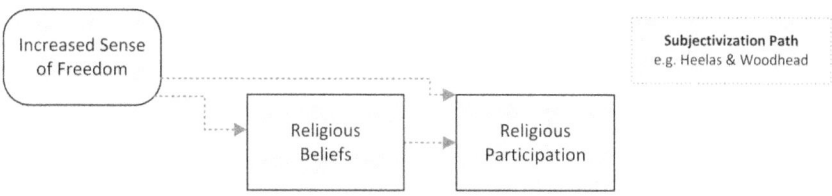

Figure 6.2 Conceptual model of the Subjectivization Path.

found in the hypotheses set out by Proulx and Inzlicht (2012), which built on the work of Festinger (1957) and others. Such theories also give social meaning to psychological concepts and plausibility structures of the sort that typically emerge as a result of education in the sciences and humanities, which tend to diminish supernaturalist religious beliefs (Dyer & Hall, 2019; Hungerman, 2014). This is one aspect of classical secularization theory that we should preserve because these psychosocial dynamics are demonstrably active in human affairs (for a defense of classical secularization theory, see Bruce, 2011, chapter 2). Indeed, meaning maintenance and the management of cognitive dissonance have become key concepts in cognitive science of religion, where they are incorporated into theories not only of the social and existential functions of religion but also of the evolutionary origins of religion (Atran, 2002; Guthrie, 1993).

Second, the *Subjectivization Path* (Figure 6.2), which is based upon the work of Paul Heelas and Linda Woodhead (Heelas & Woodhead, 2000; Davie et al., 2003; Woodhead & Heelas, 2005), also fits relatively well into the ideological-political category of theory. One of the most empirically sturdy results from these authors' research is that, as individual freedom increases, people become less wary of incurring social penalties when they express their spiritual beliefs and decide whether and how to participate in religious communities. In contexts where freedom of religious expression is strongly curtailed, on the other hand, the secularization process rarely gets started and people tend to continue believing

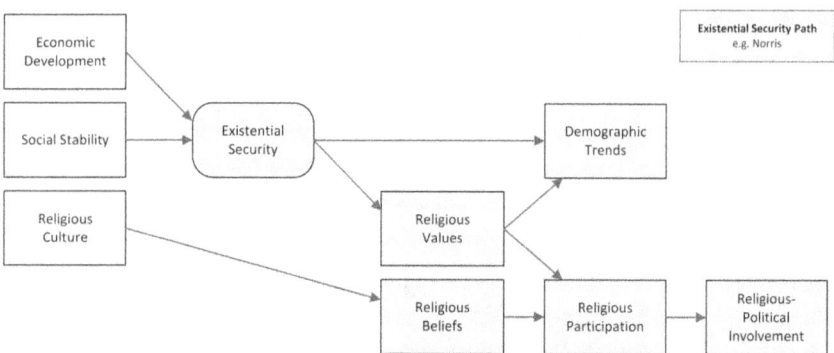

Figure 6.3 Conceptual model of the Existential Security Path.

in supernatural agents and engaging in supernatural rituals prevalent within the dominant culture. In other words, the extent to which beliefs about supernatural agents are subjectified (rather than institutionalized and monitored) impacts the extent to which individuals in a population maintain those beliefs and participate in traditional ritual practices associated with them.

The next two hypothesized pathways to Modernity fit better within what we have been calling the *material-social* type of theory. The *Existential Security Path* (Figure 6.3) is derived from theories rooted in data mined from the World Values Survey (WVS) and other datasets (e.g., Norris & Inglehart, 2011, 2015, 2019; Inglehart & Norris, 2012). According to Norris and Inglehart, differences in religious culture and changes in existential security predict shifts in personal religious values, beliefs, and behaviors. The Existential Security Path attempts to explain the way supernaturalist religiosity operates in a wide variety of cultural contexts, taking account of variations in religious cultures and demographics. It also tries to register the causally more determinate aspects of the effects of social change on religion (existential security changes religious values, which changes religious participation, which changes religiously motivated political involvement). Put simply, the basic argument here is that the more existentially secure a population feels the more likely belief in supernatural agents and participation in religious rituals will wane.

Also leaning toward the material-social category, the *Human Development Path* (Figure 6.4) is based on a structural equation model (SEM) developed by Inglehart and Norris, utilizing WVS data (Inglehart & Norris, 2012; Inglehart et al., 2008; Norris & Inglehart, 2015). We were unable to replicate the SEM loadings for want of sufficient information about construct measures in the original calculations (even after talking with the team that produced it), but the

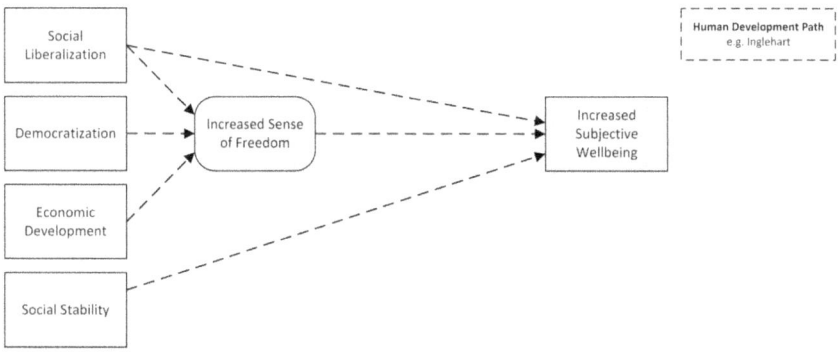

Figure 6.4 Conceptual model of the Human Development Path.

pathway makes solid theoretical sense and we incorporate it into the synthesis on that basis. This path indicates how four elements of social change (social liberalization, democratization, economic development, and social stability) produce an increased sense of freedom, which in turn increases subjective well-being. WVS data show that the most salient factor at the beginning of the Human Development Path is economic development, but with time economic development contributes less to subjective well-being than social liberalization and democratization. In other words, the processes that lead to the development of secularization begin with economic change and proceed (or intensify) with political and lifestyle change. Inglehart and Norris's original SEM standing behind the Human Development Path did not include social stability. In our architecture described below, we added social stability because it is an obviously relevant factor in individual freedom and subjective well-being, which decrease supernaturalist religious beliefs and practices. That helps us integrate the Human Development Path with the Existential Security Path. While much of the empirical warrant for these paths emerges out of analysis of similar datasets, the former path is more focused on freedom while the latter emphasizes the role of existential security.

The last two pathways fit into what we have been calling *cognitive-coalitional* theories. For scholars who prefer the *Cultural Particularity Path* (Figure 6.5) the focus is on the importance of particular religious cultures in determining religious values and religious participation. For example, Robert Putnam notes that the best predictor of religiousness in the United States is racial background (Putnam, 2001; Putnam & Campbell, 2010; Campbell & Putnam, 2011). These insights are obviously based on considerations specific to one nation. From this point of view, looking for cross-cultural causal dynamics linking social change

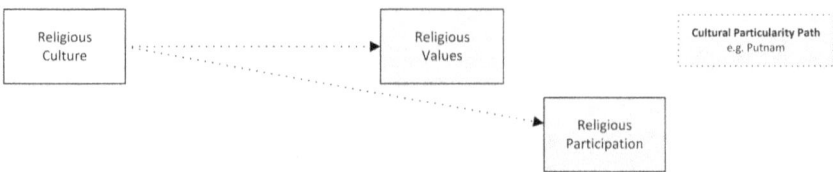

Figure 6.5 Conceptual model of the Cultural Particularity Path.

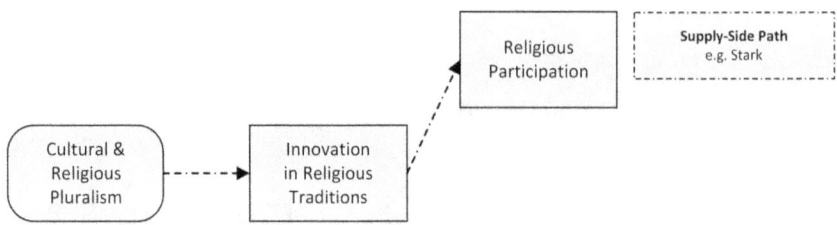

Figure 6.6 Conceptual model of the Supply-Side Path.

and supernaturalist religious beliefs and practices may be a quest merely to isolate minor influences on secularization rather than the most salient influences, the latter being more intricately tied to the historical details of each social setting. In plain language, demographic differences and sociological shifts of the sort described by Putnam and Campbell directly impact the rise or fall of supernaturalist religious values, beliefs, practices, and participation. In our view, there are some components of cultural influence that are cross-culturally generalizable to a significant degree. It is these aspects that we incorporate into the final theoretical synthesis we create. We'll say more about this momentarily.

The sixth and final path incorporated into our theoretical synthesis is meant to capture the insights of a family of supply-side sociological and economic theories (see, e.g., Finke & Stark, 1998). We call this the *Supply-Side Path* (Figure 6.6). These theories postulate a link between pluralistic cultural and religious settings and religious participation by means of competition-induced innovation in religious products and services. This helps to explain why populations in some geographical regions tend to maintain the same basic levels of religiosity (or secularity) over time although individuals (with varying levels of religiosity or secularity) are constantly moving in and out of them (Iannaccone & Makowsky, 2007). Such approaches are "supply side" (as opposed to "demand side") insofar as the dominant factors incrementing or decrementing religiosity are associated with the providers of religious services (as opposed to the needs of religious "consumers"). We argue that some aspects of these supply-side theories can be understood as complementary to—and not only as competitors of—theories that emphasize the demand-side of religious participation.

Preserving the most empirically robust elements of each theory, we synthesized all six theories into a unified conceptual model that illustrates how elements in the six theories are interconnected (Figure 6.7). FOReST has several feedback loops, so all variables interact. Nevertheless, we identify four variables (in the shaded area) as "key conditions" because they are salient mediators between generic socioeconomic conditions and supernaturalist religious or post-supernaturalist secular worldviews.

Constructing models is one thing; determining whether this synthesized causal architecture makes conceptual sense is another. Such a determination depends on the empirically validated theoretical arguments to which we have already alluded. Plausibility can also be increased by exposing this novel architecture to the conceptual rigors of implementation in a computational simulation. At this stage of the process, however, building such a model demands precise specification of how the major components of the theory fit together. That process of clarification may require us to make the model more specific in some places, or to limit the scope of its applicability.

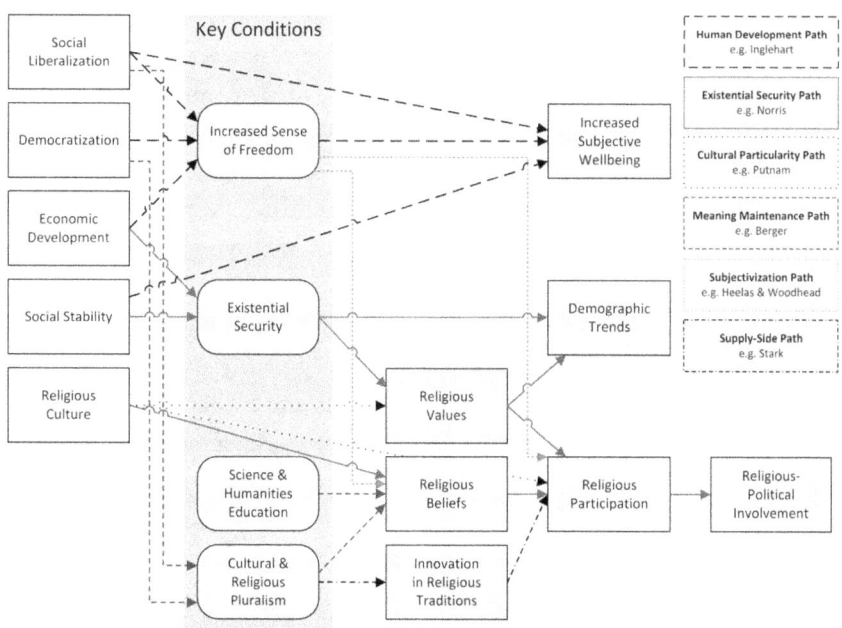

Figure 6.7 Conceptual model of synthesis of six theories of religious and secular change.

For example, the Religious Culture variable (Figure 6.7, lower left), which is critical to the Cultural Particularity Path, is vague and unimplementable in a computational architecture as it stands. We limit the scope of this variable to focus on dynamics that tend to produce liberal religious cultures or conservative religious cultures. This limited conceptualization of "religious culture" generalizes across societies well, so long as the concepts of liberal and conservative focus on more universal features of human life. Following research on the universal features of religious ideology (Wildman et al., 2023), conservative here means a religious ideology stressing the preservation of achieved human value, even if individuals must suffer as a side effect; and liberal means a religious culture emphasizing human well-being, even at the cost of damaging valuable institutions. Other aspects of ideology—say economics—do not generalize well across cultures and therefore play no role in the way we implement "religious culture" in this theoretical synthesis. We will introduce this specification of "religious culture" when we move from the conceptual model of Figure 6.7 to its implementation in a computational simulation, in the next section.

The FOReST Model

To analyze the processes that lead to changes between supernaturalist religion and post-supernaturalist secularism, we implemented the theoretical synthesis of Figure 6.7 as the Causal Nexus and linked it to the conversion process described in Chapter 3, a method also employed in Chapters 4 and 5. In this case, the conversion process depicts post-supernaturalist secular and supernaturalist religious people being born and dying, and in between possibly converting from one posture to the other. Conversion back and forth between traditional supernaturalist religious worldviews-lifeways and post-supernaturalist secular worldviews-lifeways suggests that we might simplify the corresponding phrases to religious and secular. But FOReST is more about the rise and fall of supernaturalist worldviews-lifeways, which are often but not always religious, than it is about the rise and fall of religion, which is often but not always supernaturalist. Thus, we abbreviate the two states in the conversion model as "trad" for "traditional supernaturalist religious worldviews-lifeways" and "post" for "post-supernaturalist secular worldviews-lifeways." The trad people are typically religious and the post people are typically secular but not always.

In the conversion part of FOReST, people begin life either as supernaturalist religious babies (trads) or post-supernaturalist secular babies (posts), corresponding to their dominant family and cultural heritage (these family and cultural relationships are implied, not explicitly incorporated into the model). Supernaturalist religious (trad) babies have three possible fates:

- They grow up to be supernaturalist religious (trad) adults without significant exposure to post-supernaturalist secularism (post) worldview-lifeways.
- They grow up to be supernaturalist religious (trad) adults even though they receive significant exposure to post-supernaturalist secular (post) worldview-lifeways.
- They grow up to be post-supernaturalist secular (post) adults because they receive significant exposure to post-supernaturalist secular (post) worldviews-lifeways and actually convert.

Likewise, post-supernaturalist secular (post) babies may or may not be exposed to traditional supernaturalist religious (trad) worldview-lifeways and may or may not convert after exposure.

The way people move through the conversion process is affected by a series of flow rates, increasing or decreasing the corresponding direction of flow. Six key parameters in the conversion model determine flow rates, as follows.

- Traditional Birthrate (trad_BirthRate): the birthrate of babies into supernaturalist religious families and cultural settings.
- Post-Supernaturalist Birthrate (post_BirthRate): the birthrate of babies into post-supernaturalist secular families and cultural settings.
- Exposure Rate of Traditional to Post-Supernaturalist (trad_ExposureRateToPost): the rate at which traditional supernaturalist religious people are exposed in a substantive way to post-supernaturalist secularism.
- Exposure Rate of Post-Supernaturalist to Traditional (post_ExposureRateToTrad): the rate at which post-supernaturalist secular people are exposed in a substantive way to traditional supernaturalist religion.
- Supernatural-to-Secular Conversion Rate (trad_ConvertToPost): the rate at which traditional supernaturalist religious people exposed to post-supernaturalist secularism convert.
- Secular-to-Supernaturalist Conversion Rate (post_ConvertToTrad): the rate at which post-supernaturalist secular people exposed to traditional supernaturalist religion convert.

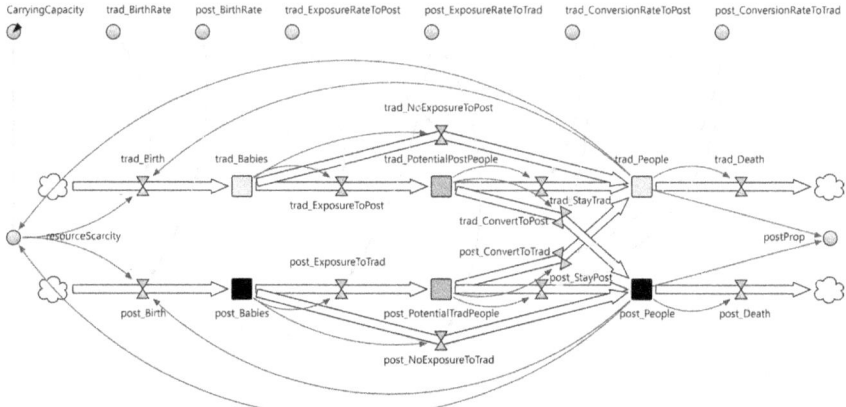

Figure 6.8 Conversion model for FOReST.

As in previous chapters, FOReST's conversion model also includes a measure of Resource Scarcity (resourceScarcity). This is impacted by the parameter Carrying Capacity (CarryingCapacity), which sets the total number of people possible in the ecology of the model. The Resource Scarcity variable is also affected by the actual population by means of feedback loops that drive the model dynamics. Figure 6.8 depicts the conversion model.

As we've seen in Chapters 4 and 5, verification is important for developing a persuasive system-dynamics computational simulation. One key question for FOReST is Does the expected range of behaviors emerge for appropriate tunings of the model? In the case of FOReST's conversion model, this means paying attention to flow rates. For almost all settings of the six flow rates, this conversion process eventually converges on an equilibrium state in which the ratio of traditional supernaturalist religious (trad) people to post-supernaturalist secular (post) people remains constant. The line graphs in Figure 6.9 depict the relative sizes of the traditional supernaturalist religious and post-supernaturalist secular subpopulations and displays the equilibrium as it emerges.

To indicate how the conversion model works, Figure 6.9 shows the population equilibrium emerging when parameters are set as follows. The maximum supernaturalist religious birthrate is 2.5 babies per person (i.e. five babies per family; the average is lower) and the average post-supernaturalist secular birthrate is 0.9 babies per person (i.e. 1.8 babies per family). The middling post-supernaturalist secular exposure rate (50 percent) and conversion rate (20 percent) suggest a social situation in which a small secular enclave exists within a larger supernaturalist population—perhaps a couple of centuries ago when secularization was still on the

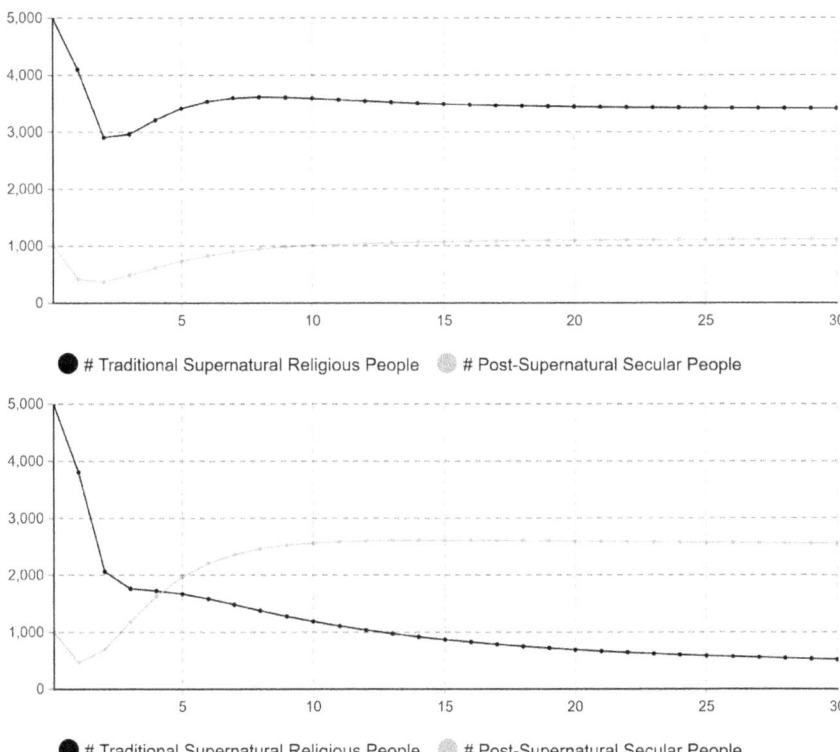

Figure 6.9a (top) The conversion process shows an emerging equilibrium between traditional supernaturalist religious (black) and post-supernaturalist secular (gray) people. The horizontal axis is model time. The vertical axis is the number of people of each type. The equilibrium depicts a social situation in which a small secular enclave exists within a larger supernaturalist religious ("traditional") population.
Figure 6.9b (bottom) The conversion model's emerging equilibrium with parameters set to yield more post-supernaturalist secular people than supernaturalist religious ("traditional") people. Only two parameters are changed between the two cases: the rate of exposure of traditional supernaturalist religious people to post-supernaturalist secular worldviews (trad_ExposureRateToPost) and the rate of conversion of traditional supernaturalist religious people to post-supernaturalist secular worldviews (trad_ConversionRateToPost).

horizon in most Western nations, or right now in countries where what appears to be a secularization process is just getting started.

Figure 6.9b shows a combination of parameter settings that yields a very different equilibrium state with more post-supernaturalist secular people than supernaturalist religious people. The social setting implied here is one in which virtually all supernaturalist religious people (95 percent) are exposed to secular modes of life and thought and a sizable minority (40 percent) convert (the other rates remain unchanged from Figure 6.9a).

This verification exercise shows that FOReST's conversion model produces the expected behavior when we control flow rates *manually*. The next challenge is to define the six flow rates *automatically* using the conceptual integration of theories of religious and secular change described in the previous section. That is, the two birthrates, the two exposure rates, and the two conversion rates must be inferred from the theoretical synthesis of Figure 6.7. That is the task of FOReST's Causal Nexus.

We describe the parameters and variables of FOReST's Causal Nexus in several stages. First, the parameters tune FOReST, enabling it to simulate countless virtual societies, which in turn facilitates the study of the Modernity transition, including when it occurs, and why it occurs when it does. Table 6.1 describes FOReST's parameters.

Second, the main loop within the Causal Nexus parallels that of NSIM (Chapter 4) and MAxiM (Chapter 5). In the case of FOReST, a variable representing modern social forms (Modernity) is incremented by the modernitypro variable and decremented by the modernitycon variable. These two variables sum the effects of the causal architecture that promote or suppress the emergence of characteristics of modern secular society, respectively. The incrementing and decrementing variables are affected by (among other things) the proportion of post-supernaturalist secular people in the population (postProp), which is supplied by the conversion model (Figure 6.8), and the degree of secular and religious political participation. The diagram illustrating the main loop is in Figure 6.10. The formulas for this critical looping structure are in Table 6.2.

Third, the computational representation of the theoretical synthesis of Figure 6.7 involves corresponding variables, parameters, and associated formulas. Figure 6.11 illustrates them and their relationships. Table 6.3 lays out the technical details.

Fourth, and finally, the Causal Nexus needs to generate the six flow rates driving the conversion model of Figure 6.8. Figure 6.12 depicts the relationships and Table 6.4 furnishes the technical details.

The dynamism of FOReST is akin to what we've already seen in Chapters 4 and 5: the population equilibrium changes as the six flow rates are altered by the Causal Nexus, and the proportion of post-supernaturalist secular people from the conversion process feeds back into the Causal Nexus, where it plays a critical role. Thus, as with NSIM (Chapter 4) and MAxiM (Chapter 5), in FOReST, the two-way conversion process stands in a feedback loop with the Causal Nexus.

Table 6.1 Definition of FOReST's parameters

Parameter	Definition and Description
PrefAfflbirthrate	This is the preferred affluent birthrate (default is 0.9 babies per person, a little below replacement) and expresses the preferred birthrate of people living with affluent levels of environmental calorie capture, and is used to calculate traditional religious and secular birthrates.
Maxbirthrate	This is the maximum birthrate (default maximum of 2.5 babies per person, with the average birthrate lower) and is used to calculate traditional religious and secular birthrates.
Technology	This refers to the technological capacity of the model world, which covers communication, transportation, agricultural, and manufacturing technologies.
Destabilization	This is a quantified expression of disasters capable of destabilizing a social order (for example, environmental disasters, nuclear war, and so on). If the destabilization parameter is above zero, well-being, existential security, and education are all negatively impacted.
ChangeRate	This speeds up or slows down the speed at which the key Modernity variable changes.
Modernitymin	This is the lowest threshold possible for the Modernity variable and expresses the irreversibility of some degree of modern culture.
PromodenityInflOfRel	This reflects the fact that some traditional religious beliefs and practices advance aspects of secular social life, as when the booming Pentecostal movement in South America accelerates processes of liberalization and democratization, or when the Protestant Reformation helped to give birth to Western Modernity by promoting individuality (see Bruce, 2011).
Libmin	This is the lowest threshold possible for liberal religious culture and reflects the irrepressibility of liberal impulses to individual liberty, social justice, and human-heartedness.
Consmin	This is the lowest threshold possible for conservative religious culture and reflects the portability of socially borne plausibility structures that keep traditional religious cultures alive regardless of how secular the surrounding culture becomes.
ResistChange	This reflects the tendency of all people, and especially conservative people, to resist new ideas and experiences, and thus to conversion.

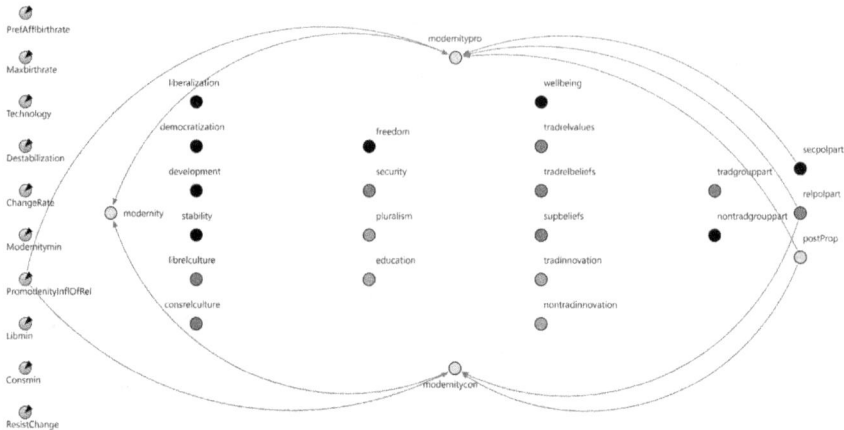

Figure 6.10 The main looping structure within the Causal Nexus of FOReST.

Table 6.2 Definition of the variables involved in the main looping structure within FOReST's Causal Nexus

Flow Rate	Definition and Description
modernitypro	*((secpolpart + (relpolpart × PromodenityInflOfRel)) / 2) × postProp* The *Modernity* variable is incremented by secular political participation (*secpolpart*) and by religious political participation (*relpolpart*) to the extent that religion has a (typically unanticipated) pro-Modernity influence (the *PromodenityInflOfRel* parameter). That combined incremental influence is magnified as the post-supernaturalist portion of the population (*postProp*) increases.
modernitycon	*relpolpart × (1− PromodenityInflOfRel) × (1 − postProp)* The *Modernity* variable is decremented by religious political participation (*relpolpart*) to the extent that religion does not possess a pro-Modernity influence (1 − *PromodenityInflOfRel*). That combined decremental influence is magnified as the supernaturalist portion of the population (1 − *postProp*) increases.
modernity	*modernity + ChangeRate × (modernitypro × (1 − modernity) − modernitycon × (modernity − Modernitymin))* The incrementing factor (*modernitypro*) and the decrementing factor (*modernitycon*) combine to change the *Modernity* variable. The entire process can be sped up or slowed down by a parameter (*ChangeRate*), and another parameter (*Modernitymin*) prevents the *Modernity* variable from dropping below a minimum threshold, reflecting the built-in tendencies toward modern forms of civilization that emerge from prior eras.

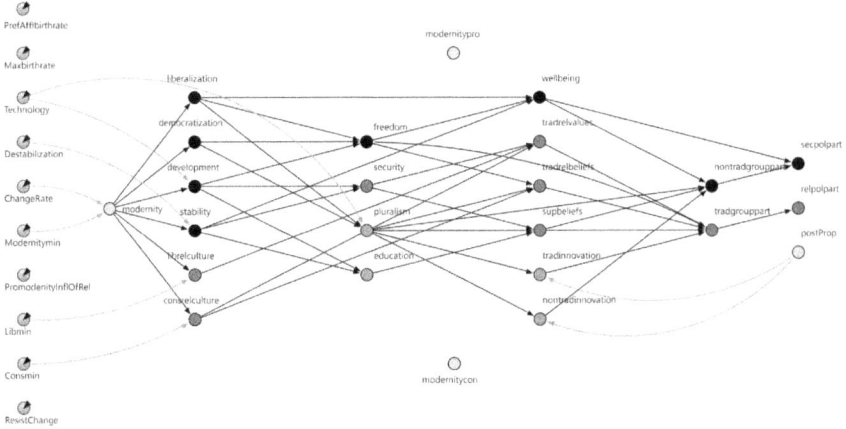

Figure 6.11 The Causal Nexus of FOReST.

Most of the nodes in the Causal Nexus (Figure 6.10) directly match constructs in the conceptual model (Figure 6.7). There are minor changes and additions, all forced by the goal of implementing the theoretical synthesis of religious and secular change in a coherent system-dynamics model. In particular, note the splitting of "Religious Culture" in the theoretical synthesis into "conservative religious culture" (consrelculture) and "liberal religious culture" (librelculture); this is in accordance with our strategy for implementing the vague idea of religious culture in a way that both generalizes well across cultures and relates fairly precisely to other elements of the causal architecture.

The mathematical formulas in FOReST's causal architecture are as natural as possible (as always, products are used when the input quantities are linked by a logical *and* while averages are used when the link is a logical *or*). Slightly more complex, but still natural, formulas express the way the modernitypro and modernitycon variables are derived and how they in turn increment and decrement (respectively) the Modernity variable. The formulas for the six variables feeding into the conversion model express commonsense interpretations of the two birthrates, the two exposure rates, and the two conversion rates.

Table 6.3 Definition of the variables within FOReST's Causal Nexus

Variable	Definition and Description
Liberalization	*Modernity* The value of the *liberalization* variable just is the value of the *Modernity* variable.
Democratization	*Modernity* The value of the *democratization* variable just is the value of the *Modernity* variable.
Development	*(modernity + Technology) / 2* The *development* variable averages the *Modernity* variable and the *Technology* parameter.
Stability	*max(modernity − Destabilization, 0)* The *stability* variable takes account of both of the current degree of Modernity (*modernity*) and of the existence of a destabilizing event, expressed in the *Destabilization* parameter.
Librelculture	*Libmin + modernity × (1 − Libmin)* As *Modernity* increases, the degree of liberal religious culture (*librelculture*) rises above a minimum (the *Libmin* parameter), expressing the built-in tendency of all cultures to prioritize human well-being to some minimum extent.
Consrelculture	*Consmin + (1 − modernity) × (1 − Consmin)* As *Modernity* decreases, the degree of conservative religious culture (*consrelculture*) rises above a minimum (the *Consmin* parameter), expressing the built-in tendency of all cultures to prioritize the preservation of achieved value to some minimum extent.
Freedom	*(liberalization + democratization + development)/3* The *freedom* variable depends equally on *liberalization*, *democratization*, and *development*.
Security	*(development + stability) / 2* The *security* variable rises and falls with both the degree of development (*development*) and cultural predictability (*stability*).
Pluralism	*(liberalization + democratization + technology) / 3* The *pluralism* variable depends equally on *liberalization*, *democratization*, and *technology*, all of which increase the free flow of information and confront people with others who may be very different in culture or religion.
Education	*(development + stability) / 2* The *pluralism* variable depends on both the degree of socioeconomic complexity (*development*) and cultural predictability (*stability*).

well-being	*(liberalization + freedom + stability) / 3*
	The *wellbeing* variable averages *liberalization*, *freedom*, and *stability*, all of which increase health and life satisfaction.
Tradrelvalues	*(max(consrelculture − librelculture, 0) + (1 − security)) / 2*
	Traditional religious values (*tradrelvalues*) are enhanced roughly equally by two factors: the extent to which conservative religious culture (*consrelculture*) dominates liberal religious culture (*librelculture*) and the extent to which the socioeconomic and political situation is insecure (*1 − security*).
Tradrelbeliefs	*(max(consrelculture − librelculture, 0) + (1 − pluralism) + (1 − freedom)) / 3*
	Traditional religious beliefs (*tradrelbeliefs*) are enhanced roughly equally by three factors: the extent to which conservative religious culture (*consrelculture*) dominates liberal religious culture (*librelculture*), the extent to which a pluralistic attitude to cultural and religious diversity is weak (*1 − pluralism*), and the extent to which there are serious religious limitations on freedom of expression (*1 − freedom*).
Supbeliefs	*1 − (education + security + pluralism) / 3*
	Supernaturalist beliefs decline in the presence of high scientific and humanistic education (*education*), high existential security (*security*), and high pluralistic embrace of cultural and religious diversity (*pluralism*).
Tradinnovation	*pluralism × (1 − postProp)*
	Religious traditions tend to innovate (*tradinnovation*) in pluralistic cultural and religious settings (*tradinnovation*), and all the more so when the number of traditionally religious people (*1 − postProp*) is high.
nontradinnovation	*pluralism × postProp*
	Innovative spiritual exploration outside the scope of religious traditions (*nontradinnovation*) tends to occur in the presence of a pluralistic embrace of cultural and religious diversity (*pluralism*) and is magnified by large numbers of post-supernaturalist people in the population (*postProp*).
Tradgrouppart	*(tradrelvalues + tradrelbeliefs + supbeliefs + tradinnovation + (1 − freedom)) / 5*
	Participation in traditional supernaturalist religious groups (*tradgrouppart*) is enhanced by a number of factors, weighted roughly equally: high traditional religious values (*tradrelvalues*), high traditional religious beliefs (*tradrelbeliefs*), high supernaturalist beliefs (*supbeliefs*), high levels of innovation within traditional religions (*tradinnovation*), and lower levels of freedom of self-expression (*1 − freedom*), penalizing people for leaving traditional religions.

(Continued)

Table 6.3 (*Continued*)

Variable	Definition and Description
nontradgrouppart	(*wellbeing* + *pluralism* + *nontradinnovation* + (1 − *supbeliefs*)) / 4 Participation in nontraditional groups of spiritual questers (*nontradgrouppart*) is enhanced by several factors, weighted roughly equally: high well-being of people so they are less in need of support from traditional religious institutions (*wellbeing*), high pluralistic embrace of cultural and religious diversity (*pluralism*), high levels of creative innovation to support spiritual quests outside of traditional religious institutions (*nontradinnovation*), and implausibility of traditional supernaturalist religious beliefs (1 − *supbeliefs*).
Secpolpart	(*nontradgrouppart* + *wellbeing*) / 2 Secular political participation (*secpolpart*) depends roughly equally on the degree to which people participate in nontraditional groups capable of informing members and catalyzing group action (*nontradgrouppart*) and on the degree of well-being in a society (*wellbeing*).
Relpolpart	*tradgrouppart* Religious political participation (*relpolpart*) depends on the degree to which people participate in traditional supernaturalist religious groups (*tradgrouppart*), thereby giving those groups political clout.

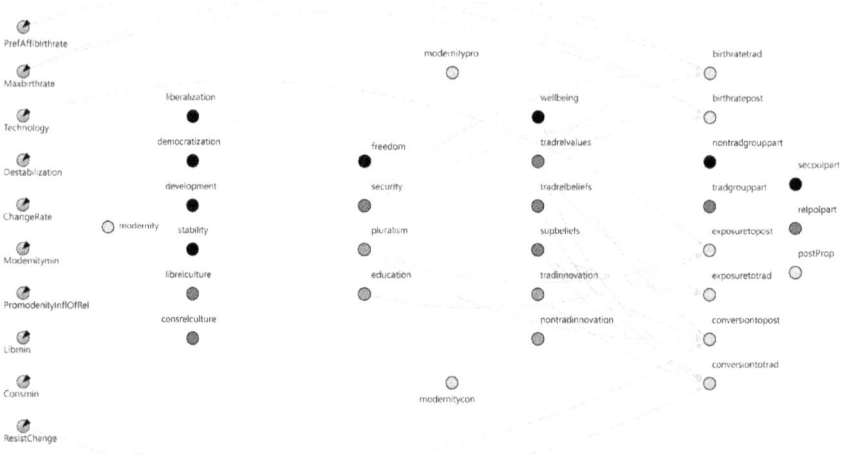

Figure 6.12 The derivation of six flow rates from FOReST's Causal Nexus.

Table 6.4 Definition of six flow rates driving FOReST's conversion model

Flow Rate	Formula
trad_BirthRate	$1 + min(max(2 \times tradrelvalues - security, PrefAfflbirthrate - 1), Maxbirthrate - 1)$ The fertility of traditional supernaturalist religious people (*trad_BirthRate*) is lifted above the preferred birthrate in affluent societies (*PrefAfflbirthrate*) and toward the maximum birthrate (*Maxbirthrate*) when traditional religious values (*tradrelvalues*) prevail and when there is significant existential insecurity (− *security*), with the former being roughly twice as important as the latter.
post_BirthRate	$1 + min(max(0.5 \times tradrelvalues - security, PrefAfflbirthrate - 1), Maxbirthrate - 1)$ The fertility of post-supernaturalist secular people (*post_BirthRate*) is lifted above the preferred birthrate in affluent societies (*PrefAfflbirthrate*) and toward the maximum birthrate (*Maxbirthrate*) when traditional religious values (*tradrelvalues*) prevail and when there is significant existential insecurity (− *security*), with the former being roughly half as important as the latter.
trad_ExposureRateToPost	$max(max(pluralism, education), Technology)$ The rate at which traditional supernaturalist religious people are exposed to post-supernaturalist secular worldview-lifeways (*trad_ExposureRateToPost*) depends on high technology to enhance the free flow of information (the *Technology* parameter) and on either *pluralism* or *education* being high.
post_ExposureRateToTrad	$min(supbeliefs, min(tradrelvalues, tradrelbeliefs))$ The rate at which post-supernaturalist secular people are exposed to traditional supernaturalist worldview-lifeways (*post_ExposureRateToTrad*) depends on the prevalence of supernaturalist beliefs (*supbeliefs*) and on both traditional religious values (*tradrelvalues*) and traditional religious beliefs (*tradrelbeliefs*).
trad_ConversionRateToPost	$(wellbeing + pluralism + education + notradinnovation + (1 - supbeliefs) / 5) \times ResistChange$ The rate at which traditional supernaturalist religious people convert to post-supernaturalist secular worldview-lifeways (*trad_ConversionRateToPost*) depends on several equally weighted factors that determine the attractiveness of post-supernaturalist secular worldview-lifeways: *wellbeing*, *pluralism*, *education*, innovation in the nonreligious spiritual sphere (*notradinnovation*), and the prevalence of post-supernaturalist beliefs (*1 − supbeliefs*). Conversion is slowed by general resistance to change (the *ResistChange* parameter).

(*Continued*)

Table 6.4 (*Continued*)

Flow Rate	Formula
post_ConversionRateToTrad	*((supbeliefs + tradinnovation + tradrelvalues + tradrelbeliefs) / 4)* × *ResistChange*
	The rate at which post-supernaturalist secular people convert to traditional supernaturalist worldview-lifeways (*post_ConversionRateToTrad*) depends on several equally weighted factors that determine the attractiveness of traditional supernaturalist religious worldview-lifeways: the prevalence of supernaturalist beliefs (*supbeliefs*), innovation in the traditional religious sphere (*tradinnovation*), and the strength of traditional religious values (*tradrelvalues*) and traditional religious beliefs (*tradrelbeliefs*). Conversion is slowed by general resistance to change (the *ResistChange* parameter).

Simulation Experiments

We ran FOReST through a parameter sweep (using Latin Hypercube sampling to identify representative combinations of parameter settings). We recorded the associated emergent equilibrium (i.e., the proportion of post-supernaturalist secular people) for each combination of parameters and then analyzed the vast dataset of results to generate insights into model dynamics and to produce comprehensible visualizations of those dynamics.

Figures 6.13a and 6.13b depict a response surface for the post-supernaturalist secular proportion of the population (SecProp). This response surface suggests that there are pathways leading to a population in which post-supernaturalist secularism becomes the dominant posture. A sensitivity analysis reveals that whether or not this transition occurs depends most strongly on high technology (the Technology parameter, which has a host of downstream consequences, including high ease of communication and population mobility, driving both pluralism and development upwards), and a high tendency among people with supernaturalist religious worldviews to create conditions conducive to the rise of post-supernaturalist secular people and societies (the PromodernityInflOfRel, or PM, parameter; recall the examples in Table 6.1 of Latin American Pentecostalism increasing liberalization and democratization and European Protestantism increasing individuality, thereby strengthening tendencies to Modernity). These pathways to the dominance of post-supernaturalist secularism are powerful enough to contend with the large disparity in birthrates, which were held at 0.9 for post-supernaturalist secular and significantly higher for traditional supernaturalist religious people in the response surfaces of Figures 6.13a and 6.13b.

As the level curves at the top of Figure 6.13a indicate, the post-supernaturalist secular population only goes past 50 percent if traditional supernaturalist religious worldviews-lifeways exercise a significant degree of indirect influence (above about 0.5) in the direction of modern ways of life, other things being equal. Similarly, the proportion of the post-supernaturalist secular population can only rise above 50 percent when technology passes a threshold around 0.4. The same information is presented in an illuminatingly different way in Figure 6.13b. This time the vertical axis displays the absolute value of the difference between the post-supernaturalist secular proportion and the traditional supernaturalist religious proportion of the population, while the other two axes remain the same. When that absolute-value

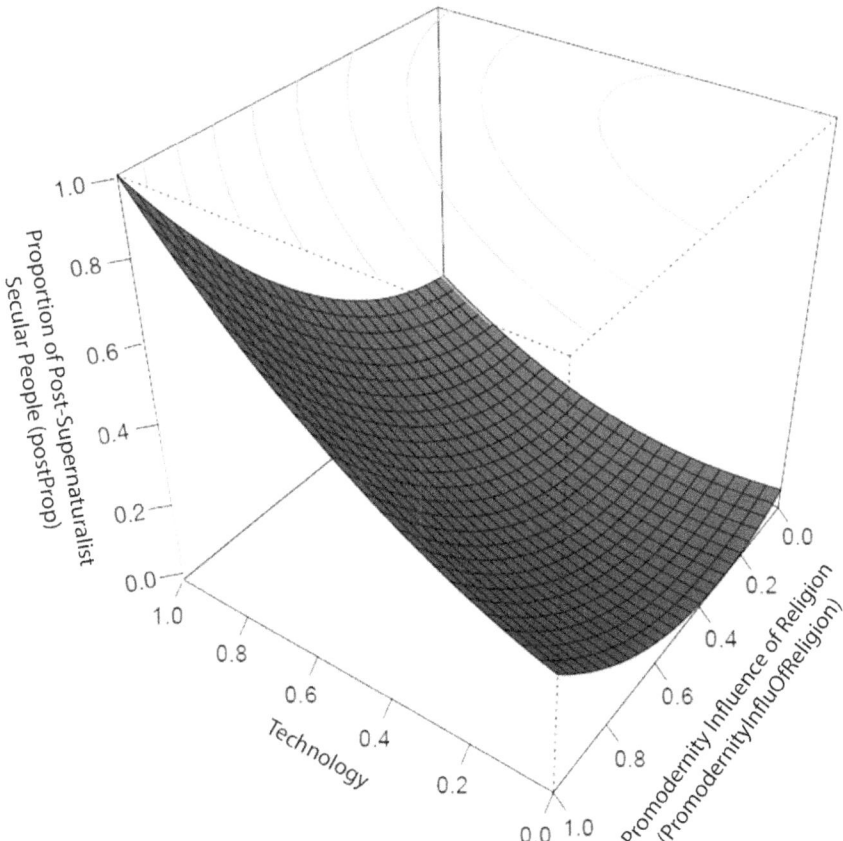

Figure 6.13a FOReST response surface for the proportion of the post-supernaturalist secular population (postProp) as a function of the level of technology (Technology) and the pro-Modernity influence of supernaturalist religious worldviews-lifeways (PM).

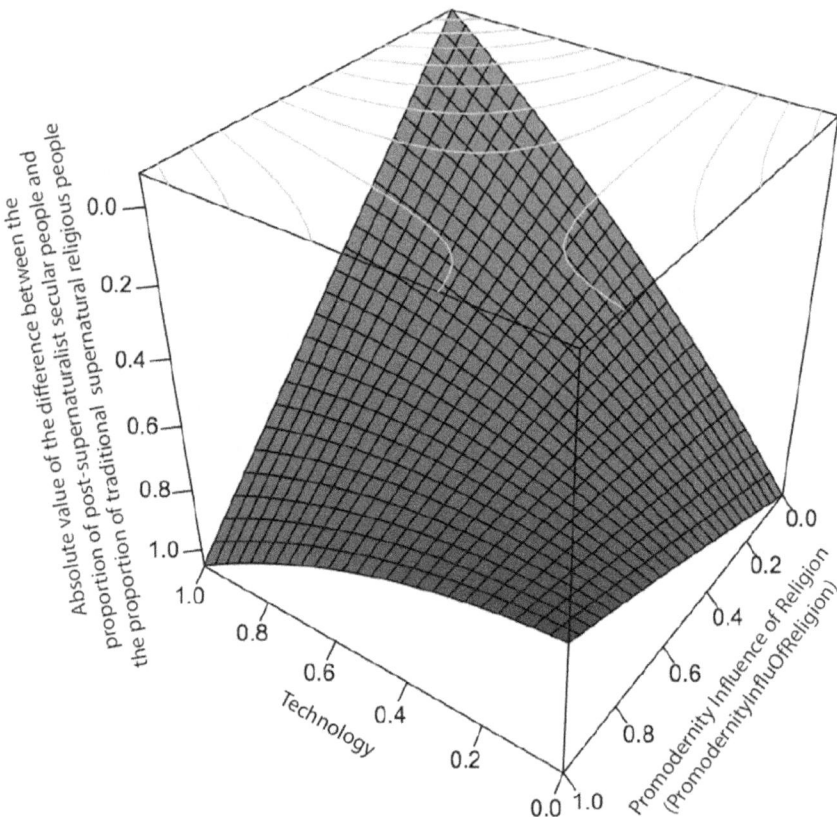

Figure 6.13b FOReST response surface for the difference between the post-supernaturalist secular population and the traditional supernaturalist religious population as a function of the level of technology (Technology) and the pro-Modernity influence of supernaturalist religious worldviews-lifeways (PM).

number is zero, the population is at a 50–50 balance. At either side of the central ridge we see the two equilibrium regimes of the FOReST system: the historically common traditional supernaturalist religious regime (on the right) and the historically rare post-supernaturalist secularist regime (on the left).

The transition from the equilibrium regime of majority supernaturalist religious to the equilibrium regime of majority post-supernaturalist secular is one of the most interesting aspects of FOReST dynamics. It is difficult to perch the system at a 50–50 split; the model gravitates toward one of the stable equilibrium regimes. To examine this highly nonlinear transition, we held all parameters constant except for technology (Technology), which we varied across its range (0 to 1). For each level of technology, we identified the equilibrium state. Figure 6.14 plots the equilibrium state for the post-supernaturalist secular (postProp) and traditional supernaturalist religious (1–postProp) populations against the technology variable.

As technology increases, driving up many of the other variables in the causal architecture, the population balance shifts, with post-supernaturalist secular people growing in number but remaining a minority in the entire population. Eventually, however, a threshold is reached (in Figure 6.14a, around Technology = 0.5) after which there is rapid transition to a new equilibrium regime with post-supernaturalist secular people in the majority. Figure 6.14b shows actual population numbers instead of percentages, allowing us to see that a dominantly post-supernaturalist secular population produces a lower overall population (due to lower secular birthrates). The transition in the other direction, from a dominantly post-supernaturalist secular population to a dominantly traditional supernaturalist religious population displays similar highly nonlinear threshold behavior.

The dynamics of real-world social change are far more complex than can be expressed in a simple simulation such as FOReST. For example, system-dynamics models often involve two equilibrium regimes with high instability between them, whereas real-world social transitions between two equilibrium states are rarely so precipitous. Nevertheless, Figures 6.14a and 6.14b offer insights into the dynamics of religious and nonreligious change.

First, the transition from a predominantly traditional supernaturalist religious to a predominantly post-supernaturalist secular population is a notably nonlinear process in the model, which matches what happens in the real world. In both cases, the change is gradual for a while but, when a threshold is passed, the entire society changes relatively quickly to one in which supernaturalist religions are the special interest of a minority and the evolved tendencies to embrace supernaturalist worldviews are more widely contested within the culture. In the model, this is expressed in the "S" shape of the transition curves of Figure 6.14a and 6.14b; the same type of transition was found in Brauer's (Brauer, 2018) study of a similar transition in the United States (not directly related to supernaturalist worldviews), and also in our own data on Norway (discussed further on).

Second, the fact that a predominantly post-supernaturalist secular population tends to be significantly smaller than a predominantly supernaturalist religious population will have important downstream implications for ecological sustainability, resource management, and economic practices.

The sensitive dependence of FOReST suggests that the conditions necessary for a majority post-supernaturalist secular population can be destabilized, after which the reverse transformation to a dominantly traditional supernaturalist

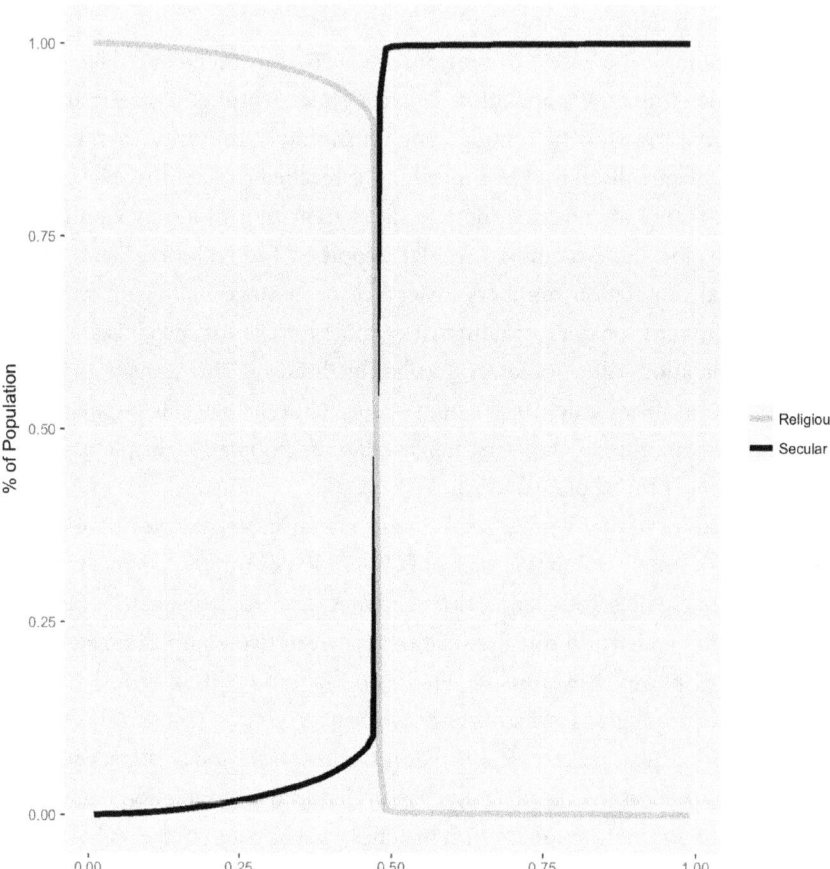

Figure 6.14a Equilibrium state for the post-supernaturalist secular (postProp, in black) and supernaturalist religious (1–postProp, in gray) population percentages plotted against the Technology parameter, showing sensitive dependence on technology at the boundary between the two equilibrium regimes.

religious population can occur. This transformation is most dramatic when the disruption significantly reduces technological capability. This possibility of two-way traffic toward and away from post-supernaturalist secular worldviews and cultures is typically not envisaged within conventional secularization theory but is a crucial aspect of FOReST. To investigate this, we sought to destabilize equilibrium states within FOReST.

The destabilization parameter simulates the kind of disaster that could interfere with the key conditions under which a population moves in large numbers toward post-supernaturalist secularism. An increase in the destabilization parameter

Figure 6.14b The same as Figure 6.14a with population numbers instead of percentages, which shows that a dominantly post-supernaturalist secular population is significantly smaller overall, with important sustainability and ecological implications.

lowers well-being, existential security, and education. The effect of these dynamics is expressed through the series of plots in Figure 6.15. Each dot represents the equilibrium state achieved in one complete run of the FOReST simulation, with the proportion of post-supernaturalist secular people (postProp) on the vertical axis, the destabilization parameter (Destablilization) on the horizontal axis, the pro-Modernity influence of supernaturalist religion (PM) determining the panels, and the shading expressing technology level (Technology).

For middling values of the pro-Modernity influence of supernaturalist religious worldviews (say, the third panel where 0.5 < PM < 0.6), destabilization

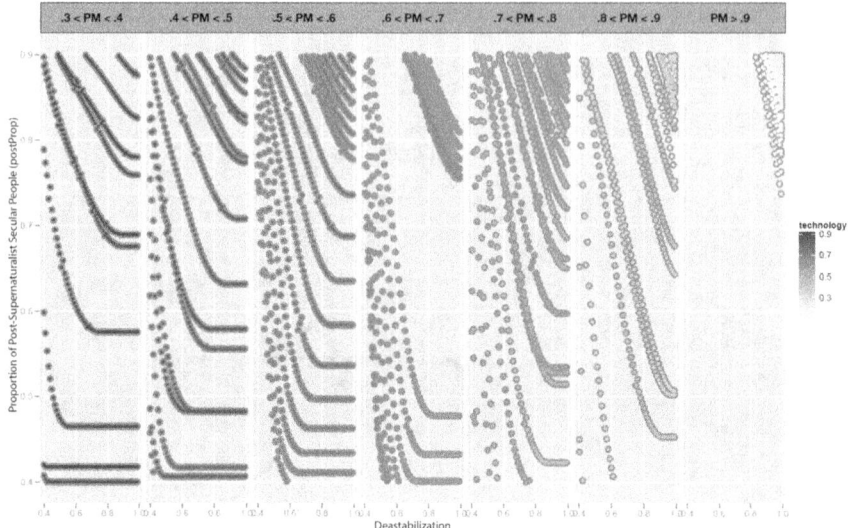

Figure 6.15 FOReST scatter plots illustrating the impact of the destabilization parameter (horizontal axis) on the proportion of post-supernaturalist secular people (vertical axis) for different levels of technology (shade intensity) and the pro-Modernity influence of supernaturalist religion (PM in the panels).

clearly drives down the post-supernaturalist secular proportion in all cases, though least when technology remains relatively high and most when the level of technology itself falls. Meanwhile, for the highest values of the pro-Modernity influence of supernaturalist religious worldviews (the seventh panel where 0.9 < PM), socioeconomic destabilization has a significant but far more limited effect, and the post-supernaturalist secular equilibrium seems more robust.

In the theoretical synthesis of Figure 6.7, four variables are shaded: freedom, existential security, education, and pluralism. Even though all variables affect all others in a looping model such as FOReST, these four are singled out for theoretical reasons. To their left are variables expressing socioeconomic conditions, and to their right are variables related to worldviews and lifeways, so these middle four are theoretically critical mediating variables in the causal architecture. Thus, it is of particular interest to understand their relationship both to the modernity variable (expressing the modern institutional form of FOReST's virtual civilizations) and the postProp variable (expressing the proportion of people with post-supernaturalist secular worldviews-lifeways). All FOReST variables are significantly correlated— so strongly that some predictors in a linear regression are redundant due to collinearity and model fit is close to perfect with $R^2 = 1$ when Modernity is the dependent variable and $R^2 = 0.982$ when postProp is the dependent variable.

Nevertheless, as with MAxiM (Chapter 5), there are other methods for examining the meaning of these four key variables for the Modernity transition.

We ran a comprehensive sweep of FOReST's parameter space, generating over 2 million artificial societies. The Modernity transition (as judged by the Modernity variable) proceeds to near completion in over 90 percent of them. Around 7 percent make it no further than 16 percent of the way to a fully modern society. The remaining 3 percent are stranded somewhere in between when the simulation terminates—had we run the simulations for longer, the Modernity variable might have crept higher or lower in those cases. A similar story applies to the proportion of people with post-supernaturalist secular worldviews-lifeways. We then divided the more than 2 million artificial societies into those that went nearly all the way to Modernity (modernity >= 0.9 and postProp >= 0.9; 1,851,828 societies) and those that did not (modernity < 0.2 and postProp < 0.2, 134,676 societies). We compared freedom, existential security, education, and pluralism in these two groups using a one-way ANOVA.

All comparisons were significant ($p < 0.001$), with the four key factors averaging roughly ten times higher in the societies that transitioned to Modernity than those that did not. Importantly, every society that made the Modernity transition was high in all four key variables, and no society transitioned that had less than high values for even one of the four key variables. This means that moderate-to-high freedom, existential security, education, and pluralism are necessary conditions for the Modernity transition to occur, but none of the four is individually sufficient. Indeed, no three of the four are sufficient for Modernity to arise within FOReST. Table 6.5 presents the details from the ANOVA (note that FOReST's values for existential security and education track one another because they both depend only on development and stability, so they are listed together in Table 6.5).

Figure 6.16 displays a scatter plot showing over 2 million artificial societies from the sweep of FOReST's parameter space, with the degree of modern institutional form (Modernity) on the horizontal axis, the proportion of post-supernaturalist secular people on the vertical axis, and 3 percent random jitter added to improve readability. Dots overlap so note that 90 percent of the societies are on the right edge of this plot, around 7 percent on the left side, and the remaining 3 percent scattered in between. The random jitter is a visualization device that helps to see the approximate positions of more of the data points, thereby increasing understanding of the data.

This portrayal of the relationship between institutional Modernity and post-supernaturalist worldview-lifeways makes several points clear. First, the presence

Table 6.5 ANOVA comparing the four key variables across two groups: Nonmodern (modernity < 0.2 and postProp < 0.2, 134,676 societies) and modern (modernity >= 0.9 and postProp >= 0.9; 1,851,828 societies)

Key Variable	Group	Descriptives				ANOVA		
		Mean	SD	Min	Max	F	p	Mean Sq
freedom	nonmodern societies	0.113	0.031	0.084	0.253	36,554,303	<0.001	78,508.860
	modern societies	0.904	0.047	0.788	0.967			
security and education	nonmodern societies	0.063	0.041	0.025	0.288	1,116,504	<0.001	37,595.800
	modern societies	0.610	0.190	0.237	0.950			
pluralism	nonmodern societies	0.110	0.050	0.067	0.352	7,366,623	<0.001	61,238.097
	modern societies	0.809	0.093	0.631	0.934			

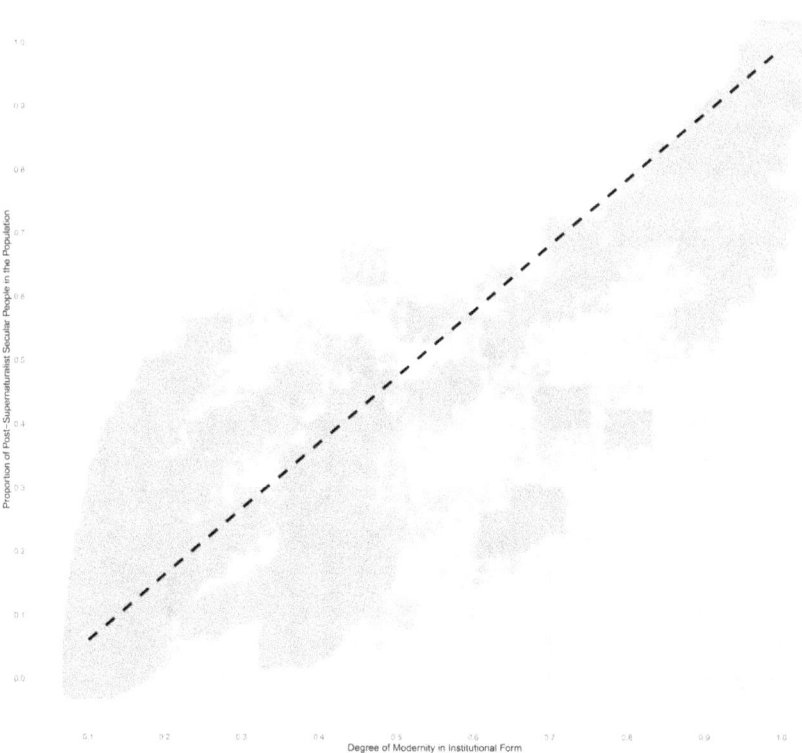

Figure 6.16 FOReST's artificial societies, with the degree of modern institutional form (Modernity) on the horizontal axis, the proportion of post-supernaturalist secular people on the vertical axis, and 3 percent random jitter added to improve readability.

in the population of post-supernaturalist secular worldviews and lifeways can push quite high, up to about 50 percent, before societies become fully Modern in form. No society gets past 50 percent of the way to becoming fully Modern unless at least 20 percent of the population embraces post-supernaturalist secular worldview-lifeways. We saw similar threshold effects in MAxiM (Chapter 5). Second, though no society achieves fully modern institutional form unless half the population has converted to post-supernaturalist secular worldviews-lifeways, there is a very strong tendency for stragglers to convert as modern institutional form takes hold (the top left of the plot in Figure 6.16 is vacant).

Figure 6.17 presents the same scatter plot with the value of the freedom variable expressed in the shading of the points (each of which corresponds to the equilibrium state of an artificial society from the sweep of FOReST's parameter space). Figure 6.18 presents the same scatter plot with the value of pluralism

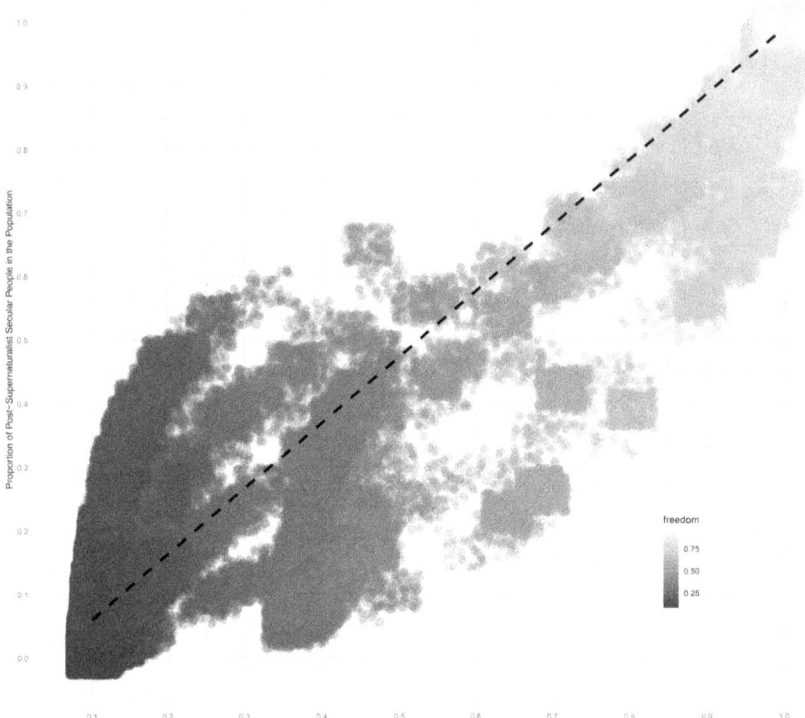

Figure 6.17 FOReST's artificial societies, with the degree of modern institutional form (Modernity) on the horizontal axis, the proportion of post-supernaturalist secular people on the vertical axis, the freedom variable determining shading, and 3 percent random jitter added to improve readability.

expressed in the shading of the points. Figure 6.19 presents the same scatter plot with the value of existential security (security) expressed in the shading of the points. Note once again that education and existential security track one another, so this plot also describes the relationship between education and Modernity within FOReST.

The dots have darker colors near the high-Modernity (top right) part of Figure 6.19 than in either Figure 6.17 (freedom) or Figure 6.18 (pluralism). To investigate this more closely, Figure 6.20 presents the same information as Figure 6.19 but faceted by degree of existential security (and education). The faceting makes clear that the Modernity transition can occur in the presence of even moderate rather than only high values of existential security and education. By comparison, it will only occur with high values of freedom and pluralism. This indicates that the Modernity transition is more sensitive to

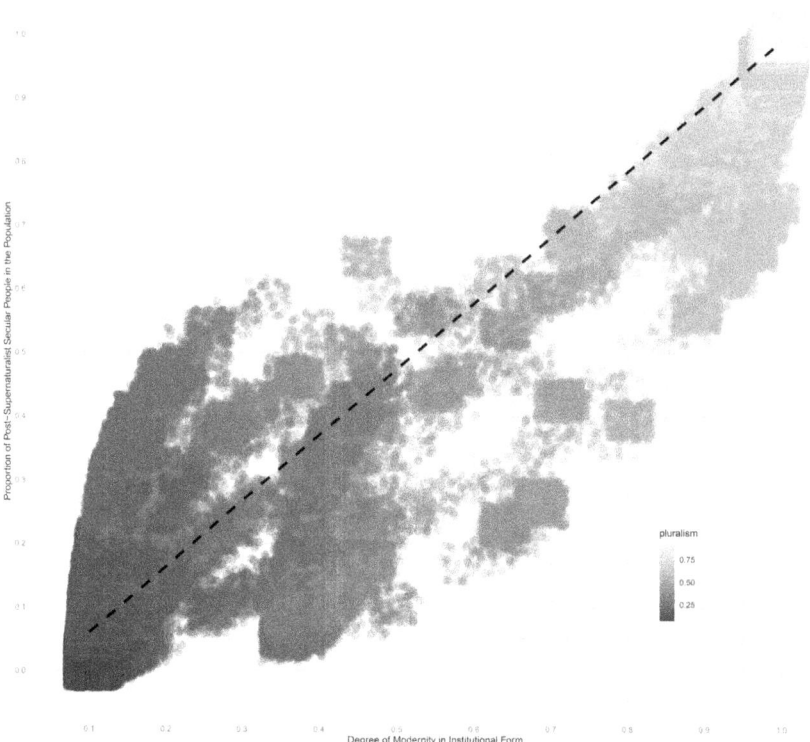

Figure 6.18 FOReST's artificial societies, with the degree of modern institutional form (Modernity) on the horizontal axis, the proportion of post-supernaturalist secular people on the vertical axis, the pluralism variable determining shading, and 3 percent random jitter added to improve readability.

freedom and pluralism than to existential security and education, though all four remain necessary-but-not-sufficient conditions. The same point is evident in the ANOVA of Table 6.5, where the mean values for existential security and education (.610) are lower than for freedom (.904) and pluralism (.809). While all four variables are necessary but not sufficient conditions for the Modern transition to occur, FOReST is less sensitive to existential security and education than to freedom and pluralism.

Significant empirical work would be required to investigate whether FOReST also describes the real world in this respect. The situation in the United States is an interesting case in point, as education (due to local control of schools) and existential security (due to a relatively weak safety net compared to other secularizing nations) are relatively lower than freedom and pluralism, and yet the United States is still moving fairly decisively toward

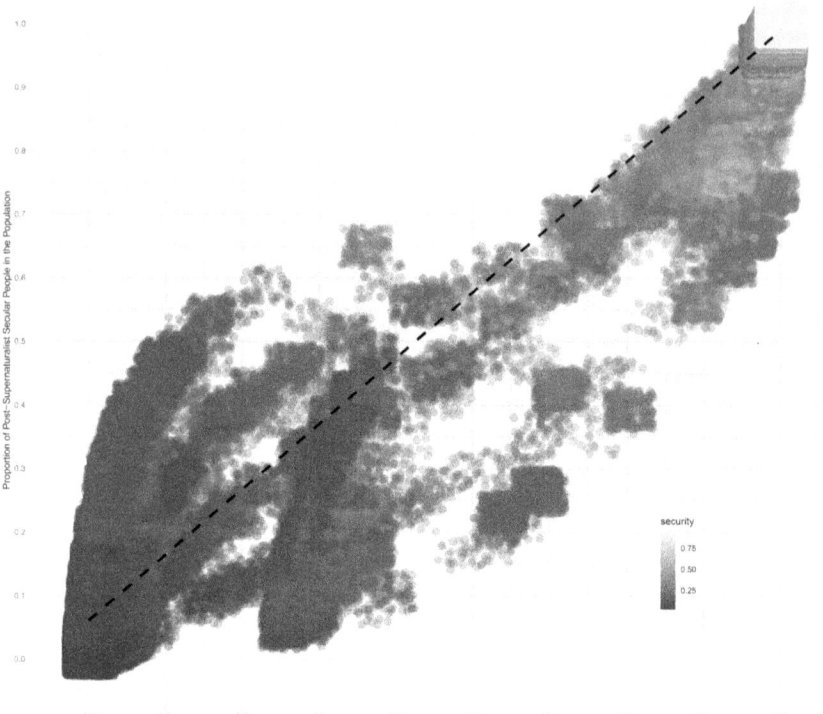

Figure 6.19 FOReST's artificial societies, with the degree of modern institutional form (Modernity) on the horizontal axis, the proportion of post-supernaturalist secular people on the vertical axis, the existential security variable (security) determining shading, and 3 percent random jitter added to improve readability.

post-supernaturalist secularism, especially in coastal regions. The movement is slower than in many other nations, probably because of the comparatively unusual arrangements for education and existential security, but it is still occurring.

Collectively, Figures 6.17–6.20 further demonstrate the key roles of freedom, existential security, education, and pluralism within FOReST's dynamics as individually necessary but not sufficient, and as jointly sufficient, for the Modernity transition to occur. They also reveal some subtle differences among the four key variables regarding the degree to which the transition is sensitive to those variables.

Finally, we simulated the process of religious change over time, to identify the effects of the key conditions first strengthening and then weakening. Figure 6.21 depicts the result, showing the number of supernaturalist religious people and

Modeling the Modernity Transition 177

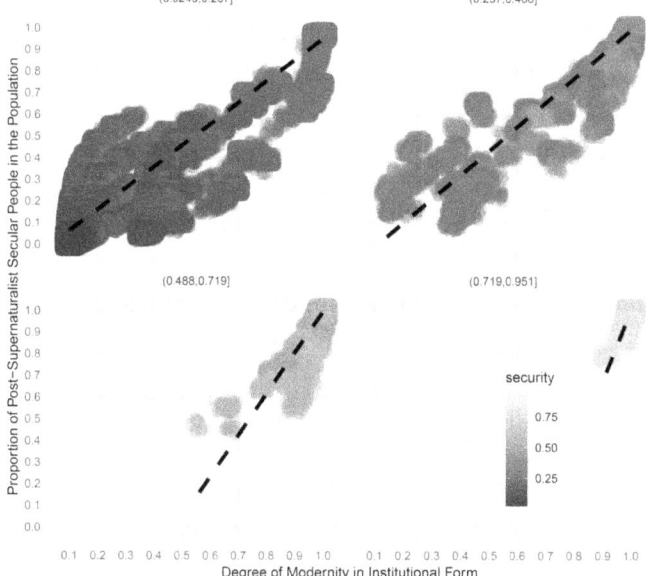

Figure 6.20 FOReST's artificial societies, with the degree of modern institutional form (Modernity) on the horizontal axis, the proportion of post-supernaturalist secular people on the vertical axis, the existential security variable (security) determining shading and faceting, and 3 percent random jitter added to improve readability.

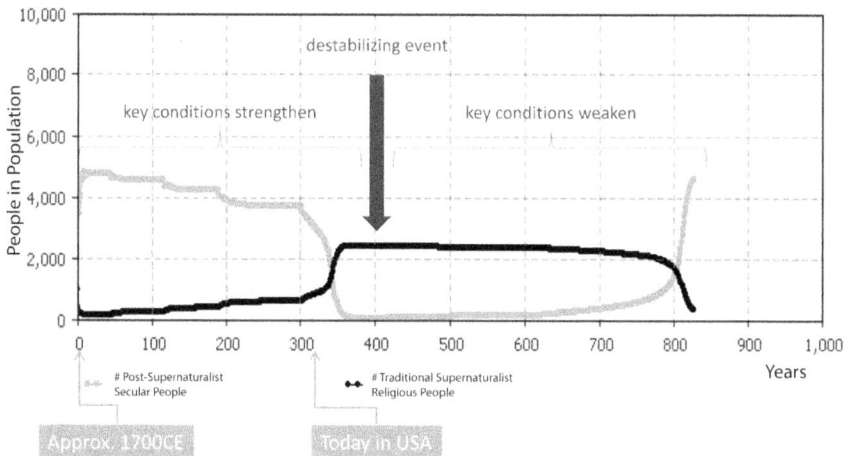

Figure 6.21 FOReST simulation results showing the effect of (1) strengthening key conditions (years 0–400) and (2) a destabilizing event that weakens key conditions (after year 400).

post-supernaturalist secular people changing with the strength of key conditions over centuries (one model cycle per year) in a Western nation that has largely navigated the transition (such as Norway) or is still in the process of navigating the transition (such as the United States). The timeline is established arbitrarily but made meaningful as a representation of change during the Modern period by periodic increases in the technology parameter (every 75 years on average) while the simulation is running. For the first 400 years, key conditions strengthen (corresponding to the increasing technology parameter), and the supernaturalist religious population declines until it drops below the post-supernaturalist secular population, following an S curve. At that point, the destabilization parameter is raised to a high level to simulate a civilization-damaging disaster, driving down the key conditions and eventually reversing the population distribution.

While this is fundamentally a theoretical research venture intended to illustrate an innovative method for synthesizing theories and exploring the dynamics of social change, we have also tried to validate the computational simulation to the extent possible. Sometimes data for validation is readily and richly available (e.g., see another of our group's models of religious change, Gore et al., 2018). In other cases we have collated it, harmonizing numerous datasets (see CMAC, 2023). In seeking to validate FOReST against real-world data, however, we have been forced to acknowledge a serious difficulty.

Data on most of the independent variables (parameters) is available for many nations since 1900 or thereabouts. The data most difficult to find is longitudinal measures of the dependent variable, which is prevalence of supernaturalist worldviews—or, failing direct measures, reasonable proxies in the form of religious service attendance or private religious practices such as personal prayer. Data sources with the required longitudinal scope, ideally running back to the beginning of the twentieth century to cover the long transition process, do not exist in convenient form for any country, including those such as Scandinavian nations that appear to have transitioned from dominantly supernaturalist religious worldviews to dominantly post-supernaturalist secular worldviews.

Data on *religious affiliation* for the past 120 years exists for several national settings, but affiliation is not what matters most in FOReST. In Norway, for example, the very large majority of people currently self-identify as Christian (Lutheran) on census forms, but the level of regular religious service attendance is extremely low. If David Voas (2009) is correct about his "fuzzy fidelity" thesis—and Brauer's (2018) analysis certainly suggests that Voas is onto something important with his claim that different aspects of religiosity change at different speeds—we would expect official religious self-identification to *mask some of the underlying dynamics of change* in religious and nonreligious worldviews and lifeways that FOReST attempts to capture.

Going beyond census religious identification, measures of personal religious faith, religious service attendance, private religious practices, and orthodoxy of religious belief do exist, fragmentarily, for some time periods within deeply secularized countries, and reasonably systematically in many countries during the past few decades. However, none of these data sources offers a close proxy for the prevalence of supernaturalism because evolutionarily stabilized tendencies in human cognition can sustain supernaturalist worldviews even when traditional religion is firmly rejected. Witness so-called New Age religion, in which so-called nonreligious people relish the exploration of supernaturalist worldviews. Hopefully data on service attendance, religious beliefs, private religious practices, and orthodoxy of religious beliefs, which has been collected for the past few decades in several national settings, will eventually accumulate to make analyzing the staggered dynamics of religious and nonreligious change possible for countries such as Norway where the post-supernaturalist secular transition is far along; for national settings such as the United States, which are not as far along in the secularization transition; and for national settings undergoing transition in the opposite direction.

Even then, however, we would still not have a direct measure of the dependent variable we most need to evaluate FOReST in detail, namely, prevalence of supernaturalist worldviews. Very few surveys have attempted to measure supernaturalism on the scale of a population, and almost none has much longitudinal depth. We are hopeful that the New Zealand Attitudes and Values Study, a longitudinal cohort study, will accumulate enough waves of the right kind of data to allow us to construct a dataset useful for validating FOReST (see New Zealand Attitudes and Values Study, 2023).

Ultimately, we decided to create a novel dataset by asking four experts in the modern history of religion in Norway to graph the prevalence of five dimensions of religiosity: personal religious faith, religious service participation, private religious practices, orthodoxy of religious beliefs, and prevalence of supernaturalist worldviews (the one of most immediate interest to us) in that country from 1900 to 2020. The data we collected, along with longitudinal census data on religious identification, is summarized in Figure 6.22.

The results suggest that (1) Norway has in fact transitioned from supernaturalism as a majority worldview to supernaturalism as a minority worldview; (2) the transition takes the form of an "S" curve, with slow decrease as supernaturalism remains dominant but decreases in prevalence, followed

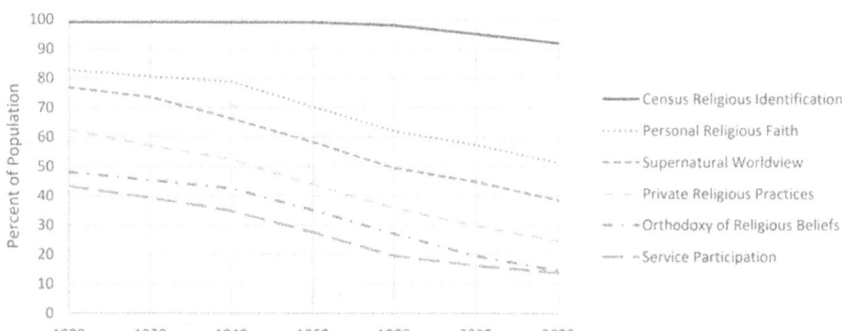

Figure 6.22 A summary of the consensus of four experts in modern religious history of Norway, estimating the change in six dimensions of religiosity over the past 120 years. Note the S curve transition with the slope steepest in decades immediately following the Second World War (ended in 1945). Also note that, for this group of experts, the average of Personal Religious Faith and Private Religious Practices serves as a reasonable proxy for the estimated level of supernaturalist worldviews.

by a period of more rapid decrease through the critical majority-minority 50 percent level, followed in turn by a period of slow decrease as supernaturalism becomes increasingly uncommon; and (3) none of the five potential proxies for supernaturalism is ideal, with census data (the easiest to obtain over a long period of time) being the worst and an average of personal religious self-identification and private religious practices being the best.

We use this expert-opinion dataset to validate *qualitatively* the transition dynamics on display in the computational simulation. In both cases, passing through the 50 percent prevalence mark, the supernaturalist worldview curve has the steepest slope, indicating a gentle S curve, so the expert consensus matches the geometry of the FOReST transition in Figures 6.14 and 6.20, as well as the findings of Brauer (2018) for the same transition in the United States.

The reason social scientists have not measured the prevalence of supernaturalist worldviews until very recently is worth noting. The importance of supernaturalist worldviews as a psychological construct only became evident with the advent of experiments in the cognitive science of religion demonstrating the presence in our species of a powerful cross-cultural tendency toward preferring supernaturalist explanations (e.g., McCauley, 2013). The maturational naturalness of the tendency to embrace supernaturalism makes it difficult for most individuals to change but it can be contested effectively, under certain circumstances (which FOReST identifies, by consolidating the six underlying theoretical pathways of religious and nonreligious change).

Figure 6.22 also presents the best simple proxy we could construct from the data we collected as an approximation to the expert estimates of the prevalence of supernaturalist worldviews, namely, the average of personal religious faith and private religious practices. The possibility that we may be able to derive a rough proxy from measures that have been collected more frequently than prevalence of supernaturalist worldviews is promising for future validation efforts of models seeking to explain the transition from traditional supernaturalist religious cultures to post-supernaturalist secular cultures. Of course, the candidate proxy itself would need to be validated in other settings and using different methodologies.

How (Non)Religion Matters in Modernity

We are still under the sway of the major civilizational shift we have been calling the Modernity transition, though some parts of the world may be in its later stages. How has religion mattered in this shift? To be more precise, how has the slow decline of religiosity in the specific sense of belief in supernatural agency mattered and how does it continue to matter in Modernity?

The results of the FOReST simulation indicate that several conditions must hold if most people in a population are to embrace a post-supernaturalist secular worldview and way of life. Though all variables interact because of feedback loops, we highlight the four most theoretically salient factors using the shaded box in Figure 6.7. The dynamics connected with these key variables are part of a complex system of interactions, but we can distinguish their effects.

- Heightened existential security, driven by effective economic and social practices, undermines the need to seek protection from supernatural agents and coalitions, decreasing the appeal of supernaturalist religious worldviews and increasing post-supernaturalist secularism.
- Heightened freedom of self-expression weakens the power of social prohibitions against acting on personal convictions, removing economic and social penalties for both supernaturalist religious and post-supernaturalist secular forms of personal self-identification.
- Heightened scientific education erodes the plausibility structures that support supernaturalist religious worldviews, while heightened humanistic education reinforces appreciation for the value of the human quest for life meaning and the feasibility of post-supernaturalist secular forms of social organization.

- Heightened pluralistic attitudes to cultural diversity diminish the plausibility of all exclusivist, supernaturally authorized coalitions. Cultural pluralism, which is perhaps the most significant factor contributing to the extraordinary period of transformation we call Modernity, has led to a global conversation about religion across cultural boundaries, rendering permeable almost all formerly internally incorrigible supernaturalist worldviews.

In the FOReST model, these conditions are strengthened when there is advanced technology, when there is high energy capture (efficient extraction of energy from the environment for healthy food, rich cultures, and high technology), and when cultural history has produced dominant religious outlooks that foster the emergence of secular forms of sociopolitical organization and high levels of scientific and humanities education. This latter point is particularly important: some supernaturalist religions help to give birth to the very conditions that undermine the supernaturalist worldviews on which traditional religious narratives depend. This point has been persuasively argued on historical grounds (Buckley, 1990) and is built into the model's Pro-Modernity Influence of Religion (PM) parameter. For example, Western religions such as Judaism and Christianity emphasize that the physical world is the creation of a rational, good deity and thus encourages its study to uncover the mind of God in the way the world works. This spurs the creation of institutions of scientific research, which yield a scientific view of the world that has no need for the hypothesis of supernatural intervention. Ultimately, there is no role for supernatural beings and the plausibility of the associated beliefs crumbles. Of course, cultural differentiation allows some people to maintain plausibility structures that resist this trend and instead support supernaturalist worldviews and beliefs in supernatural beings, of many different kinds, from gods to ghosts, and everything in between.

Someone opposed to the emergence of a social order in which most of the population holds a post-supernaturalist secular worldview could be inspired by the findings of FOReST to generate strategies of resistance, aiming to avoid or weaken such an order. Relevant resistance strategies could include ensuring that children are educated locally, under the control of school boards that can suppress an accurate understanding of cosmology or evolution; that plausibility structures remain strong within active and vibrant religious communities, so that exclusivist attitudes to religious authority can be convincingly sustained; that social media and news outlets should be so fragmented that isolated communication flows can sustain the persuasiveness of supernaturalist outlooks without having to confront types of discourse that undermine those outlooks;

and that social disincentives to leave a religious community are as large as legally possible, which is easiest to achieve outside of large cosmopolitan population centers in smaller, less cosmopolitan settings. All this is *precisely* what we see happening in the United States and the reason why that nation is more resistant to secularizing trends than many others.

A more aggressive approach is also possible, seeking to overthrow Modernity entirely, as the violent Islamic State of Iraq and the Levant (ISIL) aspires to do. Social destabilization on a scale sufficient to decrease the availability of high technology (and thereby block its downstream consequences for existential security, freedom, education, and pluralism) should be enough to reverse the trend toward post-supernaturalist secularism. By contrast, someone who favored a post-supernaturalist secular worldview would have to be on guard for precisely those kinds of destabilization maneuvers and work hard to preserve the conditions necessary for the training of each new generation of children in how to contest the maturationally natural embrace of supernaturalist religious beliefs and behaviors.

Importantly, these four key conditions also create challenges and opportunities for extant religious traditions, placing pressure on supernaturalist beliefs and practices as well as presumably opening vectors for internal institutional transformation in the direction of post-supernaturalist religious outlooks. Some religious communities may embrace the changing plausibility structures instead of resisting them, which would lead to revised conceptions of religion as post-supernaturalist. If the supply-side path has anything to commend it, and we think the empirical evidence suggests that it does, then we should expect religious communities in some contexts to adapt to changing worldviews, moving in a post-supernaturalist direction rather than standing idly by while more and more people defect. We see this especially in Unitarian Universalism in the United States, which creates effective religious homes for some post-supernaturalist people. Other post-supernaturalists maintain loyalty to dominantly supernaturalist religious communities, not making a big deal over metaphysical disagreements in exchange for benefitting from rich networks of social support. Moreover, the movement of religious naturalists—those who reject supernaturalism and religious authoritarianism and yet still detect worship-worthy spiritual depths in reality—appears to be growing among relatively highly educated people (e.g., see ReligiousNaturalism.org). Similarly, new religious groups that are secular and spiritual, and decidedly not traditionally religious, are springing up, and some of these are post-supernaturalist in orientation (Heelas & Woodhead, 2005; Langston et al., 2015).

Post-supernaturalist secular worldviews (distinguished from secular forms of social organization) have probably always existed alongside supernaturalist religious postures as a minority position within human populations. However, explicitly post-supernaturalist secular worldviews were never dominant in any civilization throughout human history until recent decades. What does the future hold, barring the kind of destabilizing ecological or technological disaster that FOReST suggests might trigger reversion to dominantly supernaturalist religious cultures? A key question here is how stable a social order could be when secular rather than religious people are in the large majority.

The FOReST model indicates that it is difficult to produce and sustain a population in which post-supernaturalist secular postures are dominant because the relevant conditions require a high level of energy input to the social system. Existential security can only remain high if energy capture is high and deprivation conditions are eliminated. Free self-expression requires technology and political practices that are robust enough to hold out against the chaos of individual opinions and the pernicious truth-denial of social media mayhem. Educational processes must train students how to overcome inborn cognitive biases toward supernaturalism. Cultural diversity, which can be confusing and draining, must be welcomed rather than avoided. All of that takes energy captured from the natural environment and spent to sustain the form of social organization and the training of human beings to embrace ways of thought and action that are in some ways contrary to what is maturationally natural for them.

Because of this need for energy input to stabilize the post-supernaturalist social equilibrium, it is reasonable to suppose that a post-supernaturalist secular social order might be more vulnerable to catastrophic collapse. If even one of these conditions (high existential security, high free self-expression, high education, high cultural pluralism) begins to disintegrate, people find it more difficult to contest the evolved proclivities that have fostered majority-supernaturalist religious social orders. Each new child is born into this world with similar cognitive-emotional mechanisms, and it is only neural plasticity and cultural entrainment that make it possible for a child to learn how to contest those tendencies, many of which all too easily lead to error (McCauley 2013). If a post-supernaturalist secular social order destabilizes to the point that existential security is threatened, for example, then the entire system can revert to the civilizational form that has characterized most of human history: the dominance of supernaturalist religious worldviews and the sequestering of non-supernaturalist outlooks to the margins of the social order. Figure 6.21 suggests that the reversion transformation might be rather dramatic, depending on other factors.

As we noted at the beginning of this chapter, post-supernaturalist secular postures (and a variety of forms of emergent social structures to support them) have expanded in several regions around the world, and especially in Scandinavian countries (Zuckerman, 2007, 2010; Zuckerman et al., 2016). On the other hand, where *any one of the four primary conditions* for the emergence of a post-supernaturalist era is weak—that is, when existential security, personal freedom, education, *or* pluralism is low—supernaturalism still dominates the religious and spiritual imaginations of the prevailing social order. We think this helps to explain why the United Sates has moved more slowly toward secularism than Northern Europe and most other North Atlantic cultures. Most importantly, even though three of the four conditions are fairly robust—freedom is strong, pluralism is fairly strong, and existential security is strong for a sizable majority—the US education system is largely regulated locally, preventing it from having the effects that high levels of scientific and humanities education have had in other, more secularized cultures. The fact that a large majority of people in the United States reject the scientific consensus of evolutionary theory (Pew Research Center, 2015) shows how effective the weakening of just one of the four necessary conditions can be in arresting the transformation toward a dominantly post-supernaturalist secular population, at least in certain regions.

With all this in mind, let us return to our heuristic matrix to explore the sense in which and the extent to which (non)religion matters (and is mattering) in Modernity (see Table 6.6).

As with in Chapters 4 and 5, let's take the matrix row by row. What do *ideological-political* theories contribute to our understanding of the dynamics that alter social systems and worldviews-lifeways such that they shift from supernaturalist to post-supernaturalist? The most obvious shift is from a population that does believe in supernatural agents to a population that no longer includes them in prevailing ontological inventories. Although belief in "God" decays faster than belief in general supernatural agents (e.g., ghosts, angels), both types of belief become less important, to the point that they no longer matter for the majority of people. Epistemologically, people are more likely to follow scientific authorities as they attempt to figure out what is true. Humans are increasingly seen as independent and capable of getting the knowledge they need without appealing to revelation or supernatural sources. The narrative that guides ethics becomes increasingly globalized, as pluralism grows in modern populations. Ethics in secular contexts cannot so easily be grounded in divine law or threats of supernatural punishment or reward and must be explained using arguments that are able to achieve a communal consensus, such as universal human rights.

Table 6.6 Modernity matrix

	Ontology	Epistemology	Ethics
Ideological-political	Gods become so cosmologically comprehensive that they lose plausibility, and humans are understood as self-determining, progressive political beings	Scientific authority becomes paramount, and humans are seen as capable of finding out what they need, healing diseases, and making sense of the world without supernatural inspiration; this also yields individualized expressions of ultimate concern	Communal consensus, global historic narrative, and shift to universal human rights
Material-social	Even more naturalism due to even more control through advanced technology, and humans are understood as consummate tool-wielders	Ever more specialized techniques are needed to learn how to manage our physical, economic, and social worlds; war is profoundly dangerous due to weapons of mass destruction	Moral responsibility and duties are conceived on global, historical scales, and compliance has multilevel requirements, from the local to the global
Cognitive-coalitional	Humans are understood as evolved social organisms equipped with cognitive tendencies and the capacity to contest them culturally	Even more self-differentiation and reflexivity as people choose how to construct life meaning; increasing dependence on science, universal literacy, information technology, printing, internet, travel, and artificial intelligence	Fractioning of doctrinal and imagistic modes of religiosity and growth of thin morality, polarized with thick morality (Haidt)

Material-social theories point our attention to the way in which ever-greater control of the environment through technology leads to an increase in naturalism, that is, in belief that whatever intelligent agencies exist and are at work in our world are biologically grounded (or perhaps grounded in AI devices). In Modernity, more specialized techniques are required for people to learn as governance and institutions are increasingly diversified and complexified. War-making capacities have grown exponentially, although on average humans are actually becoming less violent (if we accept the argument in Pinker, 2011). Ethical responsibilities are now experienced not only at local scales but also at global historical scales, as we all struggle with the moral and survival challenges related to climate change and inequalities that emerge within capitalist economic systems. In this new world, compliance is not only at the local and state levels but also at the international and global levels, for an increasing number of cosmopolitan people.

What about *cognitive-coalitional* theories? Here too the findings of FOReST foster insights into the ontological, epistemological, and ethical shifts in people's worldviews-lifeways as Modernity spreads through populations. For many secular people, the evolved tendency to appeal to supernatural agents has been comprehensively contested and is no longer relevant to them under ordinary circumstances. Humans are seen not as related to gods or spirits but as evolved social organisms. Self-differentiation and reflexivity are even further increased as more people have the time and space to choose and explore their own worldviews and lifeways. The rapid growth of information technology, from the printing press to the internet to artificial intelligence, accelerated the system dynamics that propel this transformation of civilizational form. Religions that used doctrinal forms of ritual as a means of social regulation tend to lose their dominance and imagistic styles of religiosity and ritual tend to become more prominent. Thus, doctrinal and imagistic modes of religiosity are fractionated in new ways, mixed together and overflowing one another as people become more individualist but also long for community and belonging. We also find the emergence and growth of "thinner" morality in Jonathan Haidt's sense (2012) —that is, a moral outlook that emphasizes "individualizing" over "binding" moral foundations, stressing mutual care and fairness (which work best in pluralistic cosmopolitan settings), while deemphasizing concerns for in-group loyalty, hierarchy, and purity (which require smaller scale cultural settings where in-groups are large enough to be dominant). This can drive polarization in modern societies between those with thin morality (individualizing moral foundations only) and those with thick morality (both individualizing and binding moral foundations), with dramatic expressions in politics and religion.

The FOReST model expresses the meaning of a synthesis of empirically and conceptually robust (yet partial) theories of social change relevant to the future of religion and helps to explain a great deal of what we already know from both the social and the cognitive wings of the scientific study of religion. It is important to keep in mind that the results of simulation experiments using FOReST are limited by our focus on supernaturalist and post-supernaturalist worldviews-lifeways because this is the polarity implemented in the conversion model. Even more importantly, FOReST's depiction of the dynamics of religious change is only as good as the theoretical synthesis defining its Causal Nexus. By utilizing this simulation methodology, which has forced us to provide clear definitions of concepts and relationships, we have tried to make it easier for others to contest our hypotheses and propose even better models.

The point of FOReST and of this chapter is to demonstrate the possibility and usefulness of a synthesis of social science theories of supernaturalist religious and post-supernaturalist secular transitions and to identify the key factors that determine how these transitions unfold. We have *not attempted to argue about the relative value* of the supernaturalist religious posture that has long dominated human life in comparison to the post-supernaturalist secular posture that is expanding in some parts of the world in recent decades. Rather, we have tried to show that the theoretical integration and causal architecture of the FOReST model does a serviceable job of explaining the *two-way transition dynamics* between populations that are primarily supernaturalist and those that are primarily post-supernaturalist. FOReST helps to explain why secular cultures dominated by individuals with non-supernaturalist worldview-lifeways have been so rare in the history of human civilizations, and it illuminates the pathways by which cultures move in that direction, and potentially also back again.

7

Insights and Prospects

This closing chapter first identifies key insights generated by the computational modeling of civilizational change presented in this book. It then considers the complexity and experiential intensity of transition dynamics, particularly during Modernity. Subsequently, we turn to analyzing what is likely to happen to religion and spirituality in the near-to-medium-term future, and we conclude with reflections on likely futures for the human project as a whole. These last two sections extrapolate into the future a short way based on insights gleaned from FOReST. Our extrapolations are consistent with the constraints established in the Modernity model but go into more detail than the model itself does. This extrapolation is warranted, we believe, as contemporary readers have an intense interest in both the future of religion and spirituality, and the future of the human project.

General Insights

Right at the outset, we want to state three critically important findings.

First, *there is no single silver-bullet factor that triggers the civilizational transformations* we have discussed. This implies that we are resisting a number of prominent theories of civilizational change that emphasize single-factor explanations. Because human societies are complex, adaptive, and highly nonlinear systems, we need to account for multiple triggers, of different types, as well as their interrelatedness. From our simulated reconstructions, we typically see a slow rise of new ways of thinking that passes a threshold, triggering rapid change in social and political organization, and then dragging more cautious, slow-adopting minds along for the ride. These dynamics of interaction between individuals and social settings are the fundamental reason *why* there are multiple necessary-but-not-sufficient conditions for large-scale transformations of civilizational form.

Second, *the mind-culture nexus is a vital conceptual framework for interpreting civilizational change.* As biological organisms, human beings have a suite of cognitive capabilities, with a virtually universal profile of strengths and weaknesses, stabilized across cultures due to evolutionary pressures, with variations due mainly to individual differences. At the same time, human beings live in wildly diverse cultures that realize the potential of their evolutionarily stabilized brains in stunningly different ways. This depends on learning, which takes advantage of neuroplasticity, and it requires imaginative creativity, which gives birth to socially constructed worlds that we come to take for granted within home cultures. There is no credible way to separate minds and cultures, or to reduce one to the other. In any interesting explanation of complex human behavior—and certainly of civilizational transformations—the mind-culture nexus functions as a necessary interpretative framework. This implies bidirectional nonreductionism.

Third, *making clear the internal complexity of the mind-culture nexus, and describing mind-culture interactions rigorously, requires computational modeling and simulation as a central methodology.* Computational simulation helps specify and integrate causal theories, and is an unprecedented tool for exploring alternative outcomes in artificial societies. Engineers routinely use this tool in nonhuman applications, such as building machines or designing factory assembly lines. But it can also be used to understand human beings through artificial societies, constructed as agent-based models or as system-dynamics models (we use the latter in this book). With suitable data for validation, such models can become platforms for ethical experimentation, leading both to deeper understanding and to evidence-based policy evaluation. Perhaps most importantly, this method supports causal inference in a powerful way because it employs a virtual causal system to model a real-world causal system.

We have hinted at these key findings throughout but we now state them clearly and confidently. All three have in common an emphasis on *complexity*. The mind-culture nexus is a formally complex arrangement of minds in cultures with all manner of feedback loops that amplify and dampen trajectories of change. Sometimes we can extract generalized insights at the level of a single academic discipline such as psychology or sociology or economics. But the intrinsic complexity of the mind-culture nexus resists explanation through the lens of any single scholarly discipline and calls instead for a more integrated, radically multidisciplinary approach, supported by methods tailored to handle complex dynamical systems.

Moving from overarching conclusions to specific findings, what have we learned materially from the computer models and simulation experiments discussed in Chapters 4 to 6? Fundamentally, *religion does matter*. It is not the only factor that matters, but it plays a key causal role (along with many other factors) in transformations of civilizational form. The reason *why* religion matters is its deep rooting in human cognition and sociality. Precisely *how* religion matters depends on the transformation in question.

Simulation experiments on NSIM suggest that religion helped people narrate their identity as farmers mastering their environment through domesticating plants and animals; living together in complex townships; committing to a worldview-lifeway that critically involved intense entanglement of human lives with all manner of objects, plants, animals, and resources in their environment; and activating previously unsuspected possibilities for personal and social meaning. Over nearly two millennia, these early human agriculturalists gradually drew in hunter-gatherers, enticing them with greater energy capture, predictability, safety, food security, cooperative efficiency, and cultural variety. Hunter-gatherers must have regarded the decision to move into a farming township as a close call, given how long the conversion process took, but committing to farming and township lifestyles, in all the places that it occurred, proved to be a fateful decision, setting most of our species on the path toward large-scale civilizations. In the Çatalhöyük context, the new lifestyle was facilitated by religious worldviews-lifeways that revered ancestors and drew inspiration from the wild animals of their natural environment to narrate a new identity and enshrine a new kind of moral obligation—to a collective far larger than groups of extended kin. From then until now, there have always been holdouts, people for whom intense entanglement of this kind seemed like a bad idea compared to a simpler and more vulnerable lifestyle lived close to the unpredictably fluxing circumstances of the natural environment. Over time, however, such holdouts became rare, and the associated worldviews-lifeways have almost completely died out—arguably a tragic inevitability.

Simulation experiments on MAxiM shed light on the failure of the great social experiment in which the rulers of giant militaristic civilizations exercised their allegedly supernaturally authorized right to do whatever they wanted. It took a few millennia, but eventually human beings found a way to contest the absolute power of rulers, balancing it with priestly and scholarly elites who controlled the narrative resources needed to rationalize and legitimate whatever power monarchs possessed. A change in the prevailing social contract of such magnitude could not happen merely because a few bright sparks set up an elite cabal of scholar-priests and started arguing with all-powerful rulers. It was only possible in the presence of other factors such as increased energy capture, as well as a worldview that persuasively framed the meaning of human life in a universal cosmic context. These new Axial religious worldviews were bursting with grand narratives of supernatural powers determining right and wrong, and stipulating the moral obligations of everyone—including formerly all-powerful monarchs. A significant minority of people, probably especially social elites, needed to buy into this new worldview before a critical threshold was passed, triggering a corresponding transformation in institutions and practices, and the subsequent conversion of most people into Axial worldviews-lifeways. Religious rationalizations for the prevailing sociopolitical order were less arbitrary and thus more convincing in the Axial framework, but they also presupposed cosmic-scale supernaturalist beliefs that ultimately contradicted one another. Eventually, this narrative incoherence among Axial religious worldviews-lifeways would prove to be a potent force for transformation that, along with monumental shifts in energy capture and technology, would give birth to the modern world.

Simulation experiments on FOReST indicate that Modernity, which has multiple different forms depending on cultural setting, also has core dynamics that recur everywhere the modern transition occurs. Compared to all prior eras, Modernity involves staggering levels of energy capture, technological changes that continue to revolutionize communication and travel, inventions such as the internet and artificial intelligence that upend economies, sky-rocketing levels of literacy and education, astonishing diversity of cultural expressions, and political conceptions of nation-states boasting relatively strong autonomy and at times somewhat well-functioning democracies. But Modernity also involves a confrontation among the prevailing Axial religions due to their inconsistent universalizing claims about ultimate reality. In the presence of high existential security, people needed less of the previously essential supernaturally narrated social glue, with its complex comforts and duties. Widespread education decreased the plausibility of explanations for the natural world that depended on supernatural agents. Cultural and religious pluralism made religious stories seem less like supernaturally authorized revelations and increasingly like obviously speculative folk tales. And increasing freedom from religiously rationalized social control allowed people to believe and say whatever they felt was true, and increasingly to live however they wanted so long as they did not bother others too much. The result was the dawning realization among rapidly widening circles of people that human beings do not need supernaturalist beliefs and practices to thrive, and in fact that we might all be better off if we were to relegate supernaturalist Axial worldview-lifeways to the trash basket of history, where superstition and pseudo-science should already be. As in the prior transitions, early adopters triggered a change in the form of institutions and social practices, driving toward secular civilizations that seem destined, over time, to drag almost everyone into a post-supernaturalist era of human self-determination and new moral obligations inspired by universal human rights and global awareness of the ecological conditions for sustaining the human project.

Religion, we insist, *matters*.

Transition Dynamics

The simulations presented in Chapters 4, 5, and 6 each focus on the before-and-after story of an epochal transformation in the form of civilization. There is a pre-transformation worldview-lifeway, a post-transformation worldview-lifeway, and a complex process of conversion between the two driven by a nexus of causes reflecting multiple kinds of interacting forces: ideological-political, material-social, and cognitive-coalitional. Religion plays a role in the Causal Nexus of civilizational change, though a different role in the three cases.

Each model also shed some light on transition dynamics—the process of change itself. Reading between lines of code, the simulations help us picture something of what it must have felt like for human beings to be caught in the nexus of change.

NSIM (Chapter 4) portrays a decision that hunter-gatherers faced between the relative freedom and perpetual vulnerability of life on the move in small kin-based groups and the relatively more constrained and secure lifestyle of a farming township. Once involved in the town, they needed to navigate a new form of life held together by an unfamiliar kind of religious social glue keyed into an intense form of entanglement with objects, plants, animals, and resources that the new worldview-lifeway rationalized and reinforced through complex relationships with ancestors and animal spirits.

MAxiM (Chapter 5) depicts the slow growth of a new way of thinking and acting that eventually triggered a cascade of institutional changes. The shift reflected a growing intolerance of the unchecked power of rulers and the dawning belief that there must be a better way, that wisdom teachers and religious leaders were at least as reliable as power-hungry monarchs and their groupies, and that an authority-sharing arrangement that distributed power more broadly would be safer and more productive. The Axial religions helped realize this new vision of civilizational order, offering universal, cosmic-scale narratives to both glue people together in a new way and to infuse life with a potent kind of meaning.

FOReST (Chapter 6) tells the story of the slow disintegration of the Axial equilibrium, with a secular form of social glue steadily rendering unnecessary the supernatural religious glue that had prevailed for millennia. The consolidation of nation states, the discovery of new ways to capture massive amounts of energy from the environment, the emergence of universal humanistic ethics, and a rapid pace of technological change are jointly causing dramatic institutional transformations to go along with the shift in the ways that people make meaning and bind themselves to one another, with and without religion—and all this is complicated by sometimes aggressive forms of resistance.

Modernity is especially fascinating because we are in the middle of this transition, with some regions of the planet more deeply affected by it than others, heading toward a form of civilization as yet unknown. Moreover, we are painfully aware that the entire human project is now vulnerable to catastrophic collapse, and that this, too, is the work of Modernity. The intensity of the transition is obvious when we are living through it, not least because we can't be confident about where we are headed, which increases anxiety. We can safely assume that the intensity of change was also evident to our forebears in the Neolithic and Axial transitions, and that they were similarly baffled about where they were headed, with attendant anxieties. But the pace of change makes the modern transition unprecedentedly intense, and the rise of a largely nonreligious, technocratic civilizational order makes Modernity even more fascinating and unpredictable.

We know much more about what it is like to live through the Modern transition than the Neolithic or Axial transitions, superb historical reconstructions of the deep past notwithstanding. Countless psychologists, sociologists, and anthropologists have been documenting every aspect of the modern human experience. Polls and surveys are ubiquitous, to the point that we might be forgiven for feeling we are trying to conduct our daily affairs with a psycho-socio-metric thermometer poking out of our heads. The downside of this intense self-awareness is an obscene degree of self-absorption, to the point of taking our passing intensities and anxieties with more seriousness than they deserve, and far more than prudence and virtue would suggest is wise. The upside, meanwhile, is that scholars know a lot about *what it is like to be modern humans*.

We know about the excitement of new technologies, the luxuries made possible by unprecedented levels of energy capture and engineering skill, the joys of learning and traveling, and the life-extending wonders of modern medicine. We are also intimately familiar with the despair of blue-screen loneliness, the horrors of preventable socioeconomic injustice, the desperate ignorance of xenophobia directed toward migrants forced to uproot their lives and undertake perilous journeys to survive, the catastrophic destruction of small-scale cultures, and the fearsome perils of weapons of mass destruction and climate change.

The intensely ambiguous texture of our self-awareness during the modern transition is a reminder of how intense life must have felt during past eras of civilizational change. It also prompts us not to idealize Modernity, which imperils and destroys even as it liberates and transforms.

We are particularly fascinated with what Modernity does to the experience of being religious or nonreligious. We know that Modernity tends to dissolve the plausibility structures on which the Axial religions depend, as well as supernaturalism in other forms, but what does it feel like to lose one's religion, and what kind of spirituality survives, or rises, to take the place of religion?

FOReST (Chapter 6) shows that the secularization process depends on high existential security, education, freedom, and pluralism, which implies that secular worldviews-lifeways are far from being a foregone conclusion and once in place can always revert. Nevertheless, given that people tend to appreciate cultures with high levels of existential security, education, freedom, and pluralism, it seems likely that secularization of individual worldviews-lifeways and of institutional forms will continue and spread, barring a civilization-destabilizing disruption. Therefore, something like what has happened in the more secularized societies of our planet will probably happen in the less secularized societies in due course. How is that transition experienced by religious and nonreligious people?

Sociologist David Voas (2009) set forth the "fuzzy fidelity" hypothesis to describe transition dynamics of modern religion in secularizing settings. This theory has proved to be robust in relation to data from diverse societies and it is valuable in this context because it conveys something of what it feels like to live through the modern transition as a religious person. According to this view, few people abandon religion comprehensively or precipitously. Rather, modern religiosity changes slowly, drawing people from unshakeable confidence in an enchanted religious worldview-lifeway into the zone of fuzzy fidelity, where they believe, participate, and practice religion to some extent without taking it too seriously. Most see value in religion—at least their religion—so they don't completely abandon it. But they are also not drawn to the intense forms of commitment and involvement that they may once have known, or that their parents or grandparents knew. At some point, people in the fuzzy-fidelity zone may give up on religion entirely, but it is often their children who take that step, as the transition of religiosity across generations fails to replicate previous degrees of religiosity. The fuzzy-fidelity reality applies to religious identification, public service participation, private religiosity, supernaturalist beliefs, and the subjective importance of religion, and most of the change in all these dimensions occurs in religious transmission across generations rather than within the lifetime of individuals or at critical cultural moments that impact entire populations.

It is difficult for even the most religious moderns to appreciate how intensely religiosity suffused life for most premodern people. Religious enchantment is profoundly disrupted by modern technologized lifestyles. Instead of earnestly praying for relief from pain, we pop a pill. Instead of trusting in divine protection for embarking on a potentially dangerous journey, we board a jet and barely think about risk. Instead of painstakingly performing research in purportedly divinely inspired sacred texts, we access more information than we can absorb at the click of a button from large language AI models trained on the entire internet. As more and more of blessed enchantment yields to scientific explanation and socio-technological control, the space for depending on providential protection and inspiration from supernatural agents narrows, and religion becomes compartmentalized. From there, it is a small step to discover that life can make sense without the religious compartment, or at least without taking that compartment so seriously.

The cracking of Axial religious edifices is accelerated by pluralism, which creates a situation in which credible witnesses to the deepest mysteries of reality flat-out disagree with one another. Marginalized mystics may be able to see through the cacophony of mutual disparagement to something resembling harmony across Axial religions, but many people—including many religious people—respond to the conflicting cosmic visions by not taking any of them so seriously, or by rejecting the lot of them as inspirational stories that need to be demythologized to learn anything reliable about reality. The supernatural pillars of the Axial worldviews tremble as education reveals a more evidence-based way of thinking about how the world works, and the very real human need for authority is handled without reference to supernatural forces or deities. Morality makes sense in a humanistic framework that emphasizes compassion, social justice, and individual rights, while purportedly supernaturally derived moral compasses are increasingly distrusted because of the evident lack of ordinary compassion displayed by religious groups, particularly for people marginalized relative to prevailing religious norms.

Much is lost in modern religious change, and many people grieve the losses: the intimacy of personal connection to an all-powerful and all-loving deity or supernatural force, the moral orientation afforded by aligning one's intentions and actions with supernaturally revealed information about the highest good, confidence about one's place in a cosmos that comes to feel like home instead of an implacable threat, and impressive forms of social support through religious communities that exhibit genuine care for people in the fold. These losses are painful. Yet much is gained, too, including no longer needing to hold beliefs that strain credulity, to submit to arbitrary religious authorities, or to accept the rules that cruelly exclude some in the name of religious purity.

One of the keys to the ascendancy of Axial religions was the nearly comprehensive suppression of small-scale religions, folk religions, and eclectic forms of spirituality. Correspondingly, as Axial religions lose their steely grip on the imaginations of modern people, those formerly widespread expressions of religion have begun to flourish again. Now that people are free to believe and behave according to their own lights—giving expression to what sociologist Peter Berger called the "heretical imperative" (Berger, 1979)—religious traditions driven underground by the Axial juggernaut (Druids, Wiccans, Shamans, etc.) are mounting comebacks in secular contexts, and New-Age eclecticism is running riot in many parts of modern societies. In these cases, supernaturalism still thrives, but the Axial muting of potentially chaotic ritual intensities and imposing of doctrinal orthodoxies is winding down, and in some places has already ended. Many people now just do what feels right.

Post-religious or anti-religious people often pursue spiritual quests of varied kinds. Researchers have begun to explore the territory of nonreligion, charting its spiritual inhabitants. For example, Linda Mercadante (2014) identifies five types of spiritual people outside the domain of the self-identified religious: Dissenters, Casuals, Explorers, Seekers, and Immigrants. Each has a helpful in-depth description based on qualitative research, and this helps us picture what it is like to be modern when the loss of religion does not also eliminate all interest in spiritual matters. Among other things, people prize authenticity in belief and action, while reporting loneliness due to the difficulty of sustaining long-lasting spiritual collectives outside of organized religion.

Spirituality is a word we need in a religiously transitioning world because it says a lot about how people, including nonreligious people, experience

Modernity. Admittedly, the word seems to be used in such a flurry of discordant ways that it seems useless for research purposes. However, sociologist Nancy Ammerman's qualitative research has demonstrated that the initial impression of chaotic and contradictory usage, while understandable, is misleading. In fact, spirituality takes shape in a variety of intelligible "cultural packages" based on qualitative analysis of interviews. To formalize that idea, Wesley led a team to create the Dimensions of Spirituality Inventory (DSI). The measurement strategy of the DSI was to avoid defining spirituality in advance, which is inevitably controversial, and instead to define numerous relatively uncontroversial dimensions of spirituality, measuring each one to create quantitative expressions of Ammerman's cultural packages. The twenty-one dimensions in the DSI derive from intensive engagement with religion scholars and the texts of the world's religions, both Axial and non-Axial, as well as nonreligious worldviews-lifeways. The result is something like a twenty-one-letter alphabet for spelling out cultural packages of spirituality. The DSI helps us listen to modern people as they talk about what religion and spirituality and value mean to them.

Using the DSI to deepen our understanding of modern spirituality, we ran a survey of people (N = 820) from mostly Western, educated, industrialized, rich, and democratic societies (WEIRD societies; see Henrich et al., 2010), and thus societies where secularization is strongest and the Modernity transition in full swing. Factor analysis revealed four main cultural packages of spirituality (see Wildman et al., 2023 for details). Names for the cultural packages are derived from loadings of the twenty-one dimensions on the four factors (Table 7.1).

Figure 7.1 presents word clouds for the four dominant cultural packages, with the size and recurrence of words representing the relative importance of the corresponding DSI dimension on each cultural package.

Factors 1 and 3 are Axial, theistic spiritualities, in that both are significantly positively correlated with DSI sub-dimensions Divine Beings (.537 and .574, respectively) and Spiritual Beings (.344 and .309, respectively), meaning that relating to the divine is central and belief in supernatural powers and spirits is common to both.

Despite these important similarities, there are also four major contrasts between these two theistic spiritualities. First and foremost, Factor 1 spirituality is predominantly concerned with becoming a more ethical and axiologically sensitive person in a way that Factor 3 spirituality is not. Whereas Factor 1 is very strongly positively correlated with the Self-Transformation (.779), Ethical Growth (.766), and Axiological Sensitivity (.693) sub-dimensions, Factor 3 is negligibly correlated with the same subdimensions (.102, .102, and .066,

Table 7.1 Rotated component matrix, disclosing four latent factors. the factor names are derived from the analysis of loadings. loadings at or above 0.40 are shaded in gray, or in light gray in the case of a secondary loading

Subdimension	Factor 1 Transformational Theistic Spirituality	Factor 2 Axiological Extra-Theistic Spirituality	Factor 3 Ritualistic Theistic Spirituality	Factor 4 Supernaturalistic Extra-Theistic Spirituality
Self Transformation	0.78	0.19	0.10	0.13
Ethical Growth	0.77	0.16	0.10	0.19
Meaning	0.77	0.14	0.29	0.09
Belief	0.77	0.01	0.29	0.14
Sensitivity	0.69	0.32	0.07	0.17
Practices	0.66	0.19	0.19	0.10
Nonattachment	0.60	0.42	−0.05	0.10
Connection	0.56	0.11	0.46	−0.22
Beauty	0.15	0.68	0.06	−0.04
Awe	0.12	0.66	0.08	0.14
Truth Seeking	0.24	0.66	−0.05	−0.27
Oneness-Unity	0.13	0.65	0.11	0.37
Kinesthetic	0.04	0.48	−0.01	0.40
Oneness-Transcendence	0.25	0.45	0.36	0.15
Ritual	0.17	0.16	0.74	−0.05
Tradition	0.45	0.01	0.63	−0.07
Divine Beings	0.54	−0.12	0.57	0.00
Self Discovery	0.07	0.33	−0.17	0.65
Spiritual Beings	0.34	−0.20	0.31	0.58
Dead Active	−0.06	0.12	0.53	0.55
Mystery	0.23	0.02	−0.11	0.51

respectively). Though both are strongly correlated with Connection (.555 and .461), a second difference is that Factor 1 is much more strongly correlated than Factor 3 to other sub-dimensions relating to what Ammerman labels "Belief and Belonging" spirituality: Meaning (.775 and .285), Belief (.767 and .286), and Practices (.659 and .193). Third, despite being less invested in "Belief and Belonging" spirituality, Factor 3 spirituality is more inclined to see spirituality as inextricably intertwined with a Religious Tradition (.628 and .445), much more likely to regard traditional rituals as enhancing rather than hindering

Figure 7.1 Word clouds for the four latent factors. Top row, left to right: Factor 1, Transformational Theistic Spirituality; Factor 2, Axiological Extra-Theistic Spirituality; bottom row, left to right: Factor 3, Ritualistic Theistic Spirituality; Factor 4, Supernaturalistic Extra-Theistic Spirituality.

(Ritual: .741 and .170), and far more likely to affirm that deceased people directly influence the living (Dead Active: .527 and −.056). Finally, Factor 3 is slightly negatively correlated with several sub-dimensions with which Factor 1 is significantly positively correlated: Nonattachment (−.047 and .604), Mystery (−.109 and .231), and Truth Seeking (−.052 and .237). This implies that, relative to Factor 1 spirituality, Factor 3 spirituality is less inclined to identify the acceptance of unavoidable change as important to spirituality, to admit that reality is fundamentally mysterious, or to identify the quest for intellectual understanding as central to spirituality.

In sum, the theistic spirituality reflected in Factor 1 emphasizes personal flourishing and communal belonging—becoming a better person, finding meaning through one's religious beliefs, and anchoring oneself in community through established religious traditions and practices. It is a practical, results-oriented spirituality that embraces the inevitability of change and the need to remain flexible, even while being solidly conservative, working to perpetuate established religious beliefs and practices. It might be thought of as "personal flourishing through communal belonging theistic spirituality." We label it "Transformational Theistic Spirituality."

The theistic spirituality reflected in Factor 3 is similarly conservative, concerned to secure communal belonging, and guided by established traditions and beliefs. However, it is not particularly concerned with personal axiological growth, and it is less open to viewing reality as fundamentally mysterious and less inclined to associate spirituality with open-ended quests for intellectual understanding. Factor 3 spirituality also depends more heavily upon established religious rituals and traditions to steady the spiritual journey, and it tends to regard both relations with the divine and relations with deceased persons as spiritually and practically important. This theistic spirituality is firmly oriented toward the local, heavily reliant upon tried-and-true rituals and traditions, and rather suspicious of mystery generally and of heroic personal quests, whether intellectual or ethical in nature. Factor 3 spirituality might be thought of as "security through ritual, stability through tradition theistic spirituality." We label it "Ritualistic Theistic Spirituality."

Factors 2 and 4 are two variants of extra-theistic spirituality. While they differ dramatically in terms of their positive emphases, what is most striking about these extra-theistic spiritualities is what does not matter to them: Factors 2 and 4 are both negatively correlated with the Divine Beings sub-dimension (−.125 and −.004, respectively) and weakly or negatively correlated with the Ritual (.155 and −.046), Belief (.014 and .136), Religious Tradition (.010 and −.067), Meaning (.139 and .094), and Connection (.114 and −.219) sub-dimensions. Here we see the clear rejection of "Belief and Belonging" spirituality, a rejection that Ammerman identifies as characteristic of spiritual-but-not-religious people. Though positive, these factors' weak correlation with Ethical Growth (.162 and .195) and Self-Transformation (.189 and .127) suggests that these spiritualities developing outside established religious traditions, while helpful in the struggle to become a better person, lack the axiologically transformative power of Factor 1 spirituality. Interestingly, unlike the theistic spiritualities expressed in Factor 1 and Factor 3, both of these extra-theistic spiritualities are strongly positively correlated with the Kinesthetic (.477 and .403) sub-dimension, which connects spirituality with the attempt to cultivate focused awareness of one's physical body.

Despite these notable similarities, Factors 2 and 4 also differ profoundly. Perhaps most striking, Factor 2 spirituality adds to its rejection of orientation toward divine beings a deep skepticism regarding Spiritual Beings (−.202) more generally, while Factor 4 spirituality is strongly positively correlated (.580) with belief in invisible powers and good and evil spirits. Similarly, Factor 2 spirituality is lukewarm at best regarding belief in deceased people's capacity to influence the living, while Factor 4 is strongly positively correlated with the Dead Active sub-dimension (.121 and .548, respectively). In addition to a thoroughgoing naturalism, Factor 2 spirituality tends to view the quest for intellectual understanding as an integral part of the spiritual journey, while Factor 4 is significantly negatively correlated with the Truth Seeking sub-dimension (.660 and −.279, respectively). Again, whereas Factor 2 is strongly positively correlated with a tendency to regard the experience of beautiful art and music as spiritually meaningful, Factor 4 is weakly negatively correlated with the Appreciating Beauty sub-dimension (.679 and −.040, respectively). Another key difference is Factor 2's stronger correlations with the tendency to regard experiences of Awe before cosmic vastness as spiritually energizing (Awe: .662 and .144), tendency to regard acceptance of difficult or painful changes as spiritually important (Nonattachment: .419 and .097), and tendency to associate spirituality with potent experiences of Transcendence (.455 and .148). Factor 2 spirituality is also more strongly associated with experiences of Oneness (.646) with all things, although Factor 4 is also significantly positively correlated (.369) with such experiences.

Summarizing the Factor 2 side of this contrast, this spirituality is naturalistic in flavor, unconcerned with orientation toward divine beings and skeptical regarding unseen spirits and the power of the dead to directly influence the living. In lieu of rejected supports offered by Belief and Belonging spirituality—clearly prescribed beliefs, existentially orienting meaning, deep communal connection, steadying religious rituals, and time-tested religious traditions—Factor 2 spirituality embraces the quest for intellectual understanding as central to the spiritual life and draws inspiration from a variety of profound non-supernatural experiences: beauty perceived in music and art, awe felt before the universe's immense vastness, momentary transcendence of ordinary time and space, dawning awareness of a unity embracing all things, and sober acceptance of the final transience of all that is. In sum, Factor 2 spirituality is a hopeful naturalistic spirituality, firm in its rejection of belief and belonging spirituality and supernaturalism generally, optimistic about the search for truth, and open to a variety of profoundly spiritually meaningful natural experiences. We label it "Axiological Extra-Theistic Spirituality."

Three features of Factor 4 spirituality distinguish it from Factor 2 spirituality. First, despite being as firm as Factor 2 in rejecting theistic spirituality, Factor 4 spirituality does not embrace a broader naturalism, being strongly positively correlated with belief in unseen powers and spirits (Spiritual Beings: .580) and in the power of the dead to the influence the living (Dead Active: .548). Second, Factor 4 spirituality firmly rejects the idea that seeking intellectual understanding is central to the spiritual life (Truth Seeking: −.279), instead being strongly positively correlated with the view that reality in general and the spiritual realm in particular are fundamentally mysterious (Mystery: .509). Third, while Factors 1 and 3 are strongly positively correlated (.555 and .461, respectively) and Factor 2 is weakly positively correlated (.114) with the idea that connection to one's spiritual community is essential to spirituality, Factor 4 is significantly negatively correlated with this view (Connection: −.219). Rather than focusing on connection with others, Factor 4 spirituality turns inward, emphasizing that the discovery of one's true self is key to the spiritual journey (Self-Awareness: .651). Taken together, these observations suggest that, by rejecting theistic paths toward salvation and the support afforded by belief and belonging spirituality, Factor 4 spirituality construes quests for intellectual understanding as attempts to pierce the impenetrable veil of mystery, accompanied by beliefs that we are subject to the influence of good and evil spirits as well as deceased persons; the best strategy is to turn inward, seeking liberation through knowledge of one's true self. Reminiscent of ancient Gnosticism, Factor 4 spirituality might be thought of as "pessimistic supernaturalistic extra-theistic spirituality." We label it "Supernaturalistic Extra-Theistic Spirituality."

This survey, while fairly large, was not representative, so it supplies little information about the prevalence of these views in WEIRD populations. In our sample of 820 people, all of the four cultural packages were well represented, and none was overwhelmingly dominant. If the four key conditions (existential security, freedom, education, pluralism) remain strong, then FOReST predicts that there will be a move away from supernatural worldview-lifeways, and thus toward Factor 2, Axiological Extra-Theistic Spirituality, which is the most obviously naturalist option among the four. But we would also expect secularizing modern people to increasingly reject traditional Axial religions and to explore small-scale, non-Axial religions without giving up supernaturalism, and thus we would also expect a move toward Factor 4, Supernaturalistic Extra-Theistic Spirituality, with some of those eventually moving in a naturalistic direction, to Factor 2.

Figure 7.2 is a Sankey diagram expressing how we understand the flows among these four cultural packages in secularizing societies over the twenty-first century. The figure shows estimated distribution in 2000 on the left, and projected distributions for 2050 in the middle and 2100 on the right. While the details are not predicted by FOReST, which doesn't track the distinctions among these four cultural packages of spirituality, FOReST does project the growth of naturalistic religion and spirituality (Factor 2), and the DSI study does suggest the kind of change in the prevalence of both Factor 2 (naturalist spirituality) and Factor 4 (essentially New Age spirituality) that is portrayed in the first quarter of Figure 7.2.

The story as the twenty-first century dawns has Factor 1, Transformational Theistic Spirituality, followed by Factor 3, Ritualistic Theistic Spirituality, in the ascendancy. Factor 4, Supernaturalistic Extra-Theistic Spirituality, reflecting New Age involvement, is thriving, while Factor 2, Axiological Extra-Theistic Spirituality, is a distinct minority. By 2050, a few from Factor 4 will have decided that supernaturalism has lost its charm, moving to Factor 2. Meanwhile, most of the action is in the theistic Factors 1 and 3, which will shed huge numbers of people, most to the supernaturalist Factor 4 and fewer to the naturalist Factor 2. In the final stage, by 2100, the theistic Factors 1 and 3 become small, and even Factor 4, the last refuge of supernaturalism, yields to a post-supernatural worldview, resulting in Factor 2 becoming ascendant. This expresses our view

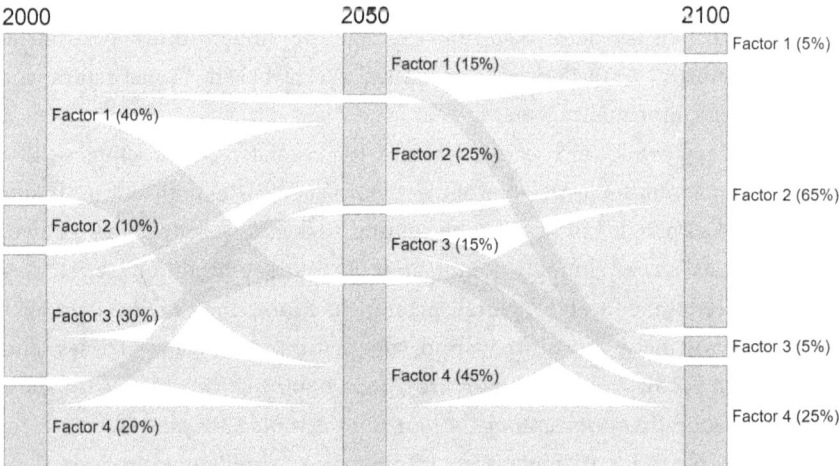

Figure 7.2 Sankey diagram showing our projection of estimated flows among four cultural packages of spirituality at 2000 (left), 2050 (center), and 2100 (right). Factor 1: Transformational Theistic Spirituality; Factor 2: Axiological Extra-Theistic Spirituality; Factor 3: Ritualistic Theistic Spirituality; Factor 4: Supernaturalistic Extra-Theistic Spirituality.

that the end of the Axial Age (marked by the decline of Factors 1 and 3) does not by itself eliminate supernaturalism. Reducing interest in such a deeply rooted cognitive reflex requires institutions to stabilize cultural habits in education and social interaction.

This portrayal of spirituality in secularizing nations tells us a lot about transition dynamics. FOReST tells us that supernaturalism will continue to decline in plausibility, gradually becoming an increasingly less compelling way of understanding the world. But this decline takes centuries to unfold, and most of the change occurs between generations rather than within individual lifespans. Moreover, supernaturalism declines more slowly than other aspects of religiosity because it is more deeply embedded in human cognition and thus requires stable structures to support educational contestation of those powerful cognitive defaults in each new generation. During the drawn-out Modernity transition, therefore, supernatural worldviews persist, but in changing forms, as Axial religions lose their powerful influence over human imaginations. Only one of the four cultural packages (Factor 2) is post-supernaturalist, focusing on the axiological depth dimensions of the natural world. Another factor (Factor 4) describes post-Axial supernaturalism in New-Age eclecticism, re-enchanting reality by conjuring invisible spirits floating through every aspect of nature and life. Two are relatively compatible with Axial worldview-lifeways, one (Factor 1) focusing on personal relationships to deity and the other (Factor 3) on socially borne ritual engagement with liminal mysteries of reality. The latter of those is also quite at home with the small-scale folk traditions and nature religions that are making an impressive comeback in the modern period.

Even if secularization continues on its current trajectory, supernaturalism will continue to remain alive and well within modern societies. During the drawn-out transition, supernatural pluralism will reign, birthing a chaotic wealth of expressions as the regulating force of Axial worldviews dissolves. In the longer run, however, supernaturalism in all its forms will steadily lose ground, and the post-supernaturalist cultural package revealed by the DSI will become ascendant: more persuasive, more prominent, and more differentiated. So what, then, is the longer term future of religion and spirituality?

Likely Futures for Religion and Spirituality

As we've seen, Modernity has given birth to secular worldviews-lifeways that wrest political and narrative control over human life from the magnificent talons of Axial religions and vest it in the hands of scientists, cultural luminaries, and popular political figures—visionaries eager yet largely untested in the business of running civilizations. The foregoing describes some of what we know about religion and spirituality right now, as the Modernity transition unfolds in significantly secularized societies. What about the mid-range or longer range future? The vast and growing numbers of "spiritual but not religious" people (SBNRs), including post-supernaturalist options, indicates that spirituality will not vanish as the Axial religions decline, though supernaturalism will be slower to decline than commitment to organized Axial religions. Can some religions adapt to the new environment? And what might religion and spirituality look like as supernaturalism—whether in a religious or nonreligious setting—is experienced as an increasingly implausible worldview? The FOReST model supports several predictions about the way the four key conditions produce effects on spirituality and religion in a dominantly post-supernaturalist secular social environment, predictions that are consistent with what we see through the lens of the DSI.

First, emerging spirituality will often resist supernaturalist worldviews, while supernaturalism will be confined to relatively small enclaves with the social clout to preserve local supernaturalist plausibility structures.

Second, post-supernaturalist forms of spirituality will often be individualistic, for want of the kind of supernaturalist social glue that has been the secret of Axial religions' success. But they may well also be corporate in nature at times, as people discover new ways to bind themselves to others who seek to share spiritual quests.

Third, traditional Axial religious communities will have the possibility of a naturalist form of spirituality as a non-traditional option, even as individual people do. Such post-supernaturalist renovators of existing Axial religions will be resisted by the traditional supernaturalists among their ranks. But it is important not to underestimate the conceptual and structural flexibility of religious narratives and the organizations that have sustained them over millennia.

It follows that religions play a critical double role in the Modernity transition. On the one hand, they play the role of dramatic resistor partly by poking holes in the pretensions of Modernity and partly by organizing rearguard action to maintain supernaturalist plausibility structures and to prevent secular worldviews-lifeways from gaining comprehensive control, reeducating the minds of their children and grandchildren. On the other hand, they play the role of a mercurial character, capable of adapting to post-supernaturalist worldviews-lifeways.

For example, throughout the Modern period, and increasingly as time has marched on, a number of prominent religious thought leaders have essentially rejected supernaturalist worldviews while remaining committed to aspects of traditional Axial belief that can be suitably reframed in a post-naturalistic way. For example, those in theistic traditions may argue against the idea of God as a supernatural divine person and instead speak of the divine as a fundamental natural principle of reason and value present in the depth structures of reality and discoverable by creatures with suitable cognitive-experiential equipment, such as human beings. Or nontheistic Buddhists might reject the supernaturalism of so many traditional practices and embrace a naturalist, scientific approach to traditional beliefs and practices. Regardless of the tradition being renovated as a post-supernatural wisdom tradition, such thought leaders tend to link the reframing of traditional beliefs to secular moral norms, such as universal human rights, global duties to preserve the ecological conditions for human life, and the cosmopolitan morality of compassion and justice. They tend to resist the socially binding aspects of morality related to in-group boundary monitoring, uncritical respect for hierarchy, and intensification of moral norms using sacred purity instincts.

The tug-of-war between supernaturalist religious people and post-supernaturalist secular people over the remnants of the major Axial religions is fascinating. It is worth pausing to consider how efforts to renovate Axial religions as demythologized and naturalized wisdom traditions relate to the four conditions that drive the Modernity transition: existential security, freedom, education, and pluralism. Figure 7.3 schematizes how we see these renovation attempts possibly occurring.

We have already discussed the effects of the four key conditions on spirituality, but it bears repeating. High existential security undermines the need to seek protection from supernatural agents and coalitions. High freedom of self-expression undermines the power of social prohibitions against acting on personal convictions. High scientific and humanistic education undermines the plausibility of supernatural-agent beliefs while maintaining sensitivity to the depths of the human spirit. And high pluralistic appreciation for cultural and religious diversity undermines the credibility of exclusivist, supernaturally authorized beliefs and coalitions.

The final column of Figure 7.3 charts the strategies we think would be necessary if the Axial worldviews are to be renovated as post-supernatural wisdom traditions.

First, high existential security drives a shift from dependence on supernatural divine agents to an embrace of human self-determination, fighting to create a

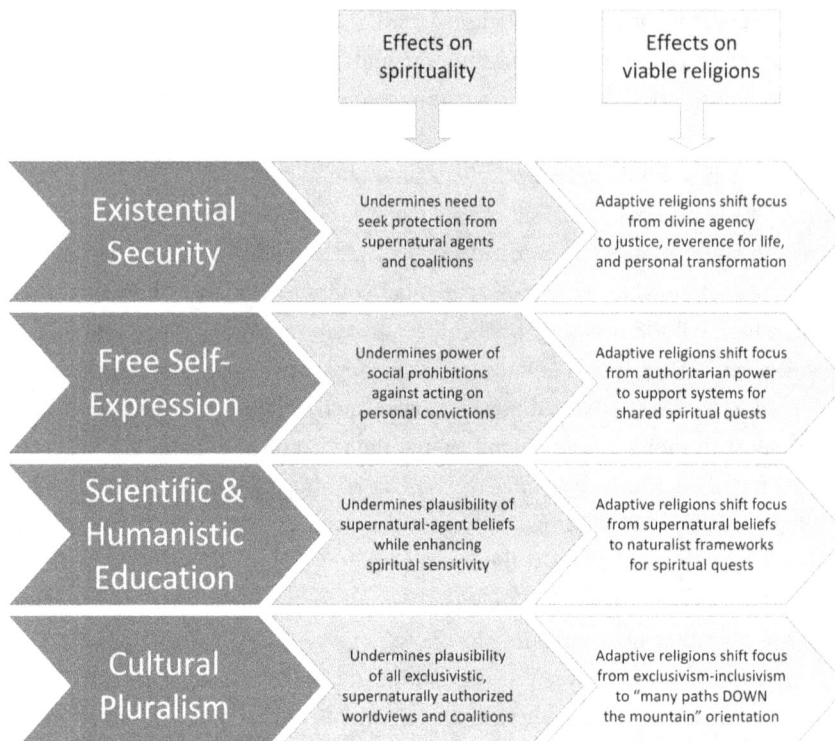

Figure 7.3 The effects of Modernity on spirituality and on religions that seek to adapt to secular, post-supernaturalistic worldviews-lifeways.

just and sustainable world that recognizes universal human rights and practices a reverence for life in all its forms, including in the ecological environment on which the human project depends.

Second, high freedom of expression drives a shift from deferring to authoritarian structures, which were critical for defining Axial orthodoxies and orthopraxies, to supporting systems for shared spiritual quests characterized by humility, curiosity, and appreciation for wisdom in whatever forms it appears.

Third, high scientific and humanistic education drives a shift from the grand supernatural worldviews that purported to explain every aspect of reality in magnificent Axial mega-narratives to a simple naturalist metaphysics. Spirituality can then be understood differently, for example, as a natural response to the depth dimension of human life rather than an urgent need to relate appropriately to sometimes compassionate but also potentially threatening supernatural entities.

Fourth, high pluralistic appreciation for cultural and religious diversity drives a shift away from both Axial exclusivity ("our universal story is the only true one") and Axial inclusivity ("our story includes you whether you know it or not"). These might be replaced by what can be called a "many paths DOWN the mountain" approach to pluralism that involves understanding all religions as a natural response to surviving and flourishing in a naturalistically conceived process of biological, cognitive, and cultural evolution, which is a shared human birthright (the mountain) and a host of culturally flexible articulations (the many paths down the mountain).

There is strong evidence that Axial traditions can be renovated in this post-supernaturalistic way. Apart from the thought leaders who have been doing just that over the past couple of centuries, these naturalistic kinds of worldviews have ancient pedigrees within the Axial traditions themselves. For example, naturalist Buddhist philosophies have existed since ancient times and radical naturalist forms of belief have sprung up repeatedly within theistic traditions, particularly among mystical philosophers. These hints of what might be possible for Axial adaptation have routinely been marginalized, and even violently suppressed, but they will surely have more room to breathe and develop if future conditions of human life continue to support high levels of the four key conditions. None of this means that institutions representing traditional Axial worldviews will rush to embrace religion without supernaturalism. Only institutional desperation joined with supply-side innovation from creative and courageous thought leaders will make it happen. Whether this kind of renovation occurs or not, the Axial Age is rapidly drawing to a close—if, we insist, the four key conditions remain robust.

Likely Futures for the Human Project

We conclude by discussing possible and likely futures for the human project as a whole. Given our emerging understanding of the complex social systems of minds in cultures—systems in which we continue to adapt—what sense can we make of the large-scale trajectories of civilizational change? And what challenges must we confront in the future?

It seems like a compelling case can be made for "progress" in human life, at least in the sense that on average people are healthier, live longer, experience less violence, and have more access to cultural richness and actionable information than ever before. Yet the progression of modern secularism in the most developed parts of the world has also led to intense challenges for religion, which has traditionally generated important glue for human societies. Are stable, just, and peaceful civilizations possible in a post-supernaturalist era where supernaturalist Axial worldviews-lifeways no longer bind us together in basic trust and common purpose? Is there a chance we can solve pressing challenges related to climate change, economic injustice, structural racism, extreme poverty, information bubbles, and artificial intelligence more effectively in post-supernaturalist civilizations? Can we regulate violent minorities who would use weapons of unthinkable power to tear down modern civilizations, if they could, sending us spiraling back into the past and resuscitating supernaturalist worldviews-lifeways within societies governed by authoritarian religious zealots? Or are post-supernaturalist religious worldviews-lifeways exercises in hubris, foolishly denying the reality of a supernatural environment and ultimately collapsing under the weight of their own pretensions? Is traditional supernaturalist religion the blessing we desperately need, now as in the past, or it is the curse from which we must free ourselves at all costs? Correspondingly, is post-supernaturalist secularism the key to our liberation and enlightenment or merely a delusional social experiment destined to fail amid a cacophony of we told you so's from religious supernaturalists?

There are scholarly versions of all kinds of answers to these questions, evidence-based variations on colorful opinions that arise easily in informal conversations. Earnest faces spring to our minds, people we respect advocating for one or another way of thinking about the role of religion in the transformation of civilizations, past, present, and future. Few people want the entire human project to collapse, relegated to a mere evolutionary footnote in the grand story of planet Earth, though a few extremist ecological activists will entertain that idea. We all have a stake in understanding the dynamics of civilizational change, in getting our advocacy choices right, in playing our part to steer our civilizations toward a healthy future. But whatever we choose, the starkest reality is that we used to do this with less understanding and with supernaturalist religion taken for granted. Now, as Friedrich Nietzsche would have it, we have awoken to the knowledge that, collectively, we have always been masters of our own destiny. There is no hiding from the severe fact that we have always been the creators, not merely the grateful recipients, of our civilizations, and that we can choose where we go next. It is a daunting choice, and a fraught one, given the extent of disagreement swirling around visions of a good human and planetary future and the stark reality of marginalized people who long for social justice and a real voice.

At this point, we must acknowledge that the past offers only slender insights into our choices for the future. The Modernity we take for granted, let alone the Modernity of generations from now, would be nearly unrecognizable to even the most imaginative of our civilizational forebears. Yet human minds have been roughly the same for thousands of years, and their intricate interactions in cultures continue, so there are relevant continuities to guide reflection on the future. With that in mind, we offer the following reflections.

First, human beings ignore or deny the depth dimension of life at their peril. The ways we create meaning and narrate our purpose as individuals and groups of people has played a key role in every phase of civilizational transformation, as this book demonstrates. The storytelling may have been supernatural in content for almost all our history, but the fundamental urge and the social need to ponder the meaning of our existence is deeper than supernaturalism, older than religion, and still as strong a factor in human life as it ever was. This is one of the wellsprings of spirituality and it will not brook neglect. Tragically, as we know all too well, humans will readily fill the void of meaning with narratives unworthy of their ultimate concern, from eager nationalist sentiment to personal ambition and political power, which has led time and again to disasters, sometimes on a civilizational scale. Whatever we do going forward, we must take the existential longings of the human mind and its ultimate concerns with extreme seriousness.

Second, human beings are bad at complexity. We instinctively oversimplify in ways that help us make fast decisions, which is how our evolutionary programming sets up our cognition. That's a gift in the sense that it confers critical survival advantages. But when it comes to making sense of monumentally complex civilizations, this gift functions more like an evolutionary curse: we are deeply stuck in a cognitive-behavioral rut and struggle to discern the ripple effects of our actions. We devise ingenious methods of energy capture with devastating environmental effects (e.g., fossil fuels) and neither see the disaster of global climate change coming nor universally accept that we're responsible—all because the climate system is so very complex, which makes inferring causes genuinely difficult. As a result, we can't generate the consensus and motivation to make the needed change. Similarly, it is all too easy to blame people for their misfortune on the grounds that they failed to exert themselves to take advantage of economic and social opportunities, without noticing that structural disadvantage can make even the most diligent and determined efforts at self-improvement unlikely to succeed. Some don't perceive the reality of structural disadvantage as a tractable policy issue and they moralize it away. Here again we are trapped by our tendency to rush to simple, actionable interpretations of complexity, resulting in the perpetuation of gross inequalities in economic opportunity and health outcomes.

As a species, very few of us can sense our way around complex adaptive social systems, drawing accurate inferences about causation, and thereby making sound decisions about what to do next. Every phase of civilizational transformation has involved an unusually intense degree of complexity—due to the associated phase transition, as this book has shown—and the Modernity transformation is orders of magnitude more complex than any our species has navigated in the past. Remaining blinded by easy assumptions, stuck in an evolutionary-cognitive rut, is a dangerous way to approach such a transition, particularly given the technological power—from weapons of mass destruction to rampant artificial intelligence—that now exists to cripple or annihilate the human project. Thus, we urgently need to teach one another about complexity, about causal inference, about historic failures of our species' perception, and about our inborn tendencies to cognitive error, and we need to cultivate the skills needed to see more deeply into complex adaptive social systems.

Third, even if we could figure out how to navigate complexity wisely and how to take seriously the human thirst for meaning, we would still require focused motivation for change. The models we presented in Chapters 4 and 5 didn't explicitly attempt to take account of this aspect of human life, admittedly. But the Modernity transition of Chapter 6 is still with us, and we have a level of awareness about it that is astronomically greater than any available during previous episodes of civilizational transformation, thanks to an unprecedented combination of rich theory, massive data, and ingenious simulation. We have more understanding, but we also are more aware than ever before that our dreams and aspirations are capable of guiding the future in a way that was never before realistic or relevant.

Therefore, we have an amplified burden of responsibility to make smart choices about how to guide our civilization, and it is a responsibility we can sense, viscerally and urgently. Unfortunately, even if we knew what to do, we may not be able to act. Our failure to curb the worst effects of climate change seems inevitable now, and not for want of engineering solutions; the crisis is spiritual, in the nonsectarian sense—directly related to meaning, moral orientation, and motivation to change. The same is true for eliminating extreme poverty, mitigating health and wealth inequality, and other so-called wicked problems: even if science can guide us toward practical solutions, we need to be morally and spiritually prepared to take the action needed. Focused motivation for change requires a vision of what is possible, clear reasoning about how the possible can be achieved, and an integrating spiritual awareness of human life meaning that furnishes the needed moral orientation.

Spirituality in this nonsectarian, post-supernaturalist, humanistic sense is not a luxury; it is critical to our survival. The rationale for including it in our interpretations of episodes of civilizational transformation goes well beyond increasing the adequacy of explanation; it was and is and will remain a vital strategic asset. However, the cultivation of this asset must now occur in a context far different from that in which our early human ancestors learned to survive and thrive. Our forebears lived in small-scale societies in which participation in repeated, emotionally arousing rituals produced what sociologist Émile Durkheim called "collective effervescence." For most of human history, this was the way in which the emotional energy related to "spirituality" (in the broad, nonsectarian sense we are using the term here) was released and regulated, reinforcing the social cohesion of relatively small and homogeneous groups. Today most of us live in large-scale societies composed of radically heterogeneous and overlapping groups of individuals whose emotional energy is released and regulated in a wide diversity of ways, from concerts to sports events to hiking in the woods with friends. We humans still need adequately cohesive civilizational forms in order to survive and thrive, but in secularizing societies emotional energy is now often mediated through somewhat intermittent and intense experiences that produce what could be called "distributive effervescence" (McCaffree & Shults, 2022).

It remains to be seen how (or whether) we humans will navigate this new and rapidly mutating context. Our goal in this book has not been to predict the future or to provide normative guidance for individuals or groups, although we could not help but throw in the occasional recommendation here and there. Rather, we have attempted to show how the development of theoretical syntheses, deployed in computational social simulations, can help to facilitate the kind of insights and conversations we believe could help our species pass some new threshold into a previously unimaginable civilizational form whose socio-ecological equilibrium could be maintained in ways that mitigate conflict and promote more sustainable cooperation in the Anthropocene.

Repositories Containing Model Details

For NSIM: https://github.com/centerformindandculture/NSIM
For MAxiM: https://github.com/centerformindandculture/MAxiM
For FOReST: https://github.com/centerformindandculture/FOReST

References

Abrutyn, S. (2014). Religious autonomy and religious entrepreneurship: An evolutionary-institutionalist's take on the Axial Age. *Comparative Sociology, 13*(2), 105–34. https://doi.org/10.1163/15691330-12341300.

Allaby, R., Brown, T., & Fuller, D. (2010). A simulation of the effect of inbreeding on crop domestication genetics with comments on the integration of archaeobotany and genetics: A reply to Honne and Heun. *Vegetation History and Archaeobotany, 19*(2), 151–8. https://doi.org/10.1007/s00334-009-0232-8.

Allaby, R. G., Fuller, D. Q., & Brown, T. A. (2010). The genetic expectations of a protracted model for the origins of domesticated crops. *Proceedings of the National Academy of Sciences of the United States of America, 105*(37), 13982–6. https://doi.org/10.1073/pnas.0803780105.

Allen, C., Varner, G., & Zinser, J. (2000). Prolegomena to any future artificial moral agent. *Journal of Experimental & Theoretical Artificial Intelligence, 12*(3), 251–61.

Alvarez, R. M. (Ed.). (2016). *Computational social science: Discovery and prediction* (Reprint ed.). Cambridge University Press.

Ammerman, N. T. (2007). Everyday religion. *Observing modern religious lives.* Oxford University Press.

Anderson, M., & Anderson, S. L. (Eds.). (2011). *Machine ethics.* Cambridge University Press.

Anderson, M., Anderson, S. L., & Armen, C. (2005). Towards machine ethics: Implementing two action-based ethical theories. In *Proceedings of the AAAI 2005 fall symposium on machine ethics* (pp. 1–7). Springer.

Anderson, S. L. (2011). Machine metaethics. In M. Anderson and S. L. Anderson, *Machine ethics* (pp. 21–7). Cambridge University Press.

Anderson, S. L., & Anderson, M. (2021). AI and ethics. *AI and Ethics, 1*, 27–31.

Armstrong, K. (2007). *The great transformation: The beginning of our religious traditions.* Anchor Books.

Asad, T. (1993). *Genealogies of religion: Discipline and reasons of power in Christianity and Islam.* Johns Hopkins University Press.

Asprem, E. (2016). Reverse-engineering "esotericism": How to prepare a complex cultural concept for the cognitive science of religion. *Religion, 46*(2), 158–85.

Assmann, J. (2012). *Cultural memory and the myth of the axial age* (R. N. Bellah & H. Joas, Eds.; pp. 366–410). Harvard University Press.

Atkinson, Q. D., & Whitehouse, H. (2011). The cultural morphospace of ritual form: Examining modes of religiosity cross-culturally. *Evolution and Human Behavior*, *32*(1), 50–62. https://doi.org/10.1016/j.evolhumbehav.2010.09.002.

Atran, S. (2002). *In gods we trust: The evolutionary landscape of religion*. Oxford University Press.

Awad, E., Dsouza, S., Kim, R., Schulz, J., Henrich, J., Shariff, A., Jean-François Bonnefon, & Rahwan, I. (2018). The moral machine experiment. *Nature*, *563*(7729), 59–64.

Axtell, R. L., Epstein, J. M., Harburger, J., Chakravarty, S., Hammond, R., Parker, J., Parker, M., Epstein, J. M., Dean, J. S., Dean, J. S., Gumerman, G. J., Dean, J. S., Gumerman, G. J., Swedlund, A. C., Harburger, J., Parker, J., Hammond, R., & Parker, M. (2002). Population growth and collapse in a multiagent model of the Kayenta Anasazi in Long House Valley. *Proceedings of the National Academy of Sciences of the United States of America*, *99*(3), 7275–9. https://doi.org/10.1073/pnas.092080799.

Barceló, J. A., & Del Castillo, F. (2016). *Simulating prehistoric and ancient worlds*. Springer.

Baumard, N., Baumard, N., Hyafil, A., Morris, I., Boyer, P., & Boyer, P. (2014). Increased affluence explains the emergence of ascetic wisdoms and moralizing religions. *Current Biology*, *25*(1), 10–15. https://doi.org/10.1016/j.cub.2014.10.063.

Baumard, N., & Chevallier, C. (2015). The nature and dynamics of world religions: A life-history approach. *Proceedings of the Royal Society B*, *282*, 20151593. http://rspb.royalsocietypublishing.org/content/282/1818/20151593.abstract (accessed December 20, 2023).

Baumard, N., Hyafil, A., & Boyer, P. (2015). What changed during the Axial Age: Cognitive styles or reward systems? *Communicative & Integrative Biology*, *8*(5), e1046657.

Bechtel, W. (2009). Looking down, around, and up: Mechanistic explanation in psychology. *Philosophical Psychology*, *22*(5), 543–64. https://doi.org/10.1080/09515080903238948.

Bell, J. A. (1987). Simulation modelling in archaeology: Reflections and trends. *European Journal of Operational Research*, *30*(3), 243–5. https://doi.org/10.1016/0377-2217(87)90065-8.

Bellah, R. N. (2005). What is axial about the Axial Age? *European Journal of Sociology*, *46*(1), 69–89.

Bellah, R. N. (2011). *Religion in human evolution: From the Paleolithic to the Axial Age*. Harvard University Press.

Bellah, R. N., & Joas, H. (2012). *The Axial Age and its consequences*. Harvard University Press.

Benioff, M. R., & Lazowska, E. D. (2005). *Computational science: Ensuring America's competitiveness*. National Coordination Office for Information Technology Research & Development. https://www.nitrd.gov/historical/Pitac/Reports/20050609_computational/computational.pdf (accessed December 20, 2023).

Berger, P. L. (1969). *The sacred canopy: Elements of a sociological theory of religion*. Anchor Books / Doubleday.

Berger, P. L. (1973). *The social reality of religion*. Penguin.

Berger, P. L. (1979). *The heretical imperative: Contemporary possibilities of religious affirmation*. Anchor Press/Doubleday.

Botero, C. A., Gardner, B., Kirby, K. R., Bulbulia, J., Gavin, M. C., & Gray, R. D. (2014). The ecology of religious beliefs. *Proceedings of the National Academy of Sciences*, *111*(47), 16784–9. https://doi.org/10.1073/pnas.1408701111.

Bowman, J. (2015). *Cosmoipolitan justice: The Axial Age, multiple modernities, and the postsecular turn*. Springer.

Boy, J. (2015). The Axial Age and the problems of the twentieth century: Du Bois, Jaspers, and universal history. *The American Sociologist*, *46*(2), 234–47. https://doi.org/10.1007/s12108-015-9254-0.

Boy, J., & Torpey, J. (2013). Inventing the Axial Age: The origins and uses of a historical concept. *Theory and Society*, *42*(3), 241–59. https://doi.org/10.1007/s11186-013-9193-0.

Boyer, P. (2002). *Religion explained: The evolutionary origins of religious thought* (Reprint ed.). Basic Books.

Brauer, S. (2018). The surprising predictable decline of religion in the United States. *Journal for the Scientific Study of Religion*, *57*(4), 654–75.

Bremner, P., Dennis, L. A., Fisher, M., & Winfield, A. F. (2019). On proactive, transparent, and verifiable ethical reasoning for robots. *Proceedings of the IEEE*, *107*(3), 541–61.

Bruce, S. (2011). *Secularization: In defence of an unfashionable theory* (1st ed.). Oxford University Press.

Buckley, M. J. (1990). *At the origins of modern atheism*. Yale University Press.

Bulbulia, J. (2004). Religious costs as adaptations that signal altruistic intention. *Evolution and Cognition*, *10*(1), 19–38.

Calhoun, C., Juergensmeyer, M., & VanAntwerpen, J. (2011). *Rethinking secularism*. Oxford University Press.

Campbell, D. E., & Putnam, R. D. (2011). Islam and American tolerance; what the experience of Jews and Catholics suggests about the future for Muslims. (Viewpoint essay). *The Wall Street Journal Eastern Edition*, A13.

Casanova, J. (2012). Religion, the Axial Age, and secular modernity in Bellah's theory of religious evolution. In R. N. Bellah & H. Joas (Eds.), *The Axial Age and its consequences* (pp. 191–221). Harvard University Press.

Cauvin, J. (2000). *The birth of the gods and the origins of agriculture* (T. Watkins, Trans.). Cambridge University Press.

Cave, S., Nyrup, R., Vold, K., & Weller, A. (2018). Motivations and risks of machine ethics. *Proceedings of the IEEE*, *107*(3), 562–74.

Chase-Dunn, C. & Lerro, B. (2014). *Social change: Globalization from the stone age to the present*. Paradigm.

CMAC (2023). ARDEMIS: Assumption Relative Demographic Information System, including the Religious Identity and Change (RICH) datasets and the Dimensions of Religiosity (DIM-R) dataset. https://mindandculture.org/projects/modeling-social-systems/modeling-religious-change/ardemis/ (accessed December 21, 2023).

Conte, R., Andrighetto, G., & Campennì, M. (2014). *Minding norms: Mechanisms and dynamics of social order in agent societies.* Oxford University Press.

Costopoulos, A., & Lake, M. W. (2010). *Simulating change: Archaeology into the twenty-first century.* University of Utah Press.

Crabtree, S. A., & Kohler, T. A. (2012). Modelling across millennia: Interdisciplinary paths to ancient socio-ecological systems. *Ecological Modelling, 241,* 2–4. https://doi.org/10.1016/j.ecolmodel.2012.02.023.

Cragun, R., McCaffree, K., Puga-Gonzalez, I., Wildman, W., & Shults, F. L. (2021). Religious exiting and social networks: Computer simulations of religious/secular pluralism. *Secularism and Nonreligion, 10*(1). https://doi.org/10.5334/snr.121.

Danaher, J., & McArthur, N. (Eds.). (2017). *Robot sex: Social and ethical implications.* MIT Press.

Davie, G., Heelas, P., & Woodhead, L. (2003). *Predicting religion: Christian, secular and alternative futures.* Ashgate.

Deacon, T. W. (1997). *The symbolic species: The co-evolution of language and the brain.* W. W. Norton & Company.

Diallo, S. Y., Shults, F. L., & Wildman, W. J. (2021). Minding morality: Ethical artificial societies for public policy modeling. *Ai & Society, 36*(1), 49–57.

Diallo, S. Y., Wildman, W. J., Shults, F. L., & Tolk, A. (Eds.). (2019). *Human simulation: Perspectives, insights, and applications.* Springer.

Diamond, J. (2003). *Guns, germs, and steel: The fates of human societies* (Revised ed.). W. W. Norton & Company.

Diamond, J. (2013). *The world until yesterday: What can we learn from traditional societies?* (Reprint ed.). Penguin Books.

Donald, M. (1993). *Origins of the modern mind: Three stages in the evolution of culture and cognition.* Harvard University Press.

Doran, J., & Palmer, M. (1995). The EOS project: Integrating two models of Palaeolithic social change. In N. Gilbert & R. Conte (Eds.), *Artificial societies: The computer simulation of social life* (pp. 103–25). UCL Press.

Doran, J., Palmer, M., Gilbert, N., & Mellars, P. (1994). The EOS project: Modelling Upper Paleolithic social change. In N. Gilbert & J. Doran (Eds.), *Simulating societies: The computer simulation of social phenomena* (pp. 195–221). UCL Press.

Dyer, K. D., & Hall, R. E. (2019). Effect of critical thinking education on epistemically unwarranted beliefs in college students. *Research in Higher Education, 60*(3), 293–314.

Edmonds, B., & ní Aodha, L. (2019). Using Agent-Based Modelling to Inform Policy – What Could *Possibly* Go Wrong? In P. Davidsson & H. Verhagen (Eds.),

Multi-agent-based simulation XIX. MABS 2018. Lecture notes in computer science (vol. 11463). Springer. https://doi.org/10.1007/978-3-030-22270-3_1.

Eisenstadt, S. N. (Ed.) (1986). *The origins and diversity of Axial Age civilizations*. State University of New York Press.

Eisenstadt, S. N. (1999). Multiple modernities in an age of globalization. *The Canadian Journal of Sociology / Cahiers Canadiens de Sociologie, 24*(2), 283–95. https://doi.org/10.2307/3341732.

Eisenstadt, S. N. (2000). The civilizational dimension in sociological analysis. *Thesis Eleven, 62*(1), 1–21. https://doi.org/10.1177/0725513600062000002.

Eisenstadt, S. N. (2001). The civilizational dimension of modernity: Modernity as a distinct civilization. *International Sociology, 16*(3), 320–40.

Eisenstadt, S. N. (2002). *Multiple modernities*. Transaction.

Eisenstadt, S. N. (2005a). Axial civilizations and the axial age reconsidered. In J. P. Arnason, S. N. Eisenstadt, & B. Wittrock (Eds.), *Axial civilizaitions and world history* (pp. 531–64). Brill.

Eisenstadt, S. N. (2005b). Religious origins of modern radicalism. *Theoria, 106*, 51–80.

Eisenstadt, S. N. (2009). *Axial visions and axial civilizations: The transformations of world histories between evolutionary tendencies and institutional formations*. Brill.

Eisenstadt, S. N. (2011). The Axial conundrum: Between transcendental visions and vicissitudes of their institutionalizations: Constructive and destructive possibilities. *Análise Social, 46*(199), 201–17.

Elkana, Y. (1986). The emergence of second-order thinking in classical Greece. In S. N. Eisenstadt (Ed.), *The origin and diversity of Axial civilizations* (pp. 40–64). State University of New York Press.

Ellis, L., Hoskin, A. W., Dutton, E., & Nyborg, H. (2017). The future of secularism: A biologically informed theory supplemented with cross-cultural evidence. *Evolutionary Psychological Science, 3*, 224–42.

Elsenbroich, C., & Gilbert, N. (2014). *Modelling norms*. Springer Netherlands.

Epstein, J. M. (2006). *Generative social science: Studies in agent-based computational modeling*. Princeton University Press.

Festinger, L. (1957). *A theory of cognitive dissonance*. Stanford University Press.

Finke, R., & Stark, R. (1998). Religious choice and competition. *American Sociological Review, 63*(5), 761–6.

Fukuyama, F. (2006). *The end of history and the last man*. Simon & Schuster.

Fuller, D. Q., Allaby, R. G., & Stevens, C. (2010). Domestication as innovation: The entanglement of techniques, technology and chance in the domestication of cereal crops. *World Archaeology, 42*(1), 13.

Fuller, D. Q., Asouti, E., & Purugganan, M. D. (2012). Cultivation as slow evolutionary entanglement: Comparative data on rate and sequence of domestication. *Vegetation History and Archaeobotany, 21*(2), 131–45. https://doi.org/10.1007/s00334-011-0329-8.

Galen, L., Gore, R., & Shults, F. L. (2021). Modeling the effects of religious belief and affiliation on prosociality. *Secularism & Nonreligion*, 1–21. https://doi.org/10.5334/snr.128.

Gavrilets, S., Anderson, D. G., & Turchin, P. (2014). Cycling in the complexity of early societies. In L. Grinin & K. Andry (Eds.), *History and mathematics: Trends and cycles* (pp. 136–58). Uchitel.

Gerbault, P., Allaby, R. G., Boivin, N., Rudzinski, A., Grimaldi, I. M., Pires, J. C., Vigueira, C. C., Dobney, K., Gremillion, K. K., Barton, L., Arroyo-Kalin, M., Purugganan, M. D., de Casas, R. R., Bollongino, R., Burger, J., Fuller, D. Q., Bradley, D. G., Balding, D. J., Richerson, P. J., Gilbert, M. T. P., Larson, G., & Thomas, M. T. (2014). Storytelling and story testing in domestication. *PNAS*, *111*(17). https://doi.org/10.1073.

Gervais, W. M., & Henrich, J. (2010). The Zeus problem: Why representational content biases cannot explain faith in gods. *Journal of Cognition and Culture*, *10*(3–4), 383–9. https://doi.org/10.1163/156853710X531249.

Gervais, W. M., & Norenzayan, A. (2012). Like a camera in the sky? Thinking about God increases public self-awareness and socially desirable responding. *Journal of Experimental Social Psychology*, *48*(1), 298–302. https://doi.org/10.1016/j.jesp.2011.09.006.

Gilbert, N., Ahrweiler, P., Barbrook-Johnson, P., Narasimhan, K. P., & Wilkinson, H. (2018). Computational modelling of public policy: Reflections on practice. *Journal of Artificial Societies and Social Simulation*, *21*(1), 1–19.

Gore, R., Lemos, C., Shults, F. L., & Wildman, W. J. (2018). Forecasting changes in religiosity and existential security with an agent-based model. *Journal of Artificial Societies and Social Simulation*, *21*, 1–31.

Graeber, D., & Wengrow, D. (2021). *The dawn of everything: A new history of humanity*. Penguin UK.

Grau, C. (2011). There is no "I" in "robot": Robots and utilitarianism. In Susan Leigh Anderson and Michael Anderson (Eds.), *Machine ethics* (pp. 451–63). Cambridge University Press.

Guthrie, S. (1993). *Faces in the clouds: A new theory of religion*. Oxford University Press.

Haidt, J. (2012). *The righteous mind: Why good people are divided by politics and religion*. Vintage.

Hall, D. D. (2020). *Lived religion in America: Toward a history of practice*. Princeton University Press.

Harari, Y. N. (2015). *Sapiens: A brief history of humankind* (1st ed.). Harper.

Harari, Y. N. (2016). *Homo Deus: A brief history of tomorrow*. Random House.

Harari, Y. N. (2018). *21 lessons for the 21st century*. Signal.

Harrison, J. M. D., & Mckay, R. T. (2013). Do religious and moral concepts influence the ability to delay gratification? A priming study. *Journal of Articles in Support of the Null Hypothesis*, *10*(1), 25–40.

Heelas, P., & Woodhead, L. (2005). *The spiritual revolution: Why religion is giving way to spirituality*. Blackwell.

Heelas, P., & Woodhead, L. (2000). *Religion in modern times: An interpretive anthology*. Blackwell.

Hegel, G. W. F. (1894). *Lectures on the philosophy of history* (2nd ed., J. Sibree, Trans.). George Bell.

Henrich, J., Heine, S., & Norenzayan, A. (2010). Beyond WEIRD: Towards a broad-based behavioral science. *Behavioral and Brain Sciences*, 33(2–3), 111–35.

Hodder, I. (1978). *Simulation studies in archaeology*. Cambridge University Press.

Hodder, I. (2006). *Catalhöyük: The leopard's tale: Revealing the mysteries of Turkey's ancient "town."* Thames & Hudson.

Hodder, I. (2010). Religion in the emergence of civilization ðCatalhèoyèuk as a case study. Cambridge University Press.

Hodder, I. (2012). *Entangled: An archaeology of the relationships between humans and things*. John Wiley & Sons.

Hodder, I. (2014). *Religion at work in a Neolithic society: Vital matters*. Cambridge University Press.

Hodder, I., & Pels, P. (2010). History houses: A new interpretation of architectural elaboration at Catalhoyuk. In I. Hodder (Ed.), *Religion in the emergence of civilization: Catalhoyuk as a case study* (pp. 163–86). Cambridge University Press.

Hungerman, D. M. (2014). The effect of education on religion: Evidence from compulsory schooling laws. *Journal Of Economic Behavior & Organization, 104*, 52–63. https://doi.org/10.1016/j.jebo.2013.09.004.

Huntington, S. P. (2011). *The clash of civilizations and the remaking of world order*. Simon & Schuster.

Iannaccone, L. R., & Makowsky, M. D. (2007). Accidental atheists? Agent-based explanations for the persistence of religious regionalism. *Journal for the Scientific Study of Religion, 46*(1), 1–16. https://doi.org/10.1111/j.1468-5906.2007.00337.x.

Inglehart, R. F., Foa, R., Peterson, C., & Welzel, C. (2008). Development, freedom, and rising happiness: A global perspective (1981–2007). *Perspectives on Psychological Science, 3*(4), 264–85.

Inglehart, R. F., & Norris, P. (2012). The four horsemen of the apocalypse: Understanding human security. *Scandinavian Political Studies, 35*(1), 71–96. https://doi.org/10.1111/j.1467-9477.2011.00281.x.

Inglehart, R., & Welzel, C. (2005). *Modernization, cultural change, and democracy: The human development sequence*. Cambridge University Press.

Jaspers, K. (1953). *The origin and goal of history*. Routledge.

Jayyousi, T. W., & Reynolds, R. G. (2014). Exploiting the synergy between micro, meso, and macro levels in a complex system: Bringing to life an ancient urban center. In P. A. Youngman & M. Hadzikadic (Eds.), *Complexity and the human*

experience: Modeling complexity in the humanities and social sciences (pp. 241–69). Pan Stanford Publishing.
Joas, H. (2012). The axial age debate as religious discourse. In R. N. Bellah & H. Joas (Eds.), *The Axial Age and its consequences* (pp. 9–29). Harvard University Press.
Johnson, A. W., & Earle, T. K. (2000). *The evolution of human societies: From foraging group to agrarian state*. Stanford University Press.
Johnson, D. (2015). *God is watching you: How the fear of God makes us human*. Oxford University Press.
Kohler, T. A., Bocinsky, R. K., Cockburn, D., Crabtree, S. A., Varien, M. D., Kolm, K. E., Smith, S., Ortman, S. G., & Kobti, Z. (2012). Modelling prehispanic Pueblo societies in their ecosystems. *Ecological Modelling, 241*, 30–41. https://doi.org/10.1016/j.ecolmodel.2012.01.002.
Lake, M. (2014). Trends in archaeological simulation. *Journal of Archaeological Method And Theory, 21*(2), 258–87. https://doi.org/10.1007/s10816-013-9188-1.
Lane, J. (2013). Method, theory, and multi-agent artificial intelligence: Creating computer models of complex social interactions. *Journal for the Cognitive Science of Religion, 1*(2), 161–80.
Lane, J. E. (2021). *Understanding religion through artificial intelligence: Bonding and belief*. Bloomsbury Publishing.
Lane, J. E., & Shults, F. L. (2018). Cognition, culture, and social simulation. *Journal of Cognition and Culture, 18*, 451–61.
Lane, J. E., & Shults, F. L. (2020). The computational science of religion. *Journal of the Cognitive Science of Religion, 6*(1–2). http://dx.doi.org/10.1558/jcsr.38669.
Langston, J., Hammer, J., & Cragun, R. T. (2015). Atheism looking in: On the goals and strategies of organized nonbelief. *Science, Religion and Culture, 2*(3), 70–85.
Langston, J., Speed, D., & Coleman, T. J. (2018). Predicting age of atheism: Credibility enhancing displays and religious importance, choice, and conflict in family of upbringing. *Religion, Brain & Behavior, 10*(1), 49–67. https://doi.org/10.1080/2153599X.2018.1502678.
Lemmen, C., Gronenborn, D., & Wirtz, K. W. (2011). A simulation of the Neolithic transition in Western Eurasia. *Journal of Archaeological Science, 38*(12), 3459–70. https://doi.org/10.1016/j.jas.2011.08.008.
Lemmen, C., & Khan, A. (2012). A simulation of the Neolithic transition in the Indus valley. In L. Giosan, D. Q. Fuller, & K. Nicoll (Eds.), *Climates, landscapes and civilizations* (pp. 107–14). American Geophysical Union
Lerro, B. (2000). *From earth spirits to sky gods: The socioecological origins of monotheism, individualism, and hyperabstract reasoning from the Stone Age to the Axial Iron Age*. Lexington Books.
Lin, P., Abney, K., & Bekey, G. A. (Eds.). (2014). *Robot ethics: The ethical and social implications of robotics*. MIT press.
Lowe, J. W. G. (1985). *The dynamics of apocalypse: A systems simulation of the classic Maya collapse*. University of New Mexico Press.

McCaffree, K., & Shults, F. L. (2022). Distributive effervescence: Emotional energy and social cohesion in secularizing societies. *Theory and Society*, *51*, 233–68.

McCauley, R. N. (2013). *Why religion is natural and science is not*. Oxford University Press.

McCauley, R. N., & Lawson, E. T. (2002). *Bringing ritual to mind: Psychological foundations of cultural forms*. Cambridge University Press.

McLaughlin, A., & McGill, A. (2017). Explicitly teaching critical thinking skills in a history course. *Science & Education*, *26*(1), 93–105. https://doi.org/10.1007/s11191-017-9878-2.

McNamara, R. A., Norenzayan, A., & Henrich, J. (2014). Supernatural punishment, in-group biases, and material insecurity: Experiments and Ethnography from Yasawa, Fiji. *Religion, Brain & Behavior*, *6*(1), 1–22.

Mercadante, Linda. (2014). *Belief without borders: Inside the minds of the spiritual but not religious*. Oxford University Press.

Mithen, S., & Reed, M. (2002). Stepping out: A computer simulation of hominid dispersal from Africa. *Journal of Human Evolution*, *43*(4), 433–62. https://doi.org/10.1016/S0047-2484(02)90584-1.

Moor, J. H. (2006). The nature, importance, and difficulty of machine ethics. *IEEE Intelligent Systems*, *21*(4), 18–21.

Morris, I. (2011). *Why the West rules – for now: The patterns of history, and what they reveal about the ruture (Reprint edition)*. Picador.

Morris, I. (2013). *The measure of civilization: How social development decides the fate of nations*. Princeton University Press.

Morris, I., Atwood, M., Korsgaard, C. M., Seaford, R., & Spence, J. D. (2015). *Foragers, farmers, and fossil fuels: How human values evolve* (S. Macedo, Ed.; Updated ed.). Princeton University Press.

Nakamura, C., & Pels, P. (2014). Using "magic" to think from the material: Tracing distributed agency, revelation, and concealment at Çatalhöyük. In I. Hodder (Ed.), *Religion at work in a Neolithic society: Vital matters* (pp. 187–224). Cambridge University Press.

New Zealand Attitudes and Values Study. (2023). https://www.psych.auckland.ac.nz/en/about/new-zealand-attitudes-and-values-study.html (accessed December 1, 2023).

Nikitas, P., & Nikita, E. (2005). A study of hominin dispersal out of Africa using computer simulations. *Journal of Human Evolution*, *49*(5), 602–17. https://doi.org/10.1016/j.jhevol.2005.07.001.

Noorman, M., & Johnson, D. G. (2014). Negotiating autonomy and responsibility in military robots. *Ethics and Information Technology*, *16*(1), 51–62.

Norenzayan, A. (2013). *Big gods: How religion transformed cooperation and conflict*. Princeton University Press.

Norenzayan, A., Shariff, A. F., Gervais, W. M., Willard, A. K., McNamara, R. A., Slingerland, E., & Henrich, J. (2016). The cultural evolution of prosocial religions. *Behavioral and Brain Sciences*, 1–86. 39:e1. doi:10.1017/S0140525X14001356

Norris, P., & Inglehart, R. (2011). *Sacred and secular: Religion and politics worldwide* (2nd ed.). Cambridge University Press.

Norris, P., & Inglehart, R. (2015). *Are high levels of existential security conducive to secularization? A response to our critics*. In S. Brunn (Eds.), *The changing world religion map*. Springer. https://doi.org/10.1007/978-94-017-9376-6_177.

Norris, P., & Inglehart, R. (2019). *Cultural backlash: Trump, Brexit, and authoritarian populism.* Cambridge University Press.

Orsi, R. A. (2002). *The Madonna of 115th street: Faith and community Italian Harlem, 1880-950.* Yale University Press.

Peoples, H., & Marlowe, F. (2012). Subsistence and the evolution of religion. *Human Nature, 23*(3), 253–69. https://doi.org/10.1007/s12110-012-9148-6.

Pew Research Center. (2015). *The future of world religions: Population growth projections, 2010-2050.* Pew Research Center.

Pinker, S. (2011). *The better angels of our nature: The decline of violence in history and its causes.* Penguin UK.

Powers, S. T., & Lehmann, L. (2014). An evolutionary model explaining the Neolithic transition from egalitarianism to leadership and despotism. *Proceedings of the Royal Society of London B: Biological Sciences, 281*(1791), 20141349. https://doi.org/10.1098/rspb.2014.1349.

Powers, T. M. (2006). Prospects for a Kantian machine. *IEEE Intelligent Systems, 21*(4), 46–51.

Proulx, T., & Inzlicht, M. (2012). The five "A"s of meaning maintenance: Finding meaning in the theories of sense-making. *Psychological Inquiry, 23*(4), 317–35. https://doi.org/10.1080/1047840X.2012.702372.

Puga-Gonzalez, I., Wildman, W. J., Diallo, S. Y., & Shults, F. L. (2019). Minority integration in a Western city: An agent-based modeling approach. In *Human simulation: Perspectives, insights, and applications* (pp. 179–90). Springer Nature.

Putnam, Robert D. (2001). *Bowling alone: The collapse and revival of American community.* Simon & Schuster.

Putnam, Robert D., & Campbell, D. E. (2010). *American grace: How religion divides and unites us.* Simon & Schuster.

Richardson, K. (2016). Sex robot matters: Slavery, the prostituted, and the rights of machines. *IEEE Technology and Society Magazine, 35*(2), 46–53.

Rounding, K., Lee, A., Jacobson, J. A., & Ji, L.-J. (2012). Religion replenishes self-control. *Psychological Science, 23*(6), 635–42. https://doi.org/10.1177/0956797611431987.

Ruiter, S., and van Tubergen, F. (2009). Religious attendance in cross-national perspective: A multilevel analysis of 60 countries. *American Journal of Sociology,* 115(3): 863–95. doi: https://doi.org/10.1086/603536.

Runciman, W. G. (2012). Righteous rebels: When, where and why? In R. N. Bellah & H. Joas (Eds.), *The Axial Age and its consequences* (pp. 317–36). Harvard University Press.

Sanderson, S. K. (2019). *Religious evolution and the axial age: From shamans to priests to prophets*. Bloomsbury Publishing.

Scheidel, W. (2017). *The great leveler: Violence and the history of inequality from the Stone Age to the twenty-first century*. Princeton University Press.

Shariff, A. F., & Norenzayan, A. (2011). Mean gods make good people: Different views of God predict cheating behavior. *International Journal for the Psychology of Religion*, *21*(2), 85–96. https://doi.org/10.1080/10508619.2011.556990.

Sheehan, O., Watts, J., Gray, R. D., & Atkinson, Q. D. (2018). Coevolution of landesque capital intensive agriculture and sociopolitical hierarchy. *Proceedings of the National Academy of Sciences of the United States of America*, *115*(14), 3628–33. https://doi.org/10.1073/pnas.1714558115.

Shults, F. L. (2010a). *Spiritual entanglement: Transforming religious symbols at Catalhoyuk*. Cambridge University Press.

Shults, F. L. (2012). The problem of good (and evil): Arguing about axiological conditions in science and religion. In W. J. Wildman & P. McNamara (Eds.), *Science and the world's religions. Volume 1: Origins and destinies* (pp. 39–68). Praeger.

Shults, F. L. (2014a). Excavating theogonies: Anthropomorphic promiscuity and sociographic prudery in the Neolithic and mow. In I. Hodder (Ed.), *Religion at work in a Neolithic society: Vital matters* (pp. 58–85). Cambridge University Press.

Shults, F. L. (2014b). *Theology after the birth of God: Atheist conceptions in cognition and culture*. Palgrave Macmillan.

Shults, F. L. (2018). *Practicing safe sects: Religious reproduction in scientific and philosophical perspective*. Brill Academic.

Shults, F. L. (2020). Computing consilience: How modelling and simulation can contribute to worldview studies. In G. Larsson, J. Svensson, & A. Nordin (Eds.), *Building blocks of religion: Critical applications and future prospects* (pp. 101–12). Equinox.

Shults, F. L. (2021). Simulating secularities: Challenges and opportunities in the computational science of (non)religion. *Secularism and Nonreligion*, *10*(1), Article 1. https://doi.org/10.5334/snr.154.

Shults, F. L. (2023). Simulation, science, and stakeholders: Challenges and opportunities for modelling solutions to societal problems. *Complexity*, *23*, 1–10. https://doi.org/10.1155/2023/1375004.

Shults, F. L., Gore, R., Wildman, W. J., Lynch, C., Lane, J. E., & Toft, M. (2018). A Generative model of the mutual escalation of anxiety between religious groups. *Journal of Artificial Societies and Social Simulation*, *21*(4), doi: 10.18564/jasss.3840.

Shults, F. L., Lane, J. E., Diallo, S., Lynch, C., Wildman, W. J., & Gore, R. (2018). Modeling terror management theory: Computer simulations of the impact of mortality salience on religiosity. *Religion, Brain & Behavior*, *8*(1), 77–100.

Shults, F. L., & Wildman, W. J. (2018). Simulating religious entanglement and social investment in the Neolithic. In I. Hodder (Ed.), *Religion, history and place in the origin of settled life* (pp. 33–63). University of Colorado Press.

Shults, F. L., & Wildman, W. J. (2019). Ethics, computer simulation, and the future of humanity. In S. Y. Diallo, W. J. Wildman, F. L. Shults, & A. Tolk (Eds.), *Human simulation: Perspectives, insights and applications* (pp. 21–40). Springer.

Shults, F. L., & Wildman, W. J. (2020a). Artificial social ethics: Simulating culture, conflict, and cooperation. *Proceedings of the SpringSim 2020 Conference*, IEEE. doi: 10.22360/SpringSim.2020.HSAA.003.

Shults, F. L., & Wildman, W. J. (2020b). Human simulation and sustainability: Ontological, epistemological, and ethical reflections. *Sustainability*, *12*(23), 10039.

Shults, F. L., & Wildman, W. (2023). The methodological naturalism and methodological secularism scale: Shedding new light on scholarship in religion. *Bulletin for the Study of Religion*, *51*(3–4), 92–102.

Shults, F. L., Wildman, W. J., Diallo, S., Puga-Gonzalez, I., & Voas, D. (2020). The artificial society analytics platform. In H. Verhagen & M. Borit (Eds), *Advances in social simulation: Looking in the mirror* (pp. 411–26). Springer.

Shults, F. L., Wildman, W. J., & Dignum, V. (2018). The ethics of computer modeling and simulation. *2018 Winter Simulation Conference (WSC)*, 4069–83.

Shults, F. L., Wildman, W. J., Lane, J. E., Lynch, C., & Diallo, S. (2018). Multiple axialities: A computational model of the Axial Age. *Journal of Cognition and Culture*, *18*(4), 537–64.

Shults, F. L., Wildman, W. J., Taves, A., & Paloutzian, R. F. (2020). What do religion scholars really want? Scholarly values in the scientific study of religion. *Journal for the Scientific Study of Religion*, *59*(1), 18–38.

Shults, F. L., Wildman, W. J., Toft, M. D., & Danielson, A. (2021). Artificial societies in the Anthropocene: Challenges and opportunities for modeling climate, conflict, and cooperation. *Proceedings of the 2021 Winter Simulation Conference*, IEEE. 1–12. doi: 10.1109/WSC52266.2021.9715391.

Smith, C., & Vaidyanathan, B. (2010). *Multiple modernities and religion*. Oxford University Press.

Sosis, R., & Alcorta, C. (2004). Is religion adaptive? *Behavioral and Brain Sciences*, *27*(6), 749–50. https://doi.org/10.1017/S0140525X04420172.

Squazzoni, F. (2012). *Agent-based computational sociology* (2nd ed.). John Wiley & Sons.

Stark, R., & Iannaccone, L. R. (1994). A supply-side reinterpretation of the "secularization" of Europe. *Journal for the Scientific Study of Religion*, *33*(3), 230–52. https://doi.org/10.2307/1386688.

Stolz, J. 2009. Explaining Religiosity: Towards a Unified Theoretical Model. *The British Journal of Sociology*, *60*(2), 345–76. doi: https://doi.org/10.1111/j.1468-4446.2009.01234.x

Strulik, H. (2016). An economic theory of religious belief. *Journal of Economic Behavior and Organization*, *128*, 35–46. https://doi.org/10.1016/j.jebo.2016.04.007.

Talmont-Kaminski, K. (2014). *Religion as magical ideology: How the supernatural reflects rationality*. Routledge.

Taves, A. (2015). Reverse engineering complex cultural concepts: Identifying building blocks of "religion." *Journal of Cognition and Culture*, *15*(1–2), 191–216. https://doi.org/10.1163/15685373-12342146.

Taves, A. (2020). From religious studies to worldview studies. *Religion*, *50*(1), 137–47.

Taves, A., & Asprem, E. (2018). Scientific worldview studies: A programmatic proposal. In A. K. Petersen, I. S. Gilhus, L. H. Martin, J. S. Jensen, & J. Sørensen (Eds.), *Evolution, cognition, and the history of religion: A new synthesis* (pp. 297–308). Brill.

Taves, A., & Asprem, E. (2020). The building block approach: An overview. In G. Larsson, J. Svensson, & A. Nordin (Eds.), *Building blocks of religion: Critical applications and future prospects* (pp. 5–25). Equinox.

Taves, A., Asprem, E., & Ihm, E. (2018). Psychology, meaning making, and the study of worldviews: Beyond religion and non-religion. *Psychology of Religion and Spirituality*, *10*(3), 207–17. https://doi.org/10.1037/rel0000201.

Taves, A., Wildman, W. J., Shults, F. L., & Paloutzian, R. F. (2022). Scholarly values, methods, and evidence in the academic study of religion. *Method & Theory in the Study of Religion*, *34*(4), 378–406.

Taylor, C. (1992). *Sources of the self: The making of the modern identity*. Harvard University Press.

Taylor, C. (2007). *A secular age* (1st ed.). The Belknap Press of Harvard University Press.

Thomassen, B. (2010). Anthropology, multiple modernities and the Axial Age debate. *Anthropological Theory*, *10*(4), 321–42. https://doi.org/10.1177/1463499610386659.

Tolk, A. (2015). Learning something right from models that are wrong: Epistemology of simulation. In L. Yilmaz (Ed.), *Concepts and methodologies for modeling and simulation* (pp. 87–106). Springer.

Tolk, A. (2017). Code of ethics. In A. Tolk & T. Oren (Eds.), *The profession of modeling and simulation: Discipline, ethics, education, vocation, societies, and economics* (pp. 35–52). John Wiley & Sons.

Tomasello, M. (2009). *Why we cooperate*. MIT Press.

Tomasello, M. (2010). Human culture in evolutionary perspective. *Advances in Culture and Psychology*, *1*, 5–52.

Turchin, P. (2007). *War and peace and war: The rise and fall of empires*. Penguin.

Turchin, P. (2010). Warfare and the evolution of social complexity: A multilevel-selection approach. *Structure and Dynamics*, *4*(3), 1–37. https://doi.org/10.5070/SD943003313.

Turchin, P. (2015). *Ultrasociety: How 10,000 years of war made humans the greatest cooperators on earth*. Beresta Books.

Turchin, P. (2016). *Ages of discord*. Beresta Books.

Turchin, P. (2018). *Historical dynamics*. Princeton University Press.

Turchin, P., Currie, T., Whitehouse, H., François, P., Feeney, K., Mullins, D., Hoyer, D., Collins, C., Grohmann, S., Savage, P., Mendel-Gleason, G., Turner, E., Dupeyron, A., Cioni, E., Reddish, J., Levine, J., Jordan, G., Brandl, E., Williams, A., … Spencer, C. (2017). Quantitative historical analysis uncovers a single dimension of complexity that structures global variation in human social organization. *Proceedings of the National Academy of Sciences of the United States of America (PNAS)*. http://discovery.ucl.ac.uk/10041342/1/PNAS-2018-Turchin-E144-51.pdf (accessed December 23, 2023).

Turchin, P., & Nefedov, S. A. (2009). *Secular cycles*. Princeton University Press.

Turchin, P., Whitehouse, H., Larson, J., Cioni, E., Reddish, J., Hoyer, D., Savage, P. E., Covey, R. A., Baines, J., & Altaweel, M. (2023). Explaining the rise of moralizing religions: A test of competing hypotheses using the Seshat Databank. *Religion, Brain & Behavior*, *13*(2), 167–94.

Van Elk, M., & Zwaan, R. (2016). Predictive processing and situation models: Constructing and reconstructing religious experience. *Religion, Brain & Behavior*, *7*(1), 85–7. https://doi.org/10.1080/2153599X.2016.1150328.

Voas, D. (2009). The rise and fall of fuzzy fidelity in Europe. *European Sociological Review*, *25*(2), 155–68. https://doi.org/10.1093/esr/jcn044.

Warner, M., Van Antwerpen, J., & Calhoun, C. J. (2013). *Varieties of secularism in a secular age*. Harvard University Press.

Watts, J., Greenhill, S. J., Atkinson, Q. D., Currie, T. E., Bulbulia, J., & Gray, R. D. (2015). Broad supernatural punishment but not moralizing high gods precede the evolution of political complexity in Austronesia. *Proceedings of the Royal Society of London B: Biological Sciences*, *282*(1804), 20142556.

Whitehouse, H. (2004). *Modes of religiosity: A cognitive theory of religious transmission*. AltaMira Press.

Whitehouse, H., & Hodder, I. (2010). Modes of religiosity at Catalhoyuk. In *Religion in the emergence of civilization: Catalhoyuk as a case study* (pp. 122–45). Cambridge University Press.

Whitehouse, H., Kahn, K., Hochberg, M. E., & Bryson, J. J. (2012). The role for simulations in theory construction for the social sciences: Case studies concerning divergent modes of religiosity. *Religion, Brain & Behavior*, 2(3), 182–201. doi: 10.1080/2153599X.2012.691033.

Whitehouse, H., Mazzucato, C., Hodder, I., & Atkinson, Q. D. (2014). Modes of religiosity and the evolution of social complexity at Çatalhöyük. In I. Hodder (Ed.), *Religion at work in a Neolithic society* (pp. 134–58). Cambridge University Press.

Wildman, W. J. (2009). *Science and religious anthropology: A spiritually evocative naturalist interpretation of human life*. Ashgate.

Wildman, W. J. (2011). *Religious philosophy as multidisciplinary comparative inquiry: Envisioning a future for the philosophy of religion*. SUNY Press.

Wildman, W. J., Rohr, D., Sandage, S., Radom, A., & DiDonato, N. (2023). The dimensions of spirituality inventory: Charting the landscape of the spiritual. *Archive for the Psychology of Religion*. https://journals.sagepub.com/doi/abs/10.1177/00846724231185180.

Wildman, W. J., & Shults, F. L. (2018). Emergence: What does it mean and how is it relevant to computer engineering? In S. Mittal, S. Diallo, & A. Tolk (Eds.), *Emergent behavior in complex systems engineering: A modeling and simulation approach* (pp. 21–34). John Wiley & Sons.

Wildman, W. J., Shults, F. L., Diallo, S. Y., Gore, R., & Lane, J. E. (2020). Post-supernaturalist cultures: There and back again. *Secularism & Nonreligion*, 9 https://secularismandnonreligion.org/articles/10.5334/snr.121.

Winfield, A. F., Michael, K., Pitt, J., & Evers, V. (2019). Machine ethics: The design and governance of ethical AI and autonomous systems. *Proceedings of the IEEE, 107*(3), 509–17.

Wittrock, B. (2005). The meaning of the axial age. In J. P. Arnason, S. N. Eisenstadt, & B. Wittrock (Eds.), *Axial civilizations and world history* (pp. 51–86). Brill Academic Pub.

Wittrock, B. (2012). The Axial Age in global history: Cultural crystallizations and societal transformations. In R. N. Bellah & H. Joas (Eds.), *The Axial Age and its consequences* (pp. 102–25). Harvard University Press.

Zuckerman, P. (2007). Atheism: Contemporary Numbers and Patterns. In M. Martin (Ed.), *The Cambridge Companion to Atheism* (pp. 47–65). Cambridge University Press.

Zuckerman, P. (2010). *Society without God: What the Least Religious Nations Can Tell Us About Contentment*. NYU Press.

Zuckerman, P., Galen, L. W., & Pasquale, F. L. (2016). *The Nonreligious: Understanding Secular People and Societies*. Oxford University Press.

Zuckerman, M., Silberman, J., & Hall, J. A. (2013). The relation between intelligence and religiosity: A meta-analysis and some proposed explanations. *Personality and Social Psychology Review, 17*(4), 325–54. https://doi.org/10.1177/1088868313497266.

Index

Abrutyn, Seth 39
agent-based modeling 44–5
agricultural draw, NSIM parameter 80
agricultural intensity, NSIM variable 81, 83
agricultural technology, MAxiM parameter 116
Asprem, Egil 10
Axial Age civilizational transition 38–40, 104–13
axiality, MAxiM model variable 115, 129
Axiological Extra-Theistic Spirituality 201–2

Bellah, Robert 39
Building Block Approach 10–11

Çatalhöyük, study of 67–8
Cauvin, Jacques 71–2
Chase-Dunn, Christopher 28–9
civilizational transformation 17–42, 189–90
  cognitive-coalitional theories of 32–40, 140–1
  complementarity of competing theories of 21
  ideological-political theories of 22–7, 139–40
  material-social theories of 27–32, 140–1
  shifts in religious worldviews as key condition of 20
contest religious cognitive defaults, NSIM variable 84
contest religious moral defaults, NSIM variable 84
contest religious ritual defaults, NSIM variable 84
contest religious social defaults, NSIM variable 85
complexity 190–1
computational modeling and simulation 14–15, 40, 43–65

computational social simulation 54–6
  in archaeology 68–71
  ethical challenges related to 57–62
  promises of 54–5
  perils of 55–6
conversion model 46–52
crisis of the humanities 53
cultural differentiation, MAxiM variable 118, 135
cultural memory, MAxiM variable 122
Cultural Particularity Path to secularization 149–50

Darwin, Charles 33
Deacon, Terrence 34
delay of gratification, NSIM variable 81, 84
depth dimension of human life 211
destabilization, FOReST parameter 157, 168–9, 183
Diamond, Jared 30–1
Dimensions of Spirituality Inventory 198–203
doctrinal rituals, MAxiM variable 121
Donald, Merlin 35–6

economic intensity, NSIM variable 81–2
Eisenstadt, Shmuel 103, 106–7
energy capture, MAxiM variable 118, 133–4
entanglement, of humans with things 73–4
ethical AI 58–9
event-driven modeling 44
evolutionary theory, majority in U.S. rejects 185
Existential Security Path to secularization 148

fitness landscape 33
FOReST computer simulation 143–88
fuzzy fidelity 9, 178, 195–6

Graeber, David 26–7

Harari, Yuval Noah 25–6
Heelas, Paul 147–8
Hegel, Georg Wilhelm Friedrich 22–3
high centrality and differentiation, MAxiM variable 121
Hodder, Ian 73–4
Human Development Path to secularization 148–9
hunter-gatherer cling, NSIM parameter 81–2

information technology, MAxiM variable 119
Inglehart, Ronald 148

Jaspers, Karl 23, 102, 106

large-scale organization 18
Lerro, Bruce 28–9
lifeways 13

Marx, Karl 28
maximum birthrate, FOReST parameter 157
McCauley, Robert 143–4
Meaning Maintenance Path 146–7
Mercadante, Linda 197
mind-culture nexus 18–19, 190
modernity, transition to 185–8, 192–3
moralizing high gods, MAxiM variable 122
Morris, Ian 31–2, 39, 72, 110, 138
Multiple Axialities Model 101–41

naturalism
  methodological tends to buttress metaphysical 62–4
  within Axial religious traditions 208–9
Neolithic civilizational transformation 67–100
Neolithic Social Investment Model 75–100, 86–100, 115–27, 147–8, 159–73, 185–7, 209–10
Norenzayan, Ara 34, 39–40
Norris, Pippa 148–9

pastoral intensity, NSIM variable 81–2
preferred affluent birthrate, FOReST parameter 157
priests, MAxiM variable 123
problem-focused determination of methods 52–3
Putnam, Robert 149–50

reflexivity, MAxiM variable 120
religion 139, 191
  working definition 75
Religious Culture, FOReST variable 152
Resource Scarcity, FOReST variable 154
Ritualistic Theistic Spirituality 198–201

Sanderson, Stephen 39
secularism, strategies to resist 182
social intensity, NSIM variable 81, 85
Stolz, Jörg 145
stress
  MAxiM parameter 116
  NSIM parameter 80
Subjectivization Path to secularization 147–8
Supply-Side Path to secularization 150–1
supernatural punishment, MAxiM variable 117, 136
Supernaturalism 143, 179–80, 204–5
Supernaturalistic Extra-Theistic Spirituality 201–3
surveyance intolerance, NSIM variable 81, 83
system-dynamics modeling 45, 113

Taves, Ann 10
Taylor, Charles 24–5
technology
  FOReST parameter 157
  NSIM parameter 81
theoretic culture, MAxiM variable 123–4
Tomasello, Michael 35
Transformational Theistic Spirituality, 198–201
transition dynamics 193–7
transmundane belief, MAxiM variable 124
transmundane importance, MAxiM parameter 116
Turchin, Peter 29–30, 108–10

Voas, David 178

warmaking capacity
    MAxiM variable 119
    NSIM variable 81, 83

Wengrow, David 26–7
Whitehouse, Harvey 36–7, 72–3, 111
Woodhead, Linda 147–8
worldviews 12–13

www.ingramcontent.com/pod-product-compliance
Lightning Source LLC
Chambersburg PA
CBHW071824300426
44116CB00009B/1419